Towns and Villages in Canada

The Importance of Being Unimportant

by

Gerald Hodge
and
Mohammad A. Qadeer

School of Urban and
Regional Planning,
Queen's University

Butterworths
Toronto

Towns and Villages in Canada

Printed and bound in Canada

The Butterworth Group of Companies

Canada:
Butterworth & Co. (Canada) Ltd., Toronto and Vancouver
United Kingdom:
Butterworth & Co. (Publishers) Ltd., London
Australia:
Butterworths Pty Ltd., Sydney, Melbourne, Brisbane, Adelaide and Perth
New Zealand:
Butterworths of New Zealand Ltd., Wellington and Auckland
Singapore:
Butterworth & Co. (Asia) Pte. Ltd., Singapore
South Africa:
Butterworth Publishers (Pty) Ltd., Durban and Pretoria
United States:
Butterworth Legal Publishers, Boston, Seattle and Austin
Mason Publishing Company, St. Paul
D & S Publishers, Clearwater

Canadian Cataloguing in Publication Data

Hodge, Gerald.
   Towns and Villages in Canada

Bibliography: p.
Includes index.
ISBN 0-409-83702-4

1. Villages — Canada. 2. Cities and towns — Canada.
3. Canada — Rural conditions. 4. Sociology, Rural —
Canada. I. Qadeer, Mohammad A. II. Title.

HT431.H6   307.7′2′0971   C83-098446-1

To our children
Brooke, Adam, and Clare
Nadra, Ahmer, and Ali

Preface

This book has grown out of an earlier (1978) study bearing the same title, which the authors prepared for the erstwhile Ministry of Urban Affairs, Government of Canada. Although many themes and ideas discussed in this book were initially formulated in that study, here they have been refined and systematized. Furthermore, many new topics have been explored in this book and most of the old ones have been extended through the incorporation of recent data. All in all, this book is not merely an updated version of the earlier study. It is largely a fresh effort that builds on the earlier findings. We are, therefore, grateful to the Ministry for helping us to get started on this venture, especially for the understanding of Chris Burke, James Maxwell, and Andrew Greiner.

This study is unique in many ways which, as we have come to realize, has its advantages and disadvantages. We are not aware of another national study of towns and villages, and we appreciate the initiative of Patricia Hodge from which it arose. This has meant that we have had a rare opportunity to explore for the first time a fundamental form of human settlement on a Canada-wide scale. It has the particular distinction of being an exploration of the nature of contemporary Canadian small communities, which are often viewed through the clichés of the past and the stereotyped images fostered by the media. One of the disadvantages is that with little or no precedent to follow it was necessary to invent the methodology to be used in analyses and to wrestle with many gaps in data about towns and villages. Another limitation of this book is that it essentially describes small communities of mainstream Canada. It does not deal with the distinguishing features of Native communities — an omission that regrettably reflects shortcomings in our knowledge and understanding.

Both because of the lack of theory and the lack of data our method has been to make several "probes" of the demographic, social, and economic bases of Canada's towns and villages. What is presented, therefore, is a mosaic of findings in which some of the pieces are still missing. It is envisioned to be an account of the patterns of growth, social and economic organization, and physical make-up of Canadian towns and villages in modern times. It could serve as a textbook for students of Regional Planning, Geography, Sociology, and Economics. On the other hand, it may be useful for officials and citizens to better understand their own small communities.

We have relied on data from diverse sources. Often the class intervals used in these divergent sources were different. For the sake of consistency, we have occasionally slightly altered the reported class intervals, wherever it was possible without affecting their values. We have benefited from insights and observations of the numerous authors cited in this book. Their guidance is gratefully acknowledged.

A number of graduate research assistants and colleagues have assisted us in various ways including collection and analysis of data, refinement of observations, and clarification of insights. We gratefully acknowledge the help of Patricia Malone, Lesley Paterson, Donald Nijsse, John Blakney, David Feldbruegge, Eric Workman, Larry Silani, Dan Berard, Jill Harris, and Professor Clarke Wilson. In getting the manuscript ready, Jackie Bell and Florence Gore not only bore most of the burden of typing, but they also patiently put up with our unscheduled deliveries and untimely demands. We appreciate their cooperation.

Anyone undertaking to write a book comes to realize the contribution of one's family. Without the sympathy and support of our families, we would have been under great strain. Patricia Hodge and Susan Qadeer gave intellectual as well as moral support. We, individually and together, acknowledge this unreserved help.

The Advisory Research Committee of the School of Graduate Studies, Queen's University, gave us "seed money" for this study. Canada Council also provided some financial help. Their contributions are fully appreciated.

We also received help and encouragement from residents and officials of small communities across Canada. To them, a special note of thanks. In this book they will find a general picture of towns and villages which, perhaps, will always be at variance with their (respective) images of their communities, but we hope that something of each community can be discerned in our description.

Contents

Tables

Chapter 3

Summary Tables

Numbered Tables

Chapter 4

Summary Tables

Numbered Tables

Chapter 5

Summary Tables

Numbered Tables

Chapter 8

Summary Tables

Numbered Tables

Chapter 10

Summary Table

Figures

Chapter 9

1 Towns and Villages in an Urban Canada

1. INTRODUCTION

. . . Argentia, Tignish, Bloomfield, Atikokan,
Springhill, Beaupre, Dalhousie, Dauphin, Bienfait, Cabri,
Hannah, Fort Nelson, Bella Coola . . .

Towns and villages have always been an important part of the settlement fabric of Canada. From the earliest Newfoundland fishing villages, to the Indian encampments of the interior, and the trading posts, grain towns, minetowns, and milltowns, we find the foundations of Canada's present settlement pattern. At best, two hundred of perhaps ten thousand of our small centers evolved to become the cities we know today in Canada. Only twenty or so made it to the metropolis stage, but their roots are undeniable.

Today, the cities and metropolises comprise two-thirds of our population; the towns and villages, only one-fifth. The promises as well as the problems of the cities attract and hold much of our attention, consume much of our resources, and generate the culture and ideas that promote Canada as an *urban* society.

Yet, today, nearly five million Canadians live in small towns and villages across the length and breadth of the country, one millon more than lived there only twenty years ago. Many small centers have lost commercial establishments; a mobile society passes them by for the lure of the city's, or even just the larger town's, stores. Yet people continue to live in towns and villages, build their homes there, raise their children there, retire there, and seemingly, treasure the habitat of the small center.

In the minds of most Canadian city dwellers, towns and villages are, at best, an anachronism and probably destined for demise. Not much thought has been given to the present situation of our small centers; even less to their future. Not much is known about our small communities, their conditions and trends, or their problems and aspirations.

There is a need to right that balance. Towns and villages are not only not dying out, but may offer some insights and benchmarks in our search for more beneficent human settlements in Canada. They may be more

1

important to us in the future just because, paradoxically, they were unimportant to us in the period of our infatuation with the metropolis.

In this book, then, the aim is to establish as clear a picture as possible of small towns in Canada and the milieu in which they exist as of the beginning of the 1980s. In the process of describing recent population trends, economic bases, social structure, and housing and land use patterns of Canada's towns and villages, it is hoped that some conventional notions about our small centers will be dispelled. But it will soon be noticed that the picture we sketch of the 9,500 Canadian towns and villages serves mostly to provide some helpful propositions about *all* these small centers. At the same time, it blurs those properties and qualities that are unique to *each* town and village.

Most of us have, in our mind's eye, one or a few favorite small towns. They may not correspond to the general dimensions identified in these chapters, and that is how it should be. It cannot be overemphasized that there is tremendous diversity among the nation's towns and villages in the 1980s, perhaps more than there has ever been. The diversity is both a fact to be absorbed about contemporary small centers and, on the other hand, the means to dispel the urbanite's conventional wisdom of the sameness of all small towns.

The effort to discern the dimensions of small centers in Canada today is, in itself, a call to recognize the diversity of settlements in what is otherwise considered an *urban* society with an *urban system*. In other words, the conclusion from the many studies of cities and their growth over the past few decades that we are an *urbanized* country comes from focusing on the dimensions that characterize urban centers. It is, as the statistician would say, a recognition of a "central tendency" of our society — urbanization. But in arriving at the conclusion that this is an urbanized country it is necessary to make two points about Canadian settlements. The first is that differences between individual cities are blurred in the perspective that labels Vancouver, Regina, and Saint John, for example, all as urban places. The second is that there is, of course, some residual of settlements which do not qualify as urban. The latter are the towns and villages which are our subject.

Thus, the picture of contemporary Canadian towns and villages rendered in the following chapters is primarily a look at the central tendencies of small centers. Many small places fall well outside these central tendencies; they are distinctive in their social structure, their growth, their economic milieu, or their physical patterns. Indeed, it could be said that each of the 9,500 towns and villages is distinctive to some degree. However, it is our contention that, regardless of the degree of "fit" of individual centers, the general dimensions derived here to describe towns and villages serve to provide an appropriate perspective for small centers. It is a perspective centered on small communities themselves rather than being the periphery of a view of cities.

Four objectives guide the development of our perspective on Canadian small communities:

(1) To affirm the integrity of towns and villages in Canada as a distinctive form of habitat;

(2) To produce a baseline of information about towns and villages in Canada in regard to their current situation and recent trends;

(3) To place towns and villages in perspective with other settlements in Canada and with contemporary trends in Canadian society; and

(4) To suggest ways in which the habitat of Canadian towns and villages may be sustained into the future.

In the succeeding sections that complete this chapter the contemporary role of towns and villages will be discussed and compared with historical situations for small centers. Current trends in population decline and shift for urban and metropolitan areas will be described and related to the trend for small centers to persist apparently independent of this. Finally, the data milieu confronting anyone wishing to study towns and villages is discussed along with the adaptations made to provide the picture presented in this study.

2. SMALL CENTERS IN CANADA'S SETTLEMENT PATTERN

Viewed at any one time, the settlement pattern of a nation is a mirror of both past and future settlement patterns. The locations that people choose to congregate their homes and shops and institutions are remarkably persistent. Economic functions and social roles may change for a place, some towns may become cities, but once established a human settlement has an identity that is seldom ever lost. Canadian planner Hans Blumenfeld cites a stanza of Goethe's in regard to the continuity of settlements:

No time, no power ever can dissolve
Created form that living will evolve.[1]

When one arrays the settlements of Canada today in a simple size-distribution, the following picture emerges.

Distribution of Canadian Settlements, 1976

	Number of Places	1976 Population	Average Population Size
Large Cities	23	12,796,000	556,348
Small Cities	148	3,920,000	26,486
Towns and Villages	9,457	4,471,000	473

One of the most striking features of these data is the sheer number of small communities in Canada. It is equivalent to one town or village for every one hundred square miles in the southern one-third of the country. Further, every one of the large and small cities is an outgrowth of a town or village at that location. Small centers may thus be considered the "foundation" of the system of settlements as well as the "seed bed" for urban development.

Population size is not the only indicator of differences among settlements. The array of functions performed by centers, especially commerical functions, is another way in which settlements differ. The basic convenience goods and services are supplied by all centers — this is the economic base of the hamlet or small village. As the goods and services become more specialized they require a larger market area, and as a result are offered by a smaller number of centers. This in turn results in a commercial hierarchy of centers, which is also positively correlated with population size.

The vast number of towns and villages is explained in large part by the commercial hierarchy, for it reflects the need to provide basic goods and services within convenient proximity to the population. The widespread provision of basic social services and institutional support (for example, schools and churches) is another part of the rationale for the ubiquity of settlements. But before we give the impression that towns and villages are mere dispensers of goods and services, it should be noted that small centers have a symbiotic relationship with the area, the people, and the activities in their locale. They are the center of economic and social communities.

This is, perhaps, easiest to grasp by looking at the traditional role of a town or village as a service center in an area where natural resources are harvested. Whether the products are from farming, fishing, forestry, or mining, such centers are an integral part of the overall economic and social functioning of these areas.

Service centers are an essential part of arrangements for efficiently producing, marketing, and distributing the output of the farms, fisheries, and similar activities. The local center brings within easy reach of the logger or farmer many of the services and facilities necessary to maintain a sophisticated enterprise: parts and repair services, sales of seed, fuel, and oil, sales and storage and, sometimes, processing of the harvested resource. In the words of regional economist Douglass North, service centers provide "external economies for the export industry."[2]

Besides providing goods and services for the farm, fishing, mining, or logging firms, towns and villages provide goods and services to the families of those engaged in natural resource industries and to the residents of the small centers themselves. People shop for food, clothing, or furniture, and obtain such services as mail delivery, medical care, or entertainment at centers within their vicinity. Small centers also provide a focus for organized community activities and informal neighborliness, in addition to their commercial functions. The elementary school and the church(es) are characteristic social facilities. Most small centers also have a community hall that is used for events such as public dances, fairs, meetings of voluntary groups, and wedding receptions. A ball park, curling rink, hockey arena, and, increasingly, a swimming pool are standard town and village assets.

This review of the functions of a town or village tends to suggest an image of a more limited, somewhat self-contained town-country community such as existed in the early phases of the settlement of Canada. Except in a few resource regions, this image is not appropriate today. Almost all rural and small-town people and their economic and social activities are linked to extensive networks of production, distribution, and socialization.[3] Nevertheless, the kinds of functional relations between towns and rural people described above are still prominent today in rural communities including those on the fringes of metropolitan areas. The changes have occurred, so to speak, in the "boundaries" of rural communities, in the trading areas of towns and villages, and in the life spaces of people. There is simply a much greater interpenetration of the activities among rural communities within any region as well as between urban and rural communities.

New kinds of people are living in rural regions — urban expatriates and retirees, among others. There are also new jobs in recreation, resources development, manufacturing, and institutions for rural people, either in rural regions or within easy commuting distance. As Harry Lash notes, "Just think of places that produce durable goods in your home: that one can get them has nothing to do with the size of [your] town, nor, beyond certain limits, with the size of the town that produces them."[4] That towns and villages are now "plugged in" to regional, national, and even international systems of production, distribution, and information is undoubtedly true. However, this should not overshadow the fact that towns and villages continue to play an essential role in satisfying the need for community and for obtaining the necessities of daily life. Small centers have persisted through a century of dramatic urban growth in Canada; their roles have changed, as have those of all centers large and small in the settlement system.

3. THE STAYING POWER OF SMALL COMMUNITIES: AN EXAMPLE

If there is one aspect of towns and villages that we find remarkable throughout all of the various probes of small centers, it is their persistence, their refusal to die out, their "staying power."[5] One facet of this came to our attention time and again: the phenomenon of *no change* in population over very long periods of time for several hundred Canadian towns and villages. The census of population for many small centers, in all parts of the country, showed that there was little or no increase or decrease in inhabitants over five or more decades. Such places provide, perhaps, the prototypical instances of small-center persistence. These places did not grow during a period, at least until the 1970s, when all settlements were urged "either grow or die," and they did not die. To varying degrees this is the story of the vast majority of towns and villages in Canada.

To illustrate the characteristics of community staying power, the results of a study of one such stable place, Newburgh, Ontario, may be instructive.[6] In the 1981 census, Newburgh is listed as having 617 inhabitants, three less than in 1971, and only three more than it had in 1901. Newburgh was not static during all this time and, of course, the region, the province, and the country also changed. But, it seems, the more things changed the more they remained the same for Newburgh. This study, which we précis here, reviewed Newburgh's historical development from its beginnings in 1820.

A review of Newburgh's 160+ years suggests that it passed through four distinct periods in its development:

The Age of Subsistence	1820-1851
The Age of Prosperity	1851-1881
The Age of Decline	1881-1921
The Age of Stability	1921-present

FIGURE 1.1
Population Changes in Newburgh, Ontario, 1820-1981

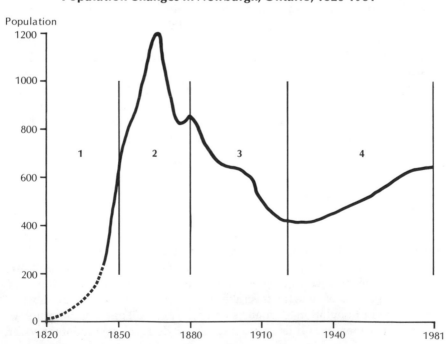

Population change throughout the four periods is shown on the accompanying chart; the highest population level (1,200) was reached in 1865 and never again equalled. These four periods also conform to several conceptual models of settlement and development.[7]

The Age of Subsistence in Newburgh, 1820-1851

Newburgh was among a half-dozen settlements founded by United Empire Loyalist settlers in the early 1800s in the region west of Kingston. All of these settlements experienced slow growth in the first thirty to forty years of their existence; their sizes remained very similar to one another, and they functioned relatively independent of one another. After 1846, a process of selection of growth centers began. Newburgh, along with its neighbor, Napanee, surged ahead on the basis of new manufacturing industries and the increasing competitiveness of agriculture in the region. By 1851, seventeen manufacturing establishments employed 52 people in Newburgh. Its population by that time was about 700 people. Napanee, about eight miles away, was slightly larger and had a more diversified manufacturing sector, probably due to its better location on water transportation routes. Land transportation to and from Newburgh was constrained by poor roads, and only by 1850 was there daily stage service from Newburgh to Kingston, about thirty miles to the east.

The Age of Prosperity in Newburgh, 1851-1881

In the first fifteen years of this period, the population of Newburgh nearly doubled to about 1,200 due, it seems, to the continued demand for sawn lumber in the United States. Newburgh was in an excellent position to respond, with its already established sawmills and proximity to the forest resources of the Canadian Shield. The 1871 census recorded 166 houses for Newburgh and a population of 828, the latter a drop from the town's peak a few years earlier. Three main reasons account for the decline: the logging boom subsided, especially as nearby timber was cut off; the Grand Trunk Railway, from Montreal to Toronto, passed to the south through Napanee in 1857; and, in 1863, Napanee was selected as the county seat. Thus, at the end of this period of development Newburgh had 182 houses and 834 residents, while Napenee, which thirty years previous had only 300 people more than Newburgh, ended the period 1851-1881 with 3,000 more people than its neighbor.

The Age of Decline in Newburgh, 1881-1921

The population of Newburgh declined by a half in this period, and other centers in the region lost comparable proportions of their residents. Indeed, the region of Newburgh as well as much of Eastern Ontario suffered through a period of major readjustment. The factors contributing to this were the end of a supply of decent farm land for homesteading in the region, sources of timber becoming more remote, a major national depression being in progress, the opening-up of Western Canada, and the growth of large cities. There was a migration from both countryside and towns in the area. For example, the population density in rural areas declined in this period from 21 per square mile to 14 in the township around Newburgh. The loss of the natural resource base affected the commercial base that had been established to service it from Newburgh. Not to be discounted in this decline was the effect of two major fires, one in 1887 (which destroyed eighty buildings) and another in 1902.

But, besides the local factors of change, Newburgh after 1881 experienced the end of the "frontier" of which it had been a part just at the time when new frontiers opened up in Canada, in the West, and in the cities. While it was a period of decline it was not a period of demise for Newburgh or the dozen other small centers in the locale. It was a period of adjustment and stabilization to the long-term realities of the natural resource base, the locational factors of transportation, and the roles of neighboring centers.

The Age of Stability in Newburgh, 1921 to the Present

During this period, Newburgh and its neighboring towns and villages either maintained their previous population levels or even showed modest growth; there were none of the spectacular rises or falls that characterized former periods. In these fifty years, Newburgh's population grew by 200. But this new population growth was based on different factors than in previous periods. As population grew, the number of manufacturing establishments declined (almost to zero), and the amount of farm land under cultivation and the number of farmers declined. The original bases of Newburgh's growth were either gone or going. By 1971, 95 residents of Newburgh, or nearly 40 percent of its labor force, worked in manufacturing plants outside the town; another 40 persons, or 16 percent, were employed in public service jobs mostly outside Newburgh. Currently, two-thirds of all the town's workers commute outside, and half of them commute to jobs in the Kingston area.

In this period, Newburgh became primarily an *exporter of labor* instead of an exporter of goods and services, as it had been in its first one hundred years. This is due in large measure to the emergence of the automobile and its use for personal transportation.[8] The automobile offered residents of towns and villages a choice of locations in which to shop, work, and seek services. The automobile, along with an almost ubiquitous rural road network largely established after World War I, served as countervailing forces to the forces of rationalization of industrial development and centralization of services and activities.

The role of a town or village as a "dormitory town" is new and, paradoxically, also enhances its traditional role as a service center for rural people. The dormitory function helps to sustain small places so that they are available to rural populations. In some ways the symbiotic relationships of city, town, and country are strengthened. As the history of Newburgh shows, small places can be viable despite a whole host of changes and, especially in the past four or five decades, have come to play two important roles in our settlement system. Further, the Newburghs of Canada are widespread. Consider, for example, Georgetown, Prince Edward Island; Broadview, Saskatchewan; Inverness, Nova Scotia; and Mundare, Alberta. All these places and many, many more of our towns and villages persist despite a long history of little or no population growth.

In subsequent chapters we discuss the nature and origins of the patterns of persistence among towns and villages in Canada. There are many variations on the theme illustrated by Newburgh. The issue is not simply one of population stability; even then, people age and move in and out of the town. The broader notion of "staying power" is probably more apt. Moreover, the various forms of persistence constitute a general phenomenon throughout the nation, occurring with comparable vigor in all regions. It appears, then, that in the 1950s and 1960s, while our attention was diverted toward the metropolis and the problems associated with its growth, towns and villages consolidated their position in the settlement system. In this predominantly urban country it might usefully be asked: what has been occurring among urban centers in this period?

4. EMERGING URBAN PATTERNS IN NORTH AMERICA

In the past few years, in both Canada and the United States, data from national census counts indicate apparently novel changes in the patterns of urbanization. In summary, the picture is one of diminishing trends in the proportion of population living in large cities, shifts in regional distributions of population and jobs, and changing concentrations of population both between and within metropolitan areas. One researcher has coined the provocative term "counterurbanization" to capture something of the nature of these new urban trends.[9] The broad outcomes of these changes in the settlement system may be discerned from the diverse Canadian research experience in this realm:

(1) *Regional Shifts in Population:* In Canada, from 1971 to 1976, both British Columbia and Alberta exhibited the highest growth rates among the provinces, nearly twice as high as Quebec and the Atlantic Region provinces. The two western provinces also experienced high in-migration from all other provinces in this period. From 1976 to 1981, all provinces east of Alberta grew at rates below the national

average. By 1981, the four western provinces had significantly expanded their share of national population over that of 1971.

(2) *Regional Shifts in Employment:* The interregional pattern of employment increase for the first half of the 1970s closely parallels the trends in population growth. The data suggest new employment shares for Ontario and Quebec are dropping relative to western provinces.

(3) *Declining Metropolitan Concentration:* In Canada, for the first time since 1941, the share of population accounted for by Census Metropolitan Areas (CMAs) failed to increase by any appreciable amount between 1971 and 1976. The share accounted for by the three largest CMAs (Toronto, Montreal, Vancouver) actually declined in this period and this performance was repeated in the 1976-1981 period. And, as in the United States, it was the smaller metropolitan areas that grew fastest.

(4) *Diminution of Urban Growth Shares:* The rate of growth of the urban population in Canada slowed to less than the national growth rate, in the 1971-1976 period, leading to a decline in the urban share of the population, the first such decline in over one hundred years; in the 1976-1981 period, the decline continued.

(5) *Expanding Metropolitan Commuting Fields:* Although there are variations by region and size of metropolis, there is a general extension of the size of commuting fields around metropolitan areas in the 1970s. Metropolitan central cities, in aggregate, grew at less than the Canadian growth rate, but their suburbs grew at 2.5 times the national growth rate from 1971 to 1976.[10]

It is not our aim to pursue further these tendencies of metropolitan decline and shift. However, in conjunction with the picture of small-town persistence already sketched out in this chapter, and elaborated on in succeeding chapters, a more complete backdrop of contemporary settlement dynamics is provided for Canada. At a glance, the array of changes occurring in our settlement system is increasingly difficult to explain with the available theories and concepts about urbanization. It is only now coming to be realized that settlement systems are not "programmed" to reach some predetermined target where, say, 80 percent of the population live in the five largest metropolitan areas. There is, clearly, the tendency for settlement systems to become progressively transformed over time, but the outcomes of subsequent stages become more and more difficult to predict as human activities and societies become more complex.[11] As both the extent and the means of interactions expand, as the innovations produced by technological and social change are adopted and adapted, further changes are stimulated in a mutuality of cause and effect.

The transformations are experienced in our settlement systems just as elsewhere in society.

It is our contention that both the urban and the small-town tendencies are two facets of the same social phenomenon. To put it another way, cities and small towns, metropolitan and nonmetropolitan populations, are subject to the same milieu of activities, values, influences, pressures, and means of adjustment. The convergence of social and cultural indices of small-town and city populations over the past several decades, which we describe in the third chapter, is clear evidence in itself that the search for explanations should encompass both urban *and* nonurban tendencies. The arbitrary distinction of urban/rural, whether based on locational or social attributes, is no longer appropriate for theory or for policy.[12]

5. SMALL CENTERS AND SETTLEMENT POLICY

Interest in a national policy for our cities, which was so prominent in the 1960s, somewhat subsided as urban growth dampened and many urban problems were dealt with. As supplies of energy became of increasing national importance in the mid-1970s, settlement patterns came under scrutiny, especially those of low-density rural regions.[13] Neither the plight nor the potential of small centers came into sharp focus in the debate over settlement policy, presumably because they weren't considered to be *urban*. If the settlement pattern again becomes a national concern in the debate over energy supplies, one may usefully reflect on whether, and to what degree, towns and villages need to be considered in any national settlement policy.

A variety of urban issues stimulated the earlier call for an urban policy, but as cogent as any was, as Bourne and Logan point out, "increasing metropolitan concentration combined with rural depopulation."[14] Concern over the quality of life at both ends of the settlement array was thus encompassed, but debate ebbed and flowed around whether the means to be used should be "growth management" of urban areas or regional development policy.[15] Our probes now show that towns and villages constitute a significant and stable form of habitat for Canadians and that urban characteristics, norms, and tastes prevail among people who reside in towns and villages. Towns and villages are, therefore, an integral part of the system of urban centers of Canada that facilitates the delivery of material and social welfare benefits to individuals in this country. They have to be included in any settlement policy debate, but their special locational and size situations also need to be accommodated in the debate.

Foremost, towns and villages are at the "outer end" of the national and provincial delivery systems. As such they suffer from a *lack of variety* in private and public goods and services, and *less than reliable* means for delivering them. Even where individual needs are relatively well-served, very often community needs are not. Many seemingly mundane problems plague small centers. Towns and villages, along with their neighboring rural areas, often "put up with" low levels of service or do without many public and private services that city dwellers take for granted. An extensive list of these meager rural services can be compiled, but a few of the categories are: fire protection, ambulance service, libraries, medical doctors, legal services, garbage collection, and street lighting.

Again, Harry Lash offers a useful place to begin considering a policy stance for towns and villages. He suggests the following primary objective for a national settlement policy:

> To bring about a settlement pattern that will give every Canadian the opportunity, if he wishes it, to enjoy the advantages that *the City* offers for his personal development, while minimizing the impediments that living in *urban centres* puts in the way of that development.[16]

This objective has two facets in regard to small-towns' policy. On the one hand, Canadians residing in towns and villages currently enjoy many of the "advantages" of the city but they are at the mercy of market forces and the bureaucratic filtering-down of urban-type policies and standards. On the other hand, while townspeople and villagers may not suffer the "impediments" of urban centers, they suffer from the impediments peculiar to small places. A small-towns' policy must make the link between each of these facets. First, it must take advantage of towns and villages being "plugged into" the urban system while not making them like, or turning them into, urban centers. Second, it must sustain and improve the living conditions of small communities.

Towns and villages are becoming urban in attitudes and activities, in most instances, not through "growth" but through being within *effective range* of cities. Improvements in the technology of communications and transportation and in their costs to residents of small centers in the past three decades are, as much as anything, responsible for integrating towns and villages into the national urban system. The critical areas of improvement were the rural road network, public telephone service, and electrical energy distribution. Although much has been done, there is still room for improvement in increasing the variety of transportation and communications options and in promoting greater reliability of service. We shall return to this issue in the final chapter and make specific suggestions regarding towns and villages in Canadian settlement policy.

6. STUDYING TOWNS AND VILLAGES: THE NEED FOR A NEW BEGINNING

This study has few direct antecedents. The customary approach of most studies of small-town trends has been to assume that the future of small towns was none too bright. These prognoses were usually based on observations of rural depopulation due to mechanization and centralization of primary production activities and the consequent decline of the commercial sector in many small towns. Thus, the accepted approach became the analysis of the strength of the town's commercial establishments. The latter, according to the traditional wisdom of central place theory, was the *raison d'être* of a center. But while the forces of change did continue to rationalize primary production in nonmetropolitan parts of Canada, small centers in these same regions showed a strong tendency to persist. Early probes provided new perspectives on the population, housing, and social characteristics of small towns and their citizens. Regardless of the conventional wisdom of the universal decline of the commercial base of small centers, towns and villages emerged as the choice of residence of a large number of Canadians (occupying many new houses, as well). Moreover, during the 1961-1971 decade it was found that close to half a million additional people had decided to call a small center "home." It seems better, therefore, to begin by acknowledging that towns and villages are a significant habitat for many Canadians.

Our approach puts the emphasis on the *people* — their numbers, characteristics, trends, and choices — rather than on the *stores* in small centers. A realistic assumption, we think, is that town and village residents have made an accommodation to the changing commercial scene in rural regions. Later probes (described more fully in Chapter 4) bear this out and also indicate that commercial decline may not be as extensive as once thought. Clearly, many people wish to maintain residence in a small community and are prepared to make the necessary "trade-offs," including, in recent years, to find ways to accommodate to higher energy costs for travel.

Charting the Study

The analytical ground this study covers is relatively uncharted. There is not, as far as we know, another nationwide study of contemporary towns and villages. There is, as well, little in the way of applicable theory about the current status of small centers. With few antecedents and little theory it was necessary for our analysis to be *inductive,* to *explore* conditions that prevail in small communities in Canada rather than *testing* hypotheses about them.

One parameter was necessary to initiate the study; this was the definition that would limit the communities to be examined. Thus, *towns and villages were felt to be included within an upper population limit of 10,000 persons.* The lower population limit was nominally 50 persons, although sometimes it was even lower. A prime criterion was that the center be recorded in the 1971 census.

It was assumed that a hierarchy of small centers existed: *towns,* those places with larger populations (up to 10,000) and more sophisticated functional arrangements; *villages*, with a small to medium-size population (up to 1,000) and a distinctive functional character; and *hamlets*, the smallest and least-developed concentrations of houses (population usually less than 100 persons). These definitions were not analytically applied, but rather were used in their commonly accepted meanings to convey a range of sizes of small communities. A special analysis in the study derived a number of specific measures to distinguish hamlets, villages, and towns; the population dimensions were essentially as stated above. *Urban settlements* were defined as those places with a population of more than 10,000, a definition slightly at odds with the census, but a more realistic view in our opinion. And, since towns and villages exist mostly outside the boundaries of Census Metropolitan Areas (CMAs), the areas where towns and villages are found have been termed *nonmetropolitan regions* (and sometimes nonurban or rural regions). Again, these latter terms are meant to be indicative rather than definitive.

It is appropriate to characterize the results of this study as a *mosaic* depicting town and village development in Canada in the 1970s. The elements of this mosaic derive to some degree from the data available. Data are not uniformly available for all the types of analysis one might wish to perform on small communities. The distinction that governs this availability most is that between *incorporated* (municipal) towns and villages and *unincorporated* (unorganized) small centers. For example, although there were nearly 9,500 towns and villages in Canada in 1976, for more than 80 percent of them there is no more than a simple population count recorded in the census for that year. The latter are almost all unincorporated.

Incorporated towns and villages, of which there are about 1,600, fall within the census category know as Census Subdivisions (CSDs). For these places there is available, theoretically, as much data as for our large cities. In practice, the data sources contain many errors and neither the full array of data nor the full number of small CSDs can be analyzed. However, it was felt that the small CSDs could be used as a valid sample to portray tendencies of all 9,500 towns and villages. The major difference between the sample of nearly 1,600 towns and villages and the total number of small places is that the latter has a higher proportion of smaller-population centers. Thus, it would be wise, when considering any of the analytical results deriving from the sample, to infer that the scale dimension is not as fully circumscribed as it might be. Though it is known that this difference does exist in the distribution by population size, the difference does not, in our opinion, seem to make a difference. In any case, there is no alternative but to accept the small CSDs as a sample if any analysis of towns and villages is to be pursued in depth.

Several other data bases had to be devised in order to delve into the nature of small-center population, economic base, physical development, community need, and so on. For the analysis of social and economic characteristics of all towns and villages we employed the broad categories of settlement types found in the census — rural farm, nonfarm, places of population 1,000-5,000, and so forth. While groupings cover all small centers, they are crude. One must, for example, subsume all villages and hamlets with populations less than 1,000 in the "nonfarm" category. Further, not all variables are defined in terms of the same settlement groups; some variables cannot be compared over time.

Special sample surveys of building statistics, questionnaire surveys of community attitudes, and a number of field studies are the sources of yet again different data. Although not statistically comparable with other facets of the study, they help to compose a reliable mosaic of Canadian towns and villages. The methods employed to obtain representative data on Canadian towns and villages are described in conjunction with the various findings.[17]

The Terrain of the Study

This study is a look at Canadian towns and villages as they appeared in a variety of perspectives during the 1970s and at many of the changes that occurred in them over the preceding decade or two. The next three chapters describe the scope, nature, and trends in town and village development. Chapter 2 is an extensive review of the population and its changes in small communities. From this chapter there emerges a picture of the stability and vitality of small centers as places to live in Canada. In Chapter 3 the discussion centers on the general question, what are the sources of income for residents of towns and villages? The opportunities for earning a livelihood in towns and villages are usually underestimated. The mix of economic activities in small centers, it turns out, is not too dissimilar from that in cities. Chapter 4 explores the regional milieux in which towns and villages participate, with the aim of determining the roles small centers currently play, their degree of dependency, and the influence of large nearby cities on them. What emerges rather strikingly is that conventional concepts of metropolitan dominance and spatial organization seem not to apply to the majority of towns and villages.

The following two chapters probe social aspects of Canadian towns and villages. Chapter 5 examines a wide array of social characteristics of the populations who live in large cities as well as in small towns and on farms. A progressive convergence of small-town characteristics with those we have come to accept as *urban* and found in big cities is the important finding of this analysis. The interpersonal relations, the power structure, and the quality of life of towns and villages is the subject of Chapter 6. It is in various aspects of community life that small communities show not only their differences from cities, but also the high degree of uniqueness among small places themselves.

The physical environment and the small community's needs for services and programs are examined in Chapters 7-9. The trends in housing development in towns and villages described in Chapter 7 show a remarkable vigor, with new dwelling units increasing at a rate more than twice as fast as the population in the average small town. Chapter 8's probes of the needs expressed by town and village residents show a modest agenda, but still many unsatisfied needs. This latter theme is carried on in Chapter 9, with the emphasis being placed on the role of community planning in satisfying community needs. Shortcomings in current planning programs and practice in regard to towns and villages suggest the need for more appropriate planning tools.

Finally, Chapter 10 provides an overview of the findings of the study and addresses their implications for policy makers. The importance of maintaining viable towns and villages in the settlement framework of Canada is a main theme of this chapter and of the entire book.

NOTES

1. As cited in Hans Blumenfeld, "Continuity and Change in Urban Form," in Larry S. Bourne, ed., *Internal Structure of the City*, 2nd ed. (New York: Oxford University Press, 1982), 47-56.
2. Douglass C. North, "Location Theory and Regional Economic Growth," *Journal of Political Economy* 67 (June 1955): 243-58.
3. This is analogous to the extension of the "vertical" dimension of community so cogently defined in Roland Warren, "Towards a Reformulation of Community Theory," in R. Warren, ed., *Perspective on the American Community* (Chicago: Rand McNally, 1966), 69-78.
4. Harry Lash, "Where Do We Start On a National Settlement Policy," *Plan Canada* 16:2 (June 1976): 94-101.
5. The evocative term "staying power" in reference to small towns is derived from Lloyd H. Douglas and Scott Shelley, *Community Staying Power*, Research Publication 171 (Manhattan, Kansas: Kansas State University, Agricultural Experiment Station, February 1977).
6. David Feldbreugge, "Newburgh, Ontario: An Historical Analysis of Village Growth" (Unpublished Master's Report, Queen's University School of Urban and Regional Planning, 1977).
7. There is a good deal of correspondence between the development history of Newburgh and that postulated in three major works on urbanization: John Friedmann, *Regional Development Policy* (Cambridge, Mass.: M.I.T. Press, 1966); C.F.J. Whebell, "Corridors: A Theory of Urban Systems," *Annals of the Association of American Geographers* 59:1 (March 1969); and Jacob Spelt, *Urban Development in South-Central Ontario* (Toronto: McClelland and Stewart, 1972).
8. *Cf.*, Norman T. Moline, *Mobility and the Small Town, 1900-1930*, Research Paper No. 132 (Chicago: University of Chicago Department of Geography, 1971).
9. Brian J.L. Berry, ed., *Urbanization and Counterurbanization* (London: Sage, 1976). See also his "The Counter-Urbanization Process: How General?" in N. Hansen, ed., *Human Settlement Systems* (Cambridge, Mass.: Ballinger, 1978),

25-50; and George Sternlieb and William Hughes, "New Regional and Metropolitan Realities for America," *Journal of the American Institute of Planners* 43 (July 1977): 227-41.

10. The leading research in Canada is reported in Larry S. Bourne, "Some Myths of Canadian Urbanization: Reflections on the 1976 Census and Beyond," *Urbanism Past and Present* 5 (Winter 1977): 1-11; R. Parenteau, "The 1981 Census and the Canadian Population" (Paper presented at the Conference on Urban Exodus, University of Montreal, April 1982); Ira M. Robinson, *Canadian Urban Growth Trends: Implications for a National Settlements Policy* (Vancouver: University of British Columbia Press, 1981); and Leroy O. Stone, "Small Community Aspects of Demographic Processes in a Steady State Economy," in *Proceedings of the Conference on Approaches to Rural Development* (Guelph: University of Guelph, 1981), 110-29.

11. See, for example, Edgar M. Dunn, *The Development of the U.S. Urban System* (Baltimore: Johns Hopkins University Press for Resources for the Future, 1980); and Alan R. Pred, *Urban Growth and City-Systems in the United States, 1840-1960* (Cambridge, Mass.: Harvard University Press, 1980).

12. *Cf.*, Gerald Hodge, "Canadian Small Town Renascence: Implications for Settlement System Concepts," *Regional Studies* 17:1 (1983) 19-28.

13. Peter Boothroyd, "The Energy Crisis and Future Urban Form in Alberta," *Plan Canada* 16 (September-December 1976): 118-34.

14. L.S. Bourne and M.I. Logan, "Changing Urbanization Patterns at the Margin: The Examples of Australia and Canada," in Brian J.L. Berry, ed., *Urbanization and Counter-Urbanization* (London: Sage, 1976), 111-43.

15. *Cf.*, Reg. Lang, "Oh Canada, A National Urban Policy?" *Plan Canada* 12: 1 (July 1972): 13-32.

16. Lash, *op. cit.*

17. The report is, of course, a compilation of many detailed studies of different aspects of Canadian towns and villages. In carrying out these studies the authors commissioned several technical studies by graduate students in the School of Urban and Regional Planning at Queen's University. The technical studies are in the form of Master's Reports. The work of these assistant researchers helped to extend our analyses significantly, and to enlarge our knowledge of towns and villages. The authors and titles follow: Donald Nijsse, "Recent Physical Development in Small Towns and Villages in Canada" (1976); Lesley Paterson and Patricia Malone, "Small Towns and Villages in Canada and Population Stability" (1977); David Feldbruegge, "Newburgh, Ontario: An Historical Analysis of Village Growth" (1977); and John Blakney, "Planning for Small Rural Communities: A Case Study of Hunter River, P.E.I." (1977).

2 The Persistence of Small Towns

A study of population is basic to one's understanding of communities of any size. Almost the first question people will ask about a place they are not familiar with is: "How big is it?" This doesn't mean its area; it means, of course, its population size. From the answer received, people will be in a position to form a picture of the community's commerce, social fabric and, possibly in their mind's eye, an image of the place. A closely related question will concern the growth, again meaning the population growth, of the place; for people are interested in a community's prospects. Using the experience of their own or of other communities, people are often implicitly asking: Is it a good place to live? How does it compare with my community? What are the prospects for a place like this?

While we cannot answer these personal questions, this chapter provides an overview of town and village development in Canada during the 1970s. By using the data on numbers and sizes of towns and villages and their population growth experience, there will be a broad basis for comparison among small communities throughout Canada. There has been such a dismal picture painted of the prospects for small communities (mostly by big-city media) that there is often a sense of urgency when small-towners ask the above questions. If anything, the picture of town and village population presented here should be reassuring to them. It is a picture of persistence, of the staying power of small communities.

1. THE SCOPE OF TOWN AND VILLAGE DEVELOPMENT

There are almost 9,500 towns and villages located throughout Canada and, in 1976, nearly 4.5 million people lived in them. Putting it another way, close to one-fifth of the nation's population lives in small communities that are no larger than 10,000 persons in size. The average size of these small-town habitats is just under 500 persons, but, as we shall see later, the majority of Canada's towns and villages actually have fewer than 200 residents. Moreover, small-town living is not a fading phenomenon; more people lived in towns and villages in 1976 than at any other time in the past.

Number of Small Towns in Canada in 1976 and Their Population

Number of Small Towns	Population in Small Towns	Average Small-Town Population	Percentage of Total Population in Towns
9,457	4,471,310	473	19.4

SOURCE: *Census of Canada*

Canada's 9,500 small communities are a pervasive form of settlement across the country. The second-largest and most urbanized province, Ontario, has the largest number of small centers, almost 1,800, while one of the smallest provinces, Nova Scotia, has over 1,500 towns and villages. The Atlantic Provinces (Newfoundland, Prince Edward Island, Nova Scotia, and New Brunswick) contain 3,700 towns and villages, or 40 percent of the nation's total. This is consistent with the much finer-grain settlement pattern and resource endowment of the Atlantic Region with its small-scale fisheries, mining, and agricultural activities. The towns are also, on the average, smaller in this region. Even in the less-densely settled western provinces (Manitoba, Saskatchewan, Alberta, and British Columbia), where nonurban resource development is characterized by large-scale agriculture, forestry, and mineral production, there are over 2,200 small centers (Table 2.1).*

The inventory of towns and villages in Canada includes both those with municipal status and those without it. The former, of which there are 1,593, are called *incorporated* centers; they possess their own local government structure. The majority of small centers, while being identifiable clusters of population, houses, and businesses, do not have their own local government but are governed by a larger surrounding territory such as a township or a county. They are, thus, called *unincorporated* centers; there are 7,864 of them. The most discernible difference between these two types is that incorporated centers are generally larger in population and tend to perform as a group, as the larger towns and villages do. Otherwise, on an individual basis, there is little to distinguish them other than their ability to govern themselves.

A highway map of any province will show just how widespread towns and villages are. A map of Saskatchewan centers is included for comparison. But to grasp more firmly how pervasive small centers are, one may calculate their *nominal* spacing in a few provinces with different settlement characteristics.[1] In Prince Edward Island, for example, towns and villages will be found nominally three miles apart. In Southern Ontario, the small centers are just over six miles apart; while in Saskatchewan's settled portion, towns and villages are twelve miles apart.

---

* All numbered tables appear at the end of this chapter.

FIGURE 2.1
Distribution of Towns and Villages in Saskatchewan, 1961

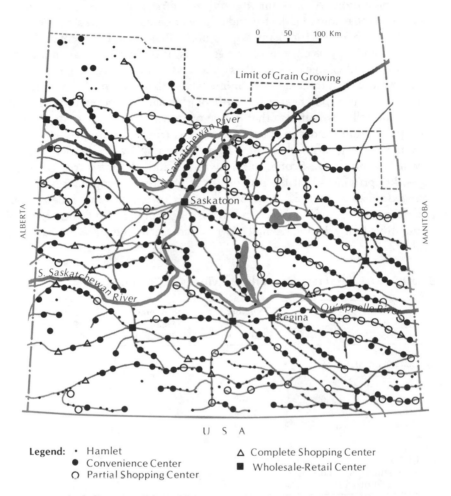

Legend: • Hamlet
         ● Convenience Center   △ Complete Shopping Center
         ○ Partial Shopping Center   ■ Wholesale-Retail Center

These relatively dense and generously distributed sets of small centers are a reflection of the settlement tendencies of the nineteenth and early-twentieth centuries. Most of today's towns and villages are found at locations that were once selected as nodal points to serve a local area's fishing, agriculture, mining, or forestry activities. They were the supply sources for producers, and outlets to markets. The more area that was developed, the greater the number of towns needed. If the area prospered from its resource development, some towns would grow apace. But since our settlement period ended, for all intents, by 1930, the rationale of extending resource-development regions has ceased as a basis for town and village development. The northern frontier is, of course, the exception. In some areas the original resource developments have become obsolete, and in others new technologies have meant that fewer people are involved in their exploitation. As a result, the *raison d'être* of providing commercial services to the resource industry and other residents of the area has declined or even disappeared for many towns and villages. But the communities remain, some only as clusters of homes; thus, it is likely there are not many fewer town and village communities today than half a century ago.

After more than three decades of intensive urbanization, the 1976 census reveals not only that nearly one-fifth of the nation's population lives in towns and villages, but also that in five provinces, one-quarter or more of their population resides in small centers. It is true these are provinces that lack many very large cities — Saskatchewan, New Brunswick, Prince Edward Island, Nova Scotia, and Newfoundland. It is also true for these and other provinces that the proportion of small-town population has not changed much since 1961 (New Brunswick is the exception). Indeed, four provinces (including Quebec and British Columbia) saw the share of population living in their small towns increase in the past two decades (Table 2.2).

Small-Town Characteristics in the Provinces of Canada, 1976

	Number of Small Towns	Average Small-Town Population	Percentage of Population in Towns
Newfoundland	617	425	47.1
Prince Edward Island	409	194	67.2
Nova Scotia	1,541	271	50.4
New Brunswick	1,132	199	33.2
Quebec	1,705	719	19.7
Ontario	1,794	603	13.1
Manitoba	359	472	16.6
Saskatchewan	660	391	28.0
Alberta	530	641	18.7
British Columbia (including the Yukon and Northwest Territories)	710	573	16.1

SOURCE: Tables 2.1, 2.2

One other facet of town and village development is the array of sizes of their populations. Using a set of eight population size categories reveals that just under one-third of all towns and villages in 1976 had less than 100 inhabitants and four-fifths had less than 500. The proportion of the small-center population accounted for by the places under 500 in size was, however, only 28 percent of the nation's town and village inhabitants. Small centers with more than 1,000 residents in 1976, of which there were nearly 900, contained the bulk of the town and village population, or 58 percent of the total (Table 2.3).

Number of Towns and Villages of Different Sizes in Canada, 1976

			Population Size				
Under 100	101-200	201-300	301-500	501-1,000	1,001-2,500	2,501-5,000	5,001-10,000
3,084	2,323	1,155	1,087	914	539	220	135

SOURCE: Table 2.3

The size distribution of centers varies somewhat among provinces. The four Atlantic Provinces have larger proportions of small centers and fewer large towns. Ontario and Quebec have the opposite sort of profile, with considerably more large towns and proportionately fewer small centers than the average. The four western provinces have slightly more small places and slightly fewer large towns when compared with the national distribution.

2. POPULATION CHANGE IN TOWNS AND VILLAGES, 1961-1976

The total population of Canada's towns and villages increased by nearly three-quarters of a million people between 1961 and 1976. This represents an increase of over 19 percent in that fifteen-year period. In the two decades prior to 1961, small-town population grew hardly at all in any part of Canada; in many regions it declined. This reversal of trends is noteworthy not only for the scale of growth it represents but also for the constancy of the new trends. In each of the three five-year periods from 1961 to 1976 the census recorded around 240,000 persons added to the small-center totals. Preliminary indications from the 1981 census are that a similar increment was added from 1976 to 1981. This would mean that the town and village population in Canada has grown by *one million* people, or more than 25 percent, in the past twenty years.

Changes in the Population Living in Canadian Towns and Villages, 1961-1976

	Total Population	Change in Numbers	Average Annual Percentage Change
1961	3,749,278	—	—
1966	3,985,483	236,205	1.26
1971	4,232,300	246,817	1.24
1976	4,471,310	239,010	1.14

SOURCE: Table 2.4

Looking at these trends by province shows that several provinces had small-center population growth rates in excess of the national growth rate for towns and villages. In the 1961-1971 decade, Newfoundland, Ontario, Alberta, and British Columbia had higher-than-average town and village growth rates. In the first five years of the 1970s, these four provinces repeated their above-average performances and were joined by Quebec. Only one province, Saskatchewan, saw its town and village population decline in the 1961-1971 period; this continued into the 1970s, but at a much-reduced rate. Two other provinces lost town and village populations between 1971 and 1976: Nova Scotia was down by less than one percent, but New Brunswick suffered a seven percent drop (Table 2.4).

(These observations, it should be emphasized, apply to the small communities in the province *as a group*. There is tremendous variation among the centers in every province, some experiencing rapid growth while others stay relatively stable or decline. These variations are discussed in more detail in Section 6 below.)

Nearly 4,800 of Canada's towns and villages added some population, or remained stable, from 1971 to 1976. That is, just over one-half of all the small centers either grew or sustained no population loss in this period. The same general trend was true for the decade of the 1960s with, again, just over 50 percent of the centers experiencing some growth or stability in their size. When one arrays the towns and villages by their different growth rates, for either the 1961-1971 or the 1971-1976 period, several points stand out. One is the large number of centers that grew by more than 30 percent — over 1,300 towns and villages — in just five years from 1971 to 1976. In the previous decade, it was found that more than 1,000 centers grew by more than 50 percent. It must also be acknowledged that a population decline of 10 percent or more was suffered by nearly one-third of all small places in the first half of the 1970s. But, looked at overall, 70 percent of all the towns and villages either grew or did not lose more than one-tenth of their population.

Distribution of Population Growth Rates Among Canadian Towns and Villages, 1971-1976

Percentage Change	Number of Towns	Percentage of Towns
over + 30.0	1,362	14.4
20.0 to 29.9	605	6.4
10.0 to 19.9	1,031	10.9
5.0 to 9.9	728	7.7
0.0 to 4.9 Growth	1,003	10.6
−0.1 to −5.0 Decline	917	9.7
−5.1 to −10.0	889	9.4
−10.1 to −20.0	1,163	12.3
−20.1 to −30.0	699	7.4
over −30.0	1,060	11.2

SOURCE: *Census of Canada*

While the growth rates for small towns are substantial, it must be acknowledged that urban settlements grew faster over the 1961-1971 period. However, if one breaks the fifteen years into three parts and examines the quinquennial census figures for each, there is a remarkable difference in the population growth trends of small towns and urban centers. In the first half of the 1960s (1961-1966), urban places grew at over twice the rate of small towns. In the second half of the 1960s (1966-1971), urban growth rates began to decline, but were still double those rates for small towns. The growth rate for towns and villages increased very slightly during the latter period. But from 1971 to 1976, urban growth rates dropped dramatically — they were less than half what they had been in the previous five-year period. Indeed, urban and small-town growth rates were nearly equal for 1971-1976, and there are indications this was true through to 1981 as well. It is notable, therefore, that the population growth of small towns, although moderate, has maintained a steady level for nearly two decades. There seems to be little doubt that towns and villages are a vigorous element in Canada's contemporary settlement fabric.

Comparative Population Growth Rates for Canadian Urban Places and Small Towns by Five-Year Periods, 1961-1976

	Percentage Population Growth		
	1961-1966	1966-1971	1971-1976
Urban Places	15.9	11.4	5.8
Small Towns	6.3	6.6	5.7

SOURCE: *Census of Canada*

3. TOWN AND VILLAGE SIZE AND POPULATION GROWTH

Population growth was a common experience in all sizes of towns and villages in Canada. But the degree of growth was not the same in each category, and some fared better than others. For example, from 1961 to 1971 in five of the size categories, more towns grew than declined. The same was true for the 1971-1976 period. The towns with populations of between 100 and 500 persons had the greatest decline, whereas towns over 1,000 population had the greatest growth. Looked at from a slightly different perspective, there were fewer people living in centers of less than 100 population, 101 to 200 population, and 301 to 500 population in 1976 than there had been in 1971. Indeed, there were substantially fewer centers in the latter two categories in 1976 than five years earlier (Table 2.5).

Percentage Change in Numbers of People Living in Canadian Towns and Villages of Different Sizes, 1971-1976

				Population Size			
0-100	101-200	201-300	301-500	501-1,000	1,001-2,500	2,501-5,000	5,001-10,000
-0.7%	-5.3%	1.9%	-5.2%	3.8%	1.8%	4.9%	25.7%

SOURCE: *Census of Canada*

Behind these general tendencies is a diversity of patterns of growth and decline within the various size categories. Centers of less than 500 population had the greatest difficulty in maintaining their previous population levels, but even here between 20 and 30 percent of centers in these classes grew by over 15 percent in only five years (from 1971 to 1976). Conversely, between 35 and 45 percent of larger towns of over 1,000 population lost up to 15 percent of their 1971 residents by 1976. Nevertheless, the modal growth rate for centers with 500 or more residents in 1971 was positive, with a between 6 and 15 percent increase (Table 2.6).

Further probing of population changes in different sizes of towns and villages offers little further illumination in this matter. It is clear, however, that the many instances of substantial growth as well as decline contribute to shifts both in the number of towns in each size class and in their aggregate population levels. Thus, major decline suffered in the 101-200 category shows up in the increase of towns of less than 100 population, to cite one instance. Also clear is the fact that each size class and, more so, each size category within it contains a diversity of centers not only from different regions in the country but also with different economic orientations and cultural backgrounds. The closer one gets to examining the growth performance of individual towns and villages, the more unique the population trends are likely to be. More will be said about this at the end of this chapter.

4. PROVINCIAL PATTERNS OF TOWN AND VILLAGE GROWTH

As one would expect from the foregoing section, those provinces whose towns and villages tend to be smaller on the average would have a greater proportion of small centers experiencing population decline. This is generally true both in the 1960s and the first half of the 1970s. Prince Edward Island and New Brunswick in the east, and Saskatchewan in the west, follow this pattern and saw well over half of their towns and villages decline in population to some degree in the fifteen-year period. An exception is Nova Scotia, whose centers also tend to be smaller on the average, but which had more centers growing than declining. Manitoba is another exception, with a high proportion of decline among its towns and villages even though they are larger on the average (Table 2.7).

If we look at these same tendencies using a finer geographical breakdown, and portrayed on a map, the provincial patterns become more distinct. The map for the 1961-1971 period (Figure 2.2) utilizes Census Divisions within provinces to display the proportions of growing and declining centers. There is, notably, the experience of widespread decline among towns and villages in a region extending from southeastern Alberta, through most of southern Saskatchewan, to western Manitoba. New Brunswick, Prince Edward Island, and western Nova Scotia fared similarly.

Two other facets of these patterns should be recognized, however. First, even within the regions of substantial decline among centers there are large areas (Census Divisions) showing more buoyant tendencies among their towns and villages. Before it is assumed that this might be due to the effects of metropolitan expansion, the same map will show that this provides little explanation. (This issue is explored thoroughly in Chapter 4.) The second facet is that within Census Divisions and provinces experiencing substantial decline, there are many small centers that have either grown or at least have not declined in population. Each of the categories of small-town decline on the map has a converse of small-town growth. Even where 60 percent of the towns and villages may have lost population, 40 percent of the small centers will have gained some population in that area.

Again, the diversity of rates of population growth we saw within different sizes of centers is also apparent within provinces. New Brunswick and Prince Edward Island, with high proportions of centers declining, also saw over one-fifth of their towns and villages grow by more than 15 percent in just five years from 1971 to 1976. One-sixth of Manitoba's small centers and one-eighth of Saskatchewan's also grew at this same high rate in the first half of the 1970s. At the same time, nearly 19 percent of Ontario's towns and villages declined in population by over 15 percent. And British Columbia experienced both extensive decline and extensive growth among its small centers (Table 2.8).

Finally, it is interesting to examine the relation between population growth in the various provinces and the growth of their towns, villages, and metropolitan areas. Typically, we have come to expect since World War II that provincial (and national) growth is due mainly to the growth of cities, especially the larger ones. In terms of numbers of people added to provincial totals, city growth is still responsible for most of the expansion into the 1970s, with the exception of Prince Edward Island. But in five provinces, from 1971 to 1976, the growth rate of small towns either equalled or exceeded the growth rate of the province. In four provinces, the small-town growth rate was higher than the metropolitan growth rate, including Alberta and British Columbia, each with very fast-growing metropolises (Table 2.9).

5. TOWN AND VILLAGE GROWTH INTO THE 1980s

A picture of population trends for towns and villages in the second half of the 1970s and the beginning of the 1980s may now be discerned from preliminary results of the latest (1981) census. In order to provide a comparable perspective with the data of previous sections, a sample of one hundred small centers across Canada is utilized. Although structured to reflect geographical and population size differences among towns and villages, the sample, of necessity, is limited to showing trends among the

FIGURE 2.2

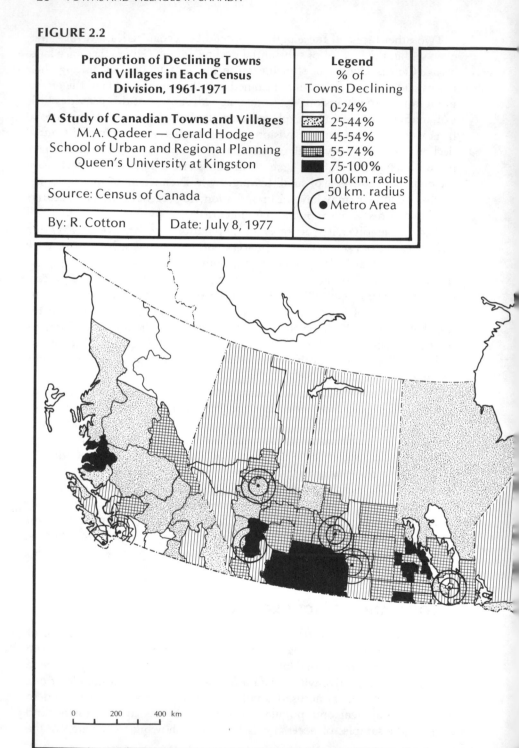

Proportion of Declining Towns and Villages in Each Census Division, 1961-1971	Legend % of Towns Declining
A Study of Canadian Towns and Villages M.A. Qadeer — Gerald Hodge School of Urban and Regional Planning Queen's University at Kingston	☐ 0-24% ▨ 25-44% ▥ 45-54% ▦ 55-74% ■ 75-100% 100 km. radius 50 km. radius ● Metro Area
Source: Census of Canada	
By: R. Cotton	Date: July 8, 1977

0   200   400 km

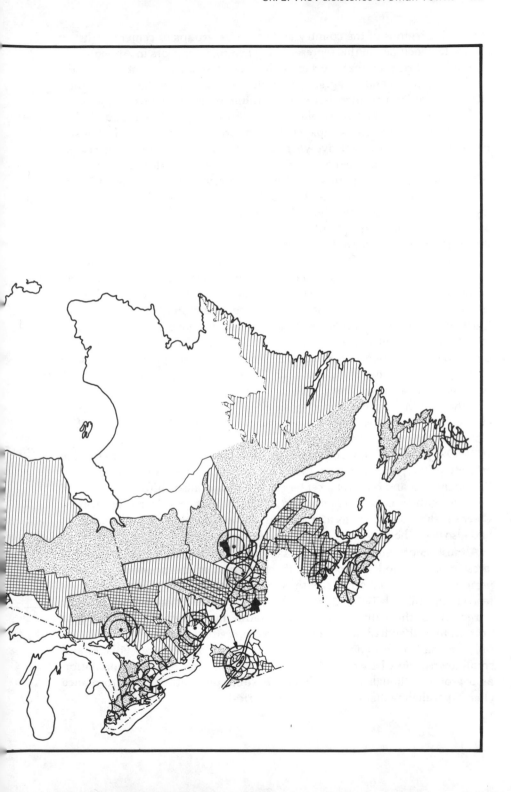

five major regions of the country and four size-groups of centers. A list of the centers included in this representative grouping appears in Appendix A, where it will be seen that the sample has fewer small-size centers than the total of all towns and villages. The results of any analyses may, therefore, slightly favor larger centers but still accurately reflect recent trends.

The general indications are of continued buoyancy of towns and villages from 1976 to 1981. The sample centers registered an increase of almost 8 percent in the most recent five-year census period. Since small-size centers are not as well represented and have weaker growth tendencies, it may be wise to discount this rate to some degree. However, it seems reasonable to assume that towns and villages equalled, or possibly slightly exceeded, the increase of 5.8 percent for the 1971-1976 period in the second half of the 1970s. On this basis, the populations of towns and villages as a group grew by a further one-quarter million from 1976 to 1981.

Among the regions of Canada in the 1976-1981 period, the Prairie Region (comprising Manitoba, Saskatchewan, and Alberta) towns and villages grew by nearly 19 percent. The small centers of the Atlantic Region (comprising the three Maritime Provinces and Newfoundland), along with Quebec and British Columbia, experienced less dramatic growth than those in the Prairies, but it was still substantial. Only Ontario's small centers declined in population as a group, and this by less than 1 percent. It is useful to keep in mind that the population of the entire country grew by 6.5 percent in the same five years.

If the data in the previous sections were grouped into the same regions as above, it could be shown that all regions, except Ontario and British Columbia, improved their town and village growth rates over those of the 1971-1976 period. It may be thought that the high rate for the Prairies is due entirely to the performance of Alberta centers, but this would not be true. Saskatchewan and Manitoba centers in the sample also showed substantial growth, with three-quarters of them experiencing some degree of growth. Over one-half of the towns and villages of the Atlantic Region declined, as had also been the case in the 1971-1976 period.

Almost 65 percent of the centers sampled added to their numbers in the latest census period, compared with 60 percent in the previous five-year period. As a group, centers with a population of less than 1,000 grew fastest, and those between 2,500 and 5,000 also had a high rate of growth. Large towns, those over 5,000 in size, had a much more moderate rate of growth than they had in any of the three preceding five-year periods, and only one-half of them actually increased in population. Large villages and small towns, those between 1,000 and 2,500 in size, decreased in population as a group, although two-thirds added some population, a performance closely paralleling that of the 1971-1976 period.

Recent Changes in Canadian Town and Village Population Levels, 1976-1981

	Percentage of Population Change	Proportion Growing
Region		
Atlantic	5.7	44.0
Quebec	5.5	75.1
Ontario	–0.1	47.1
Prairies	18.9	85.0
British Columbia	6.5	83.3
Size of Center		
Under 1,000	17.0	62.5
1,001-2,500	–0.9	64.5
2,501-5,000	11.4	76.2
5,001-10,000	7.6	50.1
100 Centers	7.9	64.4

SOURCE: *Census of Canada*

The data compiled for the one hundred centers provides a glimpse of what the 1980s seem to hold for towns and villages in Canada. The thrust of this preliminary evidence and of the more complete rendering of earlier sections is that towns and villages are viable. Small centers demonstrate that they are a significant and generally stable form of habitat in an otherwise highly urbanized, postindustrial nation.

6. THE NATURE OF TOWN AND VILLAGE PERSISTENCE

The persistence, or staying power, of small communities is clearly demonstrated for the nation as a whole and its broad-scale regions in the foregoing sections. But community persistence is a matter of individual centers surviving in their own subprovincial regions. The measure of population levels alone may not be sufficient to encompass the nature of town and village persistence. This concluding section will discuss how one's view of small-community viability is affected by seeing it through the perspective of population trends. Ways of obtaining a more complete view of town and village persistence are also explored.

Population and Persistence

The data that have been brought to bear regarding population changes in towns and villages in recent decades provide a limited view of the population dynamics of both the array of all small centers and of individual centers. One of the main limitations comes from our inability to deal with the *flows* of population in and out of small communities. Another comes from the inadequacy of the methods of comparing change in population, due to the small *size* of most towns and villages. Yet another is connected with the *time span* over which change in population is viewed. By examining each of these briefly the milieu of town and village persistence will be better understood. It is a complex phenomenon, as will be demonstrated.

First of all, with regard to *flows* of population: in every community in Canada, small or large, residents leave and newcomers arrive on a fairly frequent basis. However, there are no complete data available about these actual flows for use in deriving a picture of population change for all small communities. At best, the picture of population change attained when comparing a population count for one census year with that of a previous year is of the *net change*. It is, in other words, like a bank balance. Many population transactions may take place in any census period — births, deaths, as well as migrations — but all we know for certain is the net result. To take a distinctive small-town example, in a resource extraction center, there are usually large flows of population in and out, but the total population may register little or no change.

Some analysts maintain that a good measure of the viability of a place is whether it is growing at a pace equivalent to its own natural increase (the excess of births over deaths). This does not mean that a community is actually retaining its natural increase in population, and it will not satisfy the perennial concern of small-towners about their "young people having to leave." But it is an indication that a community could hold onto the increase due to its own population characteristics.

Data gathered by Canadian demographer Leroy Stone provides a partial rendering of current patterns. It indicates that the rate of natural increase for rural municipalities located more than forty-five miles from a metropolitan central city to be, on the average, 5.8 percent for the 1971-1976 period.[2] We know from the data for all towns and villages that their population growth rate was 5.7 percent in this same five-year period. From this it appears that most small towns are not quite able to "hold" their population; that is, more people must leave than enter to account for the difference. However, it must be emphasized that this conclusion is based on net changes and says nothing about *who* will be moving.

One striking feature of the picture of town and village persistence is provided by the latter data. There now appears to be nearly a balance in the inflow and outflow of population from small communities. This had not been the case for the three or four decades before 1961. The constancy of aggregate growth rates for small centers over the past two decades suggests that there is a basis in demographic tendencies for expecting the "staying power" of towns and villages to continue well into the future.

Second, regarding the *size* of centers and population change: in a broad-scale study of settlement change there needs to be a recognizable and reasonably precise basis of comparison. Percentage rates of change fit these criteria and were used throughout previous sections. But there is also the question of whether the base of comparison is realistic and germane. For describing aggregate trends as was done with *all* the centers in a province or in a size category it is probably sufficient. But within these aggregates, as we have noted, there is diversity in the growth experience of towns and villages in different regions, in different size groups, and in combinations of the two.

Percentage rates of change are used to offset the bias of size differences when making comparisons between centers. But when dealing with individual small centers, size may be a crucial factor in understanding changes. For example, it takes the addition of only five families to a village of 150 people to amount to as much as a 12 percent increase in population. This would be considered a healthy rate of growth over a ten-year period in comparison with other centers. However, it was only five families or, possibly, eighteen persons who were added. Thus, the absolute change is likely to be small in small centers even though the percentage rate is large. This raises the point about how best to express population changes in towns and villages. Underlying the analyses in this study is the position that any addition of population is an affirmation of the integrity of the small community as a place to live. There is much to commend some very general categories of population change, such as growth, stability, and decline, at least until much more is known about growth processes and their impact on towns and villages.

A third aspect is the *time span* over which population change is observed. As the interest in small communities is reasserted, various analyses of population trends are being offered, and more will come. There is an important reason why, in the case of towns and villages, the results of different analyses of population trends may seem disparate. It has to do with the great *variability* of actual growth performance as between individual centers over almost any period of time in the past few decades. The accompanying chart (Figure 2.3) plots the census counts for ten centers from 1961 through to 1981. The centers were chosen so as to include two places from each major region in Canada. The variability in their individual population growth performances is evident.

Three points must be made about this variability. First, it is easy to grasp how different the interpretation of population trends would be if the time span of the observations differed. Second, regardless of the time span chosen, any aggregation of centers by such criteria as size will contain a diversity of individual growth trends that may offset one another or reinforce an abberation, for example. Third, in reviewing many hundred centers' population tendencies, we are struck by the high incidence among Canadian towns and villages of *no predominant growth trends*. Over relatively long periods, fifteen or twenty years, a very high proportion of

FIGURE 2.3
Comparative Population Trends for Ten Towns and Villages, 1961-1981

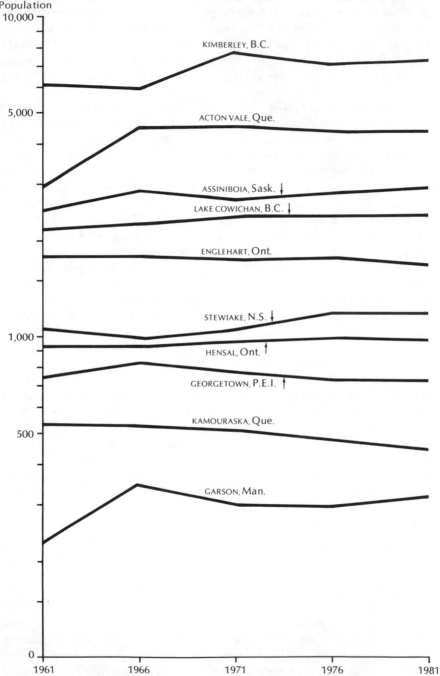

centers have individual population levels that either grew very little or declined very little. For upwards of one-third of all towns and villages, it is not realistic and possibly not germane to discuss their performance in terms of either growth *or* decline — they are essentially stable.

Other Indicators of Persistence

Population growth performance is the common measure of vitality of a town or city, but it is not the only measure. Two other indicators just as relevant for towns and villages are the change in commercial establishments and the growth in housing stock. Each of these is discussed more fully in Chapters 4 and 7 respectively; however, it will be useful to compare them briefly at this point with population growth. This will help enlarge the view of what is involved in the milieu of town and village persistence.

The national sample of one hundred small centers referred to earlier was used to record changes in both commercial establishments and in housing stock. The decade from 1971 to 1981 was chosen for each of the probes, and population data was gathered to match. Changes in commercial establishments are from counts obtained from Dun and Bradstreet data, from which only the number and type of firm can be discerned. Note was taken of changes in the total number of all commercial firms, as well as changes in the number of retail firms within this total. Changes in housing stock are from the national building statistics series. In the accompanying table, performance in these indicators is compared for each of the major regions of Canada and for the country as a whole.

Comparison of Changes in Population, Housing Stock, and Commercial Establishments in Canadian Towns and Villages, 1971-1981

| | Percentage Change in | | | |
	Population	Housing Stock	Retail Firms	Total Commercial Firms
CANADA	16.7	41.3	32.7	40.5
Atlantic	–0.2	17.5	31.3	40.1
Quebec	21.9	39.1	20.3	23.8
Ontario	1.2	27.7	11.2	16.2
Prairies	34.9	66.7	45.9	52.9
British Columbia	12.0	59.6	62.6	80.4

SOURCE: Tables 2.4, 4.2, 4.3, 7.1

These comparisons highlight three features of towns and villages at the present time. First, towns and villages are experiencing higher rates of growth in housing and commercial firms than in population in all regions of the country. Second, even in regions of low population growth in the past decade, as in Ontario and the Atlantic region, the small communities experienced substantial growth in housing and commerce. Third, there is considerable variability in the set of growth rates in the different regions. The latter two observations are a reflection of differences within individual centers, with some seeing their stores grow faster than their population or their housing stock, or *vice versa*, as well as many other combinations. Indeed, a simple correlation analysis of the data gathered for each center showed a very low degree of association between any of the pairs of variables (less than 10 percent of the variance accounted for).

One view of these findings might be that it seems peculiar that there is not a higher degree of coincidence of the components of growth. However, the variability must be examined in terms of individual town or village characteristics. Depending on the regional relations of a place (a subject discussed fully in Chapter 4), it plays different roles: it may be a shopping center for a surrounding area, or it may be a good place to live but shopping is done elsewhere. The economic growth, or lack of it in a region, may affect some components but not others. A community may possess a viable retail sector or an excess of housing and not need to grow even if demand increases.

The nature of town and village persistence is bound up in both the overall growth rates and the variability of individual cases. On the one hand, the growth rates for such things as housing and population are the net changes for all centers (the central tendencies in statistical terms) and represent the potential for growth or decline in which a center might share. On the other hand, the variability, or dispersion, of actual rates of change that individual centers experience within the housing, commercial, or population sectors represents their separate capacities to absorb change as well as the conditions existing within their own locales. The buoyant growth rates in all four sectors bode well for town and village persistence generally, and the various combinations of change indicate that the persistence of a particular place will be determined locally.

7. CONCLUSION

Despite the difficulties of realistically assessing either aggregate or individual small-center growth trends, there does appear ample reason to be optimistic about the present state and future prospects of towns and villages in Canada. Indeed, because of the complexities involved in making adequate comparisons, we have chosen to couch our optimism in terms of the *persistence* of towns and villages. This is, we believe, a valid view that can be applied generally to small centers. However, the form of this persistence for any particular center, which may even include decline in some periods or sectors, is a very individual matter. And it is to local people that the persistence of their community is ultimately important. The thrust of the analyses in this chapter is to establish that small communities need not start from a pessimistic point of view about their prospects.

NOTES

1. "Nominal spacing" is the distance that towns would be apart if each were located at the center of an area equal to the average number of square miles per town in the province (or the settled portion thereof).
2. The source and derivation of this rate is explained fully in Chapter 4.

TABLES/CHAPTER 2

TABLE 2.1

Number and Population of Canadian Towns and Villages, 1976

	Small Towns			
	Number	Percent	Total Population	Average Population
Newfoundland	617	6.5	262,224	425
Prince Edward Island	409	4.3	79,535	194
Nova Scotia	1,541	16.3	418,341	271
New Brunswick	1,132	12.0	225,293	199
Quebec	1,705	18.1	1,225,784	719
Ontario	1,794	18.9	1,081,224	603
Manitoba	359	3.8	169,553	472
Saskatchewan	660	7.0	258,302	391
Alberta	530	5.6	344,148	649
British Columbia*	710	7.5	406,906	573
CANADA	9,457	100.0	4,471,310	473

*Includes the Yukon and Northwest Territories

SOURCE: *Census of Canada*

TABLE 2.2

Proportion of Provincial Population Residing in Canadian Towns and Villages, 1961, 1971, 1976

	Percentage of Total Population Residing in Towns and Villages		
	1961	1971	1976
Newfoundland	44.1	46.6	47.1
Prince Edward Island	67.8	68.8	67.2
Nova Scotia	49.4	53.1	50.4
New Brunswick	39.6	38.1	33.2
Quebec	19.6	19.2	19.7
Ontario	14.5	13.1	13.1
Manitoba	17.1	16.6	16.6
Saskatchewan	29.6	28.3	28.0
Alberta	19.8	18.1	18.7
British Columbia*	15.0	16.0	16.1
CANADA	20.6	19.6	19.4

*Includes the Yukon and Northwest Territories

SOURCE: *Census of Canada*

TABLE 2.3
Distribution of Towns and Villages in Canada by Population Size, 1976

	Population		Towns	
	Numbers	Percent	Numbers	Percent
0-100	195,520	4.4	3,084	32.6
101-200	335,001	7.5	2,323	24.6
201-300	284,437	6.4	1,155	12.2
301-500	421,064	9.4	1,087	11.5
501-1,000	637,781	14.3	914	9.7
1,001-2,500	816,127	18.2	539	5.7
2,501-5,000	791,405	17.7	220	2.3
5,001-10,000	989,975	22.1	135	1.4
Total	4,471,310	100.0	9,457	100.0

SOURCE: Census of Canada

TABLE 2.4
Population Change in Canadian Towns and Villages, 1961-1976

	Total Population			Average Annual Population Change**	
	1961	1971	1976	1961-71	1971-76
Newfoundland	201,965	243,538	262,224	1.46	1.53
Prince Edward Island	71,307	77,085	79,535	0.59	0.64
Nova Scotia	363,710	418,761	418,341	0.51	-0.02
New Brunswick	236,857	242,107	225,293	0.03	-1.39
Quebec	1,028,628	1,158,808	1,225,784	1.25	1.16
Ontario	902,210	1,012,425	1,081,224	1.58	1.36
Manitoba	157,506	164,119	169,553	0.54	0.66
Saskatchewan	273,380	261,798	258,302	-0.42	-0.27
Alberta	264,249	295,181	344,148	1.99	3.32
British Columbia*	249,466	358,478	406,906	3.60	2.70
CANADA	3,749,278	4,232,300	4,471,310	1.29	1.14

SOURCE: Census of Canada   *Includes the Yukon and Northwest Territories
                                  **Arithmetic average of the growth rate of the period

TABLE 2.5
Proportion of Canadian Towns and Villages Experiencing Population Growth and Decline by Size of Place, 1961-1971, 1971-1976

	1961-1971		1971-1976	
Population Size	Growing	Declining	Growing	Declining
0-100	51.9	48.1	50.3	49.7
101-200	44.2	55.8	45.8	54.2
201-300	43.8	56.2	47.9	52.1
301-500	49.5	50.5	49.5	50.5
501-1,000	56.3	43.7	52.8	47.2
1,001-2,500	72.4	27.6	60.1	39.9
2,501-5,000	80.2	19.8	65.8	34.2
5,001-10,000	79.2	20.8	50.8	49.2
ALL SIZES	50.9	49.1	50.2	49.8

SOURCE: Census of Canada

TABLE 2.6

Distribution of Rates of Population Change Among Canadian Towns and Villages of Various Sizes, 1971-1976

Population Size, 1971	Rate of Decline				Rate of Growth				Total Percent
	over −25	−16 to −25	−6 to −15	0 to −5	0 to 5	6 to 15	16 to 25	over 25	
0-100	19.0	11.4	13.6	5.7	7.8	10.7	7.5	24.3	100.0
101-200	17.6	11.6	16.8	8.2	8.1	11.7	9.1	16.9	100.0
201-300	14.4	9.9	17.8	10.0	11.1	14.5	9.4	12.9	100.0
301-500	11.0	9.0	19.5	11.0	12.8	15.4	9.2	12.1	100.0
501-1,000	6.3	5.8	19.5	15.6	13.9	21.2	7.4	10.3	100.0
1,001-2,500	1.2	3.1	18.4	17.2	18.4	20.0	7.0	14.7	100.0
2,501-5,000	0.5	0.5	15.6	17.6	19.0	20.9	5.8	20.1	100.0
5,001-10,000	1.8	0.9	20.6	25.9	11.6	23.2	5.4	10.6	100.0

SOURCE: *Census of Canada*

TABLE 2.7

Proportion of Canadian Towns and Villages Experiencing Population Growth and Decline by Province, 1961-1971 and 1971-1976

	1961-1971		1971-1976	
	Growing	Declining	Growing	Declining
Newfoundland	52.2	47.8	63.7	36.3
Prince Edward Island	43.4	56.6	45.0	55.0
Nova Scotia	52.7	47.3	50.2	49.8
New Brunswick	42.0	58.0	37.6	62.4
Quebec	53.3	46.7	50.0	50.0
Ontario	62.3	37.7	57.4	42.6
Manitoba	39.0	61.0	44.2	55.8
Saskatchewan	31.3	68.7	33.4	66.6
Alberta	46.1	53.9	55.5	44.5
British Columbia*	61.9	38.1	57.1	42.9
CANADA	50.9	49.1	50.2	49.8

*Includes the Yukon and Northwest Territories

SOURCE: *Census of Canada*

TABLE 2.8

Distribution of Rates of Population Change Among Canadian Towns and Villages in Different Provinces, 1971-1976

	Rate of Decline			Rate of Growth					
	over −25	−16 to −25	−6 to −15	0 to −5	0 to 5	6 to 15	16 to 25	over 25	Total Percent
Newfoundland	6.4	6.1	15.7	8.1	15.1	20.6	13.3	14.7	100.0
Prince Edward Island	18.0	10.8	17.2	9.0	7.7	11.9	8.7	16.7	100.0
Nova Scotia	13.9	8.9	18.1	8.9	8.0	14.9	8.6	18.7	100.0
New Brunswick	28.0	13.1	14.5	6.8	7.0	9.5	8.8	12.3	100.0
Quebec	9.3	8.5	18.2	14.0	11.7	14.2	8.0	16.1	100.0
Ontario	11.0	7.8	14.4	9.4	12.0	14.6	8.4	22.4	100.0
Manitoba	13.6	9.8	20.8	11.6	12.4	13.3	7.2	11.3	100.0
Saskatchewan	16.7	15.0	24.0	10.9	11.1	11.1	3.9	7.3	100.0
Alberta	10.8	11.4	13.4	8.9	11.9	18.0	7.9	17.7	100.0
British Columbia*	17.2	7.3	11.5	6.9	9.3	11.5	8.0	28.3	100.0
CANADA	14.0	9.5	16.6	9.7	10.4	13.9	8.3	17.6	100.0

*Includes the Yukon and Northwest Territories

SOURCE: *Census of Canada*

TABLE 2.9

Comparison of Population Growth Rates 1971-1976 for Provinces, Metropolitan Areas, and Towns and Villages

	Average Annual Growth Rate 1971-76		
	Province	Metropolitan Area(s)	Small Towns
Newfoundland	1.4	1.7	1.5
Prince Edward Island	1.1	−0.3**	0.6
Nova Scotia	1.0	1.4	−0.02
New Brunswick	1.3	1.2	−1.4
Quebec	0.7	0.6	1.2
Ontario	1.5	1.5	1.4
Manitoba	0.7	1.0	0.7
Saskatchewan	−0.01	1.3	−0.3
Alberta	2.6	2.8	3.3
British Columbia*	2.6	1.7	2.7
CANADA	1.3	1.3	1.2

*Includes the Yukon and Northwest Territories
**Charlottetown Census Agglomeration

SOURCE: *Census of Canada*

3 Town and Village Economies

The persistence of towns and villages in Canada and their recent spurt of growth raise questions about the structure and performance of their economies. One is prompted to ask, what sort of job opportunities do these communities offer? How are incomes distributed? What are the economic bases of these communities? To answer these questions, the scale and mix of economic activities in these localities have to be analyzed, and incomes derived therefrom have to be examined. These are the problems addressed in this chapter.

1. ECONOMIC BASES OF SMALL COMMUNITIES

Historically, small towns and villages have served as trade and service centers for the surrounding countryside. Not only did farmers travel to such centers to market their produce, they also converged on them for supplies, medical help, information, education, amusement, and politicking. In the conventional sense of the term, goods and services exported from these centers constituted their economic bases and laid the ground for their role as the central places for surrounding areas. A general idea of the type and range of economic activities in the villages and towns of East-Central Alberta in the late 1940s is provided by Burnet. She remarks that "the villages were community centres after the ideal type of the agricultural village in North America . . . . They afforded a convenient gathering place, and such occasions for getting together as shows, concerts, dances, lectures, and sermons."[1] Among many services available in Oyen (pop. 400 in 1946), according to Burnet, were two large general stores, a dress shop, five implement dealers, three large garages, a branch of the Bank of Toronto, a flour mill, a first-class motion picture theater, a lumber yard, four churches, a new fully equipped hospital, and a large dormitory unit in conjunction with the high school.[2] Hanna (pop. 1,800 in 1950), a town on the rail line, was distinguished for establishments such as "big implement and automobile dealers, garages, two egg-grading plants, a liquor store . . . specialized dress stores . . . a Special Areas office, a courthouse. . . ."[3]

Today's small towns and villages would, on the surface, appear to be little different from Burnet's descriptions of thirty-five years ago. A small village usually has a grocery and hardware store, gas stations and, depending upon its setting, a feed depot, farmers' co-op, furniture barn, used-car lot, or a nursing home, but occasionally it might also have a tea house or a summer theater, if it is on the tourist's beat. A town might have a few supermarkets, fast-food outlets, department stores, banks, restaurants, motels, perhaps a hospital, industrial plants, and even such trendy establishments as health-food stores and video-game arcades. Yet there have been some notable changes since the late 1940s.

The small communities have been integrated into Corporate Canada. Franchises and chain stores have filtered down to villages. Esso and Shell signs beckon from cross-road hamlets, and Woolworths, Robinson Little, and Loblaws stores dot small-town main streets. Undoubtedly local businesses continue to thrive in these places, but even they have no regional fare to offer. These are signs of the weakening of lateral links between centers and the surrounding area on the one hand, and increasing vertical integration of economic activities on the other. A farmer orders supplies from, and trucks his produce to, a wider circuit of places. A household may stock monthly groceries from a discount suburban supermarket, its working members may commute to a plant in the open country, and its family doctor may be in a nearby resort town. These examples illustrate the fact that in contemporary times the centrality of small centers has been scrambled, and their links with the surrounding countryside and other settlements have taken variegated forms. Though continuing to be places of concentrated activities (and establishments), small communities are ceasing to be singular focal points for surrounding populations. This emerging spatial organization has been described as the "dispersed city," in that different centers have specialized in one or two functions and operate as elements of an interlinked system of places, usually places of equal standing.[4] Hart has vigorously argued that "traditional farm trading centers seem to be sorting themselves out into specialized centers dominated by one or a few activities" and he contends that there is no reason why this should be considered unusual. "City dwellers expect to live, work, and shop in different places, and they spend a fair portion of their time travelling from one functional area to another. Why should anyone expect dwellers in the country to be any different?"[5] It appears that small communities may still serve as trade and service centers, but they now have overlapping jurisdictions and operate more as poles of a magnetic field than as "capitals" of small regions.

Two or more centers and their intervening countryside constitute a spatial block for daily economic transactions. These blocks (or clusters of such units) constitute labor market areas for employment purposes. This is the situation at the base or lower limb of the urban hierarchy. Certainly towns and higher-level settlements retain a greater degree of centrality and functional specialization, but in settlements with a population of up to 10,000, dissipation of focus and the emergence of systems of interdependent centers are evident. For example, Dahms found that in Wellington County, Ontario, "it is possible to shop, work and live in spatially separate settlements linked by their mobile inhabitants. Access to economic functions within these places is often as convenient as access to work or shopping for residents of congested population areas."[6] From a sample survey of county residents, he found that their median commuting time was 43 minutes, and that they headed to 28 different destinations to work.[7] This dispersion of centrality contrasts with the increased complementarity of centers at present times.

Nucleated settlements of concentrated activities, much like villages and towns, are bound to be central places for some purposes. Yet, large numbers of small Canadian communities essentially have supra-local functions. They are the minetowns, milltowns, railtowns, resort places, and retirement villages of Canada. They exist not to serve the immediate area, but as production sites of commodities and services of national and even international demand. Elliot Lake (Ontario), Kitimat (British Columbia), and Churchill Falls (Labrador) are among the better-known examples of such towns.

As Canada's mineral resources are generally found in the north while its population is concentrated in a narrow band of territory along the southern border, it has an unusually large number of independent, single-industry communities on resource frontiers. Lucas suggests that there were 636 such communities in the late 1960s, accommodating about 903,401 people.[8] About one million people living in railtowns, minetowns, and milltowns constituted almost 30 percent of the population of small communities in Canada in the 1960s. The Department of Regional Economic Expansion estimates that in 1971 there were 811 single-industry communities in Canada, of which only 32 had populations greater than 10,000.[9] Given the estimate that in 1971, 3.8 millon people lived in towns and villages, about 24 percent of the population was living in single-industry communities essentially engaged in secondary-type activities. An idea of the economic bases of these communities can be obtained from Table 3.1.* Undoubtedly the table presents a partial picture of towns and villages, namely Single-Industry (SI) communities, where at least 30 percent of a locality's employment was concentrated in one industry. However, the summary table, below, does give an idea about the types of economic activities most commonly found in this segment of Canadian towns and villages.

---

*All numbered tables appear at the end of this chapter.

Dominant Activities in Canadian Single-Industry Towns and Villages,* 1971

	Manu-facturing	Mining and Refining	Dominant Activity Wood and Wood Products	Fish Processing	Public Administration	Other Industries
Percentage of Towns	6.4	16.6	37.7	16.8	8.2	15.2

*A total of 779 communities

SOURCE: Table 3.1

The two largest groups of SI communities specialized in wood products and fish processing — about 55 percent of the whole set. Metal mining and refining and public administration were the third- and fourth-ranking industries sustaining SI communities. This brief review of the economies of SI communities, a segment of towns and villages, illustrates that the processing of natural resources and administrative activities have come to be the predominant economic activity. Primary production plays an insignificant role in the economic life of these towns and villages. But do the other towns and villages manifest similar patterns? To answer this question we turn to census data. The cross-sectional profile of Canada's labor force in Table 3.2 reveals some interesting facts about the national economic structure and about the economic bases of small communities. The striking fact revealed by the table is that there was a relative uniformity across the Canadian settlement system regarding the labor force's industrial pursuits.

To the extent that the industrial distribution of labor is an index of the economic structure of an area, it appears that small towns are almost indifferentiable from big cities. The rural farm, being more of a sector than a settlement type, may be set aside. On comparing industrial distribution of the labor force in towns and villages with corresponding data for cities, a fair degree of correspondence between the two types of settlements can be observed.

The proportion of the labor force engaged in manufacturing was about 18 percent in towns of less than 5,000, it reached a peak of 24 percent for middle-sized cities (30,001-100,000), and then slid back to 19 percent for metropolises. The variation in these proportions is small, and fluctuates neither directly nor indirectly in relation to the size of settlements. It could, therefore, be inferred that the manufacturing employment was almost uniform across the Canadian settlement system. The mining activities were concentrated in small towns as indicated by a greater concentration of the labor force in such places. Trade and finance on the one hand, and community business and services on the other, are activities manifesting direct relationships between the proportion of labor force thus engaged and the size of settlements. It must be noted that ranges of variation of proportions for trade, business, and services are very narrow, namely up to five percentage points — excluding the rural sector. All in all, the labor force's industrial distribution has a very narrow range of variation approaching a constant in some sectors. Such relative uniformity of the economic activities of the labor force suggests an overall convergence towards uniform economic structures across the Canadian settlement spectrum. This characteristic has been observed in other western industrialized societies. Table 3.2 also suggests that small communities are not merely places of primary production; they have a wide variety and mix of activities. This is the generalized conclusion deducible from aggregated national data. It does not preclude provincial and regional variations, or elements of uniqueness among individual towns and villages. To observe such differences and to systematically examine economic bases of towns and villages, we have computed Location Quotients for settlements of different sizes by provinces (Table 3.3).

A Location Quotient (LQ) is a succinct measure of an area's economic base.[10] LQs reported in Table 3.3 have been computed by using provincial data for labor-force distribution by industries as denominators. An LQ value of more than 1 represents a relative specialization of an area in activities listed at the head of the column, and *vice versa*. Overall, Table 3.3 suggests that Canadian towns and villages specialized in mining as well as in manufacturing activities. This can be inferred by looking down columns 1 and 2 of the table and noting that LQs in these columns are mainly greater than 1. Trade, business, and public administrative services seem to play secondary roles in the economic bases of small communities. Closer examination of provincial LQs reveals significant regional peculiarities. In Newfoundland, centers with a population of less than 5,000 specialized in mining and manufacturing, whereas the economies of towns of 5,001-10,000 population were based on administrative activities and to a lesser extent on trade and personal services. The nonfarm countryside and hamlets were notably below provincial norms (indicated by LQs significantly less than 1), with the singular exception of manufacturing.

Prince Edward Island's hamlets and villages specialized primarily in manufacturing, although among villages and towns of less than 5,000, a modest concentration of trade and service activities are evident (LQs 1.21 and 1.08 respectively).

The economic bases of Nova Scotia's nonfarm countryside, and of hamlets and villages of less than 5,000, were essentially comprised of manufacturing activities (LQs 1.22 and 1.36 respectively), while towns with populations of 5,001-10,000 specialized in trade, services, and public administration. New Brunswick's towns and villages and even its countryside specialized in manufacturing. The countryside and small villages were venues of mining activities, while economic bases of towns of 5,001-10,000 were significantly strengthened by administrative activities.

Economies of towns and villages in the Atlantic Provinces manifested a well-defined pattern in 1971. Manufacturing was the most common basic activity, with mining following closely behind. Towns of a relatively larger size (5,001-10,000) also served as centers of administrative, educational, and health services, but trade and transportation activities seldom amounted to a specialty in local economies.

Quebec and Ontario, the two most populous and industrialized provinces, manifest similarities in the economic bases of their small communities. In both provinces, towns and villages of all sizes had significantly high LQs for mining and mineral processing, thus indicating a high degree of specialization in these sectors. Towns with a population of 5,001-10,000 also had a mild concentration of service and administrative activities.

Towns and villages in the Prairie Provinces had two divergent sets of activities constituting their economic bases. On the one hand, mining was the predominant economic activity for all centers in Manitoba, Saskatchewan, and Alberta — except in Manitoba towns of 5,001-10,000, where mining was almost nonexistent; on the other hand, trade and service activities, which have historically defined prairie service centers, also dominated the economic bases in towns. British Columbia's towns and villages were primarily mining centers with a sprinkling of manufacturing activities.

All in all, it appears that mining and manufacturing were the staples of town and village economies everywhere in Canada, and that regional variations were manifested by the contribution of other activities to the economic bases. Towns and villages of the Atlantic Provinces and Central Canada also served as administrative and health and educational centers, particularly the relatively larger towns; while in the Prairie Provinces, small communities came closest to playing the conventional roles of trade and service centers.

2. ECONOMIC TYPOLOGY OF TOWNS AND VILLAGES

By now we have a fairly good idea of the economic bases of towns and villages; however, a bit of further probing to elaborate upon the economic differences among small communities of varying sizes may be fruitful. With this objective in mind, we assembled a data set of socioeconomic variables about Census Subdivisions designated as towns and villages. There were 1,582 such towns and villages for which separate information was available from Census Subdivision data tapes, but the total varied according to the variable being examined. Obviously the unincorporated places were not in this data, but usually such places are of small size, having less than 500 persons. There is no reason to expect that the industrial distribution of the resident labor force in unincorporated places would be significantly different from the corresponding distribution for incorporated villages of similar sizes. With this assumption, we proceeded to look for distinguishable patterns of economic activity in small towns and villages of varying sizes.

National Labor-Force Distribution by Industrial Sectors, Canada, 1971

Sector	Percentage of Labor Force
Primary	8.4
Secondary	33.8
Tertiary	49.9
Unspecified	7.9

SOURCE: *Census of Canada*

Using the national labor-force distribution as "minimum requirements" to measure the economic bases of centers, we can classify towns and villages by their specialization. Activities in which a center's labor force exceeds the national norm are assumed to be its export or specialized activities. This procedure yielded the following six types of towns and villages.

Types of Local Economies

Type	Concentration of Labor Force	Economic Typology Criterion	Examples
I	Primary Sector	Percentage of labor force in primary industries *more than* 8.4, and in secondary and tertiary sectors, less or equal to 33.8 and 49.9 respectively.	Agriculture, Forestry, *and* Mining Centers
II	Secondary Sector	Percentage of labor force in secondary industries *more than* 33.8, and in primary and tertiary sectors equal to or less than 8.4 and 49.9 respectively.	Manufacturing and Processing Centers
III	Tertiary Sector	Percentage of labor force in this sector *more than* 49.9 correspondingly, primary and secondary sectors less than 8.4 and 33.8 respectively.	Commercial and Administrative Centers
IV	Primary & Secondary Sectors	Percentage of primary- and secondary-sector labor force *more than* 8.4 and 33.8 respectively. Tertiary-sector labor force equal to or less than 49.9.	Agricultural, Processing, and Mining Centers

Type	Concentration of Labor Force	Economic Typology Criterion	Examples
V	Primary & Tertiary Sectors	Percentage of labor force in primary and tertiary sectors *more than* 8.4 and 49.9 respectively. Secondary-sector labor force equal to or less than 33.8.	Agricultural and Commercial Centers
VI	Secondary & Tertiary Sectors	Percentage of labor force in secondary and tertiary sectors *more than* 33.3 and 49.9 respectively. Primary-sector labor force equal to or less than 8.4.	Manufacturing and Administrative or Commercial Centers

Each center was assigned to one of the above categories. On cross-tabulating the size of center by the economic type, Table 3.4 has been obtained. Table 3.4 indicates that the modal group of the smallest centers (pop. 0-500) specialized in the production of primary goods (agriculture, forestry, mining), although a substantial proportion (23 percent) also served as locales of tertiary services (Type V). Larger hamlets (501-1,000) do not manifest any well-defined pattern of specialization. Centers specializing in primary, secondary, and tertiary activities (Types I, II, and III) are found in similar proportions.

With the increasing size of villages and towns, the secondary sector (manufacturing and processing) becomes predominant, so much so that about 40 percent of the towns with populations of 5,001-10,000 were of Type II, that is, specializing in secondary activities.

Although manufacturing stands out as the basic economic activity of the modal group of centers with populations of more than 1,000, commerce and service (tertiary) activities constituted the economic bases of a respectable second-largest set of centers. From the preceding analysis, the following profile of economies of towns and villages can be deduced.

Profile of Economic Activities for Towns and Villages of Different Size, Canada, 1971

Size	Population Type	Basic Economic Activities	Supportive Activities
100			
•			
•			
•			
•	Hamlets	Agriculture, Mining, Forestry, Local Services	Trade
•			

Profile of Economic Activities for Towns and Villages of Different Size, Canada, 1971

Size	Population Type	Basic Economic Activities	Supportive Activities
• • • 1,000 • • • • • • 2,500 • • • • 5,000 • • • • 10,000 •	Villages Villages and Towns Towns	Mining, Forestry, Manufacturing, Education, Administration, Tourism, Commerce Manufacturing, Education, Health Services, Administration, Commerce Manufacturing, Education, Health Services, Administration, Commerce	Trade and Services Trade and Services Trade and Services

3. TOWNS AND VILLAGES IN THE NATIONAL SETTLEMENT SYSTEM

Canadian towns and villages are not autonomous entities. They are elements of the national settlement system which strings together centers of all sizes ranging from somnolent hamlets to booming metropolises. As it is the overarching system that defines functional roles of individual elements, economies of small communities tend to be shaped by their respective positions in a settlement system. Simmons suggests that Canada can be viewed as a set of interrelated urban-centered regions.[11] Each region not only has an internal hierarchical order but also is linked with other regions through flows of goods, services, information, and people. This view of the Canadian settlement system leads to two deductions. First, the increasing integration of the national economy, and consequently the settlement system, would have brought about certain uniformities in the functional roles of towns and villages. Second, since the Canadian settlement system is regionally focused, small communities are likely to reflect some differences from region to region. Both these deductions have been affirmed by the findings of the preceding sections. Nationwide similarities among towns and villages are evident, but so are regional divergences.

By viewing spatial interrelations of villages and cities as a system, contemporary theory has gone beyond the conventional notions of central-place hierarchy, which present a static picture of the relationships among settlements. It has come to be recognized that business organizations and public agencies act as channels of interaction among centers, and that they have considerable influence on the functional specializations as well as the sizes of various settlements. As Hansen succinctly paraphrases the contemporary viewpoint: "The intricate web of economic interdependence contradicts simple central-place hierarchy depictions of city systems; empirical evidence indicates that growth-inducing innovation linkages run not only from large cities to smaller cities but also from large cities to even larger cities, from smaller to larger cities and between cities of comparable size."[12] These notions reflect the new configurations of human settlement arising from electronic technology, motorized transport, national and global corporations, and increased public presence in national affairs, among other contemporary social trends. As Friedmann maintains, the basic territorial unit in contemporary times has come to be an urban field which is a "multicentred region having a relatively low density, whose form evolves from a finely articulated network of social and economic linkages."[13] The question, then, arises as to what roles small communities play in this multifocal and diffused settlement system.

On an aggregate level, economies of towns and villages seem to be indistinguishable from those of cities. The analyses reported in the previous sections bear out the fact that villages, towns, and cities all have a similar mix (not scale) of economic activities. In the same vein, it can be said that towns and villages as a group do not manifest any particular sectoral specialization, though individually they may be markedly different. This convergence to common economic characteristics across the settlement system is a reflection of the erosion of conventional central-place hierarchies. It is also a manifestation of the urbanism that has come to pervade everywhere, within as well as outside cities. Even farming has largely become a corporate business.

4. THE MODULAR SOCIETY

The infusion of secondary and tertiary activities in towns and villages has been facilitated by the pervasiveness of national (or regional) corporate structures, standardization of production processes, and a consolidation of consumption markets. With the exception of remote communities, almost everywhere people consume the same products, earn similar union-negotiated wages, are entitled to similar federal and provincial services, and are subject to the same rules.

Chain stores and franchises have permeated every segment of the settlement systems, and national or international corporations have set up branch plants to manufacture brand goods in cities as well as in the country. For example, in Canada chains and franchises constituted 72 percent of grocery and meat outlets, 100 percent of department stores, 80 percent of general merchandise and 54 percent of women's clothing stores in 1978.[14] The welfare state has ensured that the basic needs of Canadians will be provided irrespective of where they live. From Old Age Pension to governmental subsidies for education, a variety of public payments maintain a basic minimum of living standards at all locations. These factors have promoted a modular society wherein a bundle of basic goods and services is available, frequently produced on the site for a sizeable population. As an illustration, it may be assumed that every 1,000 persons create enough demand for, say, a dairy plant or a soda bottling establishment, a post office, and a public school. Similarly, a vehicle license bureau or a road maintenance crew may have to be maintained wherever, say, 2,500 people live. These are mere hypothetical examples of a bundle of basic goods and services required to maintain a population cohort. On the production side, these goods and services expand employment opportunities and add to local income. They are often financed from common national (or provincial) resources and are autonomous of the local demand-supply equilibrium. Such activities have come to constitute modules of contemporary economic activities which have come to be stamped across the national landscape. A reflection of the modular society is discernible in the distribution of federal employees.

Federal Government Employment in Nonmetropolitan Areas, Canada, 1961-1981

Year	Number of Employees	Percentage of Total Federal Employees
1961	68,217*	33.9
1971	85,533	31.9
1981	141,976	32.2

*1961 figures exclude employees of agency and proprietary corporations.

SOURCE: Statistics Canada, *Federal Government Employment in Metropolitan Areas, 1981* (72-205)

The accompanying table shows a high degree of consistency in the proportion of federal employees located in nonmetropolitan areas over two decades, 1961-1981. Almost one-third of the federal work force is spread out in nonmetropolitan Canada — including the countryside and the north. By and large, it is "serving" nonmetropolitan populations and managing national resources. Regardless of the question of whether or not nonmetropolitan areas were receiving their fair share, the fact that the proportion has remained almost constant over two decades testifies to the universality of public services in the country. Incidentally, approximately

141,000 federal jobs distributed in nonmetropolitan areas injected around 202 million dollars into local economies.[15] Similarly, concentrations of population generate commercial activity which in turn becomes a source of local employment and economic stability. A few specific examples will further illustrate the role that provisions of basic goods and services play in providing jobs and incomes for small communities.

Wolfe Island is a rural township of about 1,000 people across from Kingston on Lake Ontario. Its economy is an exquisite illustration of how the services provided for the local population become the primary elements of the economic base of a locality. Although the island is an agricultural area, employment in local schools, the post office, and churches, on provincial highways and ferries, and in federal customs and environmental agencies has been the main source of livelihood on the island.[16] Thus the services required by the local population are the main source of employment for the residents.

New Liskeard is a Northern Ontario town of about 5,500, located on Lake Temiskaming. Although the town has seven manufacturing plants including a creamery and ice cream establishment, three factories to make wood products (paneling and furniture), and two plants fabricating iron and steel products, public institutions meant to serve the local and regional population are the major employers. Among these institutions are federal and provincial departments of manpower, agriculture, the Liquor Control Board, Ministries of Natural Resources and Communication, Northern Affairs, and Ontario Hydro. Furthermore, schools, a hospital, a two-year agricultural college and a regional school for the mentally retarded employ large numbers of workers.[17] If one includes three banks, several trust and finance companies, ten churches, telephone and telegraph establishments, and building contractors, one can readily observe that the bulk of employment is in activities meant to serve the local population, through the market as well as by externally funded public agencies.

Weyburn, a town of about 9,000, is located in southeastern Saskatchewan. It has an oil field and is surrounded by farms. Nevertheless, it is public employment that constitutes the largest block of jobs. Two hospitals, nine schools, municipal and provincial agencies, and Saskatchewan Power and Telephone companies employed almost 30 percent of the workforce in 1973-1974. The share of oil establishments and manufacturers of food products was 7 percent of local employment, whereas auto dealers, traders of durables, and building contractors were among the leading "private" employers.[18]

The northeastern Alberta town of St. Paul has a population of about 5,000 people. A cheese factory, a concrete block plant, a packaging and processing plant, and a machine shop are major manufacturing establishments. There are about twenty provincial agencies (Departments of Health, Culture, Liquor Control) and seven federal agencies (Departments of Indian Affairs, Farm Credit, Canada Manpower, R.C.M.P., etc.) maintaining establishments of varying sizes in the town. A hospital, a health unit, five schools, and a school for the mentally retarded are also among the larger employers.[19] Banks, contractors, builders, auto dealers, and repair garages provide the second-largest employment sector.

These brief sketches of the economic activities and employment opportunities in four small communities illustrate a certain uniformity in the provision of daily goods and community services, which in turn become sources of local employment. This is a concrete manifestation of the modularity principle. It also explains the persistence and continual viability of towns and villages, particularly those that are not single-industry or company towns.

Reprise

At this juncture, we may compose an overall picture of town and village economies emerging from the analyses reported so far. To begin with, it should be remembered that towns and villages generally are manufacturing and service centers, though there are notable regional differences in economic specialization.

In the Atlantic Provinces, towns and villages are essentially mining and manufacturing communities, though relatively larger centers also seem to be focal points of administrative activities. Quebec and Ontario's towns and villages specialize in manufacturing, although a sprinkling of trade and administrative centers is also observable. The small communities of the Prairie Provinces have retained their historical role of area-wide service centers, whereas British Columbia's small communities are primarily mining and mineral-processing centers. Although these observations are useful, they only provide a generalized view of the economic bases of towns and villages. By examining economic profiles of individual communities, we found that many manufacturing and service activities were meant to meet local demand. Ice cream and dairy plants, furniture and building component factories, and auto repair establishments are not "export" activities. Similarly hospitals, schools, Canada Manpower offices, or field establishments of provincial ministries can be classified as local services, despite being funded from nonlocal sources. Apparently wherever there is a sizeable concentration of population, retail, manufacturing, and service establishments appear to meet local needs. It is the clustering of population that gives advantage to towns and villages in attracting these establishments. It can then be concluded that to some extent, towns and villages in contemporary Canada generate their own employment. This does not mean that they are closed and self-contained economies. In fact a large subclass of towns and villages, that is, single-industry centers and company towns, are primarily exporting places. Yet most town and village economies are structured around the provision of local needs maintained from shared national (or regional) resources.

In order to ascertain the extent to which towns and villages actually generate jobs, a test was made of one hundred small centers in Canada (see Appendix A). Data are available for 1971 on the total employment in these centers, which range from 200 to 9,000 in population and are located in all provinces. It was found that about 70 percent of the labor force in these places was employed locally and did not have to commute outside the community. Further, when the data on locally provided employment are matched with the population level of each center, a strong and significant correlation is found. The regression equation obtained in this test is as follows:

$$\text{Employed Labor Force, } 1971 = 212.8 + 0.26 \text{ (Population 1971)}$$
$$(r = 0.608 \text{ and } F = 60)$$

It seems reasonable to suggest a general rule of thumb for towns and villages above 300 in population: *such centers can be expected to generate jobs at a level equivalent to one-quarter of their population.* In other words, one should not be surprised to find 250 or more jobs available in a small town of 1,000 persons.

Another aspect worthy of note is that town and village economies are not bound within territorial limits of individual centers. It seems that the territorial unit of local economies is a complex of interrelated centers and the intervening countryside. A set of linked centers and the countryside constitutes the daily circuit of the resident population for commercial and employment purposes. This finding has been independently affirmed by other observers of small-town Canada, and it implies a modification of conventional notions of central-place hierarchy. Currently, a system of centers seems to be the more relevant concept to describe the spatial organization at the lower level of the actual settlement hierarchy. Towns and villages have been incorporated in regionally focused settlement systems where functional and trade transactions do not flow primarily along a rank-size network but follow corporate channels which, for example, may link a mining community directly with an international metropolis. Examples of such linkages are almost endless. Uranium City, Saskatchewan or Bancroft, Ontario may have more linkages with New York or Toronto than with higher-order cities nearby.

Towns and villages have been integrated in the multichannelled national spatial system and washed over by urbanism. These features are reflected in the economic structures of their economies. In small communities, the single most common sources of employment are federal, provincial, and local agencies, national corporations, and regional chains. The incomes afforded by such opportunities are considered in the following section.

5. LABOR FORCE AND UNEMPLOYMENT

Economic activities pave the way for households and individuals to earn incomes, but earnings also depend upon the proportion of population available for work (labor force) and on the employment (or conversely, unemployment) levels. The labor-force participation ratio and unemployment rate are, thus, two intervening variables whose incidence should be examined before analyzing personal incomes obtainable in towns and villages.

Labor Force and Unemployment by Size of Settlement, Canada, 1971

Place of Residence	Labor Force as Percentage of Population 15 years and over	Percentage of Labor Force Unemployed
500,000 +	59.1	8.1
100,001-500,000	61.0	7.9
30,001-100,000	58.0	8.8
10,001-30,000	56.9	8.4
5,001-10,000	55.7	8.0
Under 5,000	52.9	7.6
Rural Nonfarm	50.2	8.7
Rural Farm	64.2	2.7

SOURCE: *Census of Canada*

Although the accompanying table presents a cross-sectional view of the labor-force participation and unemployment rates, it points out two significant facts. First, there seems to be only weak positive correlations between the settlement size and the two rates. For example, the Spearman rank correlation coefficients between the settlement size and the labor force as a percentage of population (15 years and over), and between the former variable and the unemployment rate, are 0.37 and 0.42 respectively. These weak positive correlations suggest that the larger or small size of communities has some, but not too much, bearing on the unemployment levels or labor-force participation. The former are determined by the mix and share of local industries, and the latter by factors such as proportions of retirees, children, housewives, and other nonworking persons in the local population, and by the education and occupational expectations of residents. On these scores, towns and villages are not necessarily greatly divergent from metropolitan areas. Undoubtedly, they are more vulnerable to business cycles due to fewer establishments and, frequently, to the predominance of a single industry.

The second observation suggested by the table is that the ranges of variation in the labor-force participation and unemployment rates, particularly in the urban sector of the settlement system, were very narrow. Leaving aside the rural sector, particularly farm areas, which are a case apart, the labor-force participation rate has a range of 8 percentage points around a median value of 57.5 and the unemployment rate varies over a range of 0.5 percentage points around the median 8.5. Further, towns and villages do not manifest an overly low labor-force participation rate or high unemployment rate compared with larger settlements. It appears that by 1971 a fairly integrated structure had come to characterize the national economy. Undoubtedly, there were regional variations which weighed more as determinants of labor-force participation and employment than did the size of settlements.

Tables 3.5 and 3.6 present labor-force participation rates and unemployment rates for provinces by size of settlements. By using the national labor-force participation rate as the differentiating criterion and by looking for settlements and provinces that fall below it, the regional influences can be discerned. A similar procedure may be followed for the unemployment rate, except in this case we look for settlements and provinces having higher rates than the corresponding national proportion.

It appears that provinces which lagged economically, until 1971, had lower labor-force participation rates — an indication of a below-normal working population (Table 3.5). The Atlantic Provinces and Quebec stand out by these criteria. Conversely, labor-force participation in Ontario, the Prairie Provinces, and British Columbia were generally equal to or above the national level. Towns and villages conformed to regional trends: labor-force participation rates were lower in the Maritime Provinces and Quebec, and comparatively higher in the West.

Table 3.6 confirms that the regional setting was an important determinant of unemployment rates. Towns and villages in Newfoundland, Nova Scotia, New Brunswick, Quebec, and British Columbia had about 8 to 9 percent of the labor force unemployed in 1971 (which was above the national level), whereas towns and villages in Prince Edward Island, Ontario, and the Prairie Provinces had lower unemployment rates. What may be noted is that the level of unemployment in towns and villages is directly correlated with high or low levels of employment for the whole settlement spectrum of the respective provinces. All in all, it can be concluded that the labor-force participation rate and the level of unemployment in towns and villages were generally in line with the corresponding rates for provincial settlement systems. We should expect to find that personal incomes in towns and villages vary with the economic status of respective provinces.

6. FAMILY AND INDIVIDUAL INCOMES

Finally we come to the question of personal incomes in towns and villages. Given that manufacturing, commercial, and service activities constitute the bases of town and village economies, it may be expected that incomes in these places would parallel national levels. Yet a cross-sectional account of per capita income by the type of settlement (Table 3.7) reveals a consistent pattern of direct positive correlation between the size of a place and the average income.

The per capita income in 1971 was the lowest in rural farm areas ($3,561) and highest in metropolises of 500,000 or more population ($5,641). Incomes in towns and villages were about 81 to 96 percent of the national average.

The provincial distributions of individual incomes present the same continuum-like regularity, that is, incomes increasing directly with the size of settlement (Table 3.8). The amplitude of income variation is seemingly defined by a province's economic standing. The lower limits of individual incomes in the economically depressed regions of 1971, the Atlantic and Prairie Provinces, dipped low and the upper limits did not even reach the national average levels. The reverse was the case of the income range in prosperous provinces. For example, New Brunswick's farm areas had individual incomes of $2,907 per year, whereas for Ontario the corresponding value was $4,067. The highest per capita income in New Brunswick was $4,601 in cities with a population of 30,001 to 100,000, while the upper limit of individual incomes in Ontario reached $6,009 in metropolises of 500,000 or more. The evidence points out that towns and villages had systematically lower individual incomes than metropolises and other larger cities, while they had higher incomes than rural areas. The average incomes obtainable in towns and villages seem to be the function of provincial economic performance.

The regularity of the positive relationship between the size of a place and the individual (or household) income holds even within the narrow range of the size of towns and villages. The following table was composed by cross-tabulating household incomes and sizes of towns and villages from 1971 Census Subdivision data.

Average Household Income of Residents in Incorporated Canadian Towns and Villages, 1971

		Population of Center		
0-500	501-1,000	1,001-2,500	2,501-5,000	5,001-10,000
$5,721	$6,786	$7,478	$8,762	$8,699

SOURCE: *Census of Canada*

The table suggests an unequivocal conclusion that the smaller a center, the lower the household incomes. For example, the average household income in hamlets of 500 or less population was $5,721 in 1971, which was 65 percent of the income in towns of 5,001-10,000 population. The relationship between the center size and household income is strikingly consistent. It could be attributed to the local-industry mix or sectoral specialization.

To sort out these possibilities, household incomes were correlated with the variable "percentage of labor force" in primary, secondary, and tertiary industries, to arrive at the accompanying table.

Correlation Between Income Level and Labor-Force Mix in Towns and Villages in Canada, 1971

Primary Industries	Percentage of Labor Force in Secondary Industries	Tertiary Industries
$r = -0.21*$	$r = 0.17*$	$r = 0.12*$

* = significant at 99 percent or above level

It appears that the industry mix as indicated by the percentage of the labor force in different sectors has a very small influence on household incomes. Product-moment correlation coefficients (4) range between .12 and .21. Obviously, the size of a center is a more significant determinant of household incomes than the economic specialization. This can be explained by referring to the contemporary mode of production. Although modular society has brought a standard package of activities to towns and villages, the economic control and decision-making functions often remain in larger centers. Perhaps it is the concentration of the upper echelons of corporations, chains, and franchises in cities and larger towns that consistently makes higher incomes possible in such communities. It is the hierarchy within sectors and activities, not their mix as such, that lends an advantage to the larger places in household incomes. This hypothesis is borne out by the accompanying table.

Proportion of Labor Force in Managerial and Professional Occupations in Canadian Towns and Villages, 1971

		Population of Center		
0-500	501-1,000	1,001-2,500	2,501-5,000	5,001-10,000
12.4%	13.0%	15.2%	15.7%	17.0%

SOURCE: Census of Canada

Within the sample of small centers, there is a mild, direct relationship between the size of a center and the percentage of the labor force in managerial/professional occupations. Hamlets and villages stand out as having significantly lower proportions of residents in such occupations. This suggests that smaller places have lower proportions of positions of influence and prestige, which is indicative of the truncated nature of their social structure — a concept to be elaborated in Chapter 5.

An overview of the longitudinal trends in household and individual incomes can be obtained from data series other than the decennial census compiled by Statistics Canada. Table 3.9 presents comparisons of families and unattached individuals' median incomes by areas for the period 1971 to 1979.

During the period in question, it appears that the gap between incomes in nonmetropolitan areas, including towns and villages, and incomes in metropolitan areas narrowed considerably. This trend is evident for Canada as a whole, as well as for various regions of the country. For example, while in 1971 the median income of families and unattached individuals residing in nonmetropolitan areas was .73 of the metropolitan average, by 1979 the ratio had increased to .89. For British Columbia by 1979, this ratio was more than 1 and the Prairie Provinces' nonmetropolitan incomes were almost level with the metropolitan median.

These are very significant findings because they suggest that over the eight-year period 1971-1979 the incomes in towns and villages and other parts of nonmetropolitan Canada increased at a higher rate (20 percent per annum in current dollars) than the metropolitan income (14 percent per year). It is a reflection of the rapidly improving opportunities of earnings in nonmetropolitan areas, a fact that is all the more amazing in view of the slowing down of the national economy in the late 1970s. This finding fits in very well with the spurt of growth manifested by towns and villages during this period.

Within the Canadian settlement system, towns and villages have fared very well economically during the 1971-1979 period. Small urban areas (centers with a population of less than 15,000) reported in Table 3.9 are representative of the towns and villages as defined in this book. Ratios of median incomes of small urban areas to the incomes of metropolitan areas registered increases ranging from 1 percent for the Atlantic Provinces to 18 percent for the Prairie Provinces over the period 1971-1979 (Table 3.9). Yet the nonmetropolitan areas on the whole, including intermediate cities and the countryside, registered greater gains. The ratios of small urban area incomes to metropolitan incomes in 1971 were greater in all cases than ratios of nonmetropolitan incomes to metropolitan incomes. In 1979, with the exception of Ontario, the small urban area ratios were lower than the nonmetropolitan/metropolitan ratio, thereby suggesting that other parts of nonmetropolitan areas gained even more in incomes than did towns and villages.

In order to further confirm the above-described trends, data from another Statistics Canada source have been examined. The accompanying table shows household incomes after income tax for Canada for 1971 and 1979. The table confirms that ratios of nonmetropolitan and small urban centers' median incomes to metropolitan median incomes increased by 7 to 14 percentage points over the eight-year period. It also affirms the finding that nonmetropolitan areas as a whole had the highest rates of income increase, followed by small centers, with the metropolitan areas being third (see ratios of 1979 to 1971 incomes in the accompanying table).

Household Income Trends in Metropolitan and Nonmetropolitan Areas, Canada, 1971-1979

| | Median Income after Tax | | |
	1971 ($)	1979 ($)	Ratio of 1979 to 1971 Income
Metropolitan Area	7,472	15,987	2.14
Nonmetropolitan Area	5,807	14,614	2.52
Small Urban Centers	6,205	14,483	2.33
Ratio of Nonmetropolitan to Metropolitan Median Incomes	0.77	0.91	—
Ratio of Small Urban Centers to Metropolitan Median Incomes	0.83	0.90	—

SOURCE: Statistics Canada, *Income After Tax, Distributions by Size in Canada* (1971, 4-1302-502), (1979, 13-210)

The evidence is unmistakable that the 1970s witnessed a sharp increase in family and individual incomes in towns and villages and other parts of nonmetropolitan areas, so much so that the difference between incomes in metropolitan and nonmetropolitan areas has been reduced to about 10 percentage points, although in British Columbia and the Prairie Provinces practically no difference remained by 1979. These findings provide further evidence of convergence tendencies within the national settlement system, and point out that although income opportunities in towns and villages are less rewarding than in metropolitan areas, the differences have been sharply pared down.

7. POVERTY AND AFFLUENCE

One is tempted to regard towns and villages as places whose serenity masks mundane existence, and frequently pervasive poverty. Do towns and villages bear a larger burden of poverty and have proportionally fewer affluent households? To answer this question we turn to Table 3.10. To begin with, it can be observed from the table that nonmetropolitan areas, which include towns and villages, have more than their share of families and unattached individuals in the lowest income quintile. Yet, having noted this, it should be observed that remarkable improvement on this score has occurred over the eight-year period 1971-1979. Not only did the nonmetropolitan share of households in the lowest quintile decrease from 46.6 in 1971 to 35.5 in 1979, it came quite close to the proportion of total population (32.7 percent) living in these areas. The same trend is observable up to the third quintile; thereafter the trend reverses itself.

The nonmetropolitan proportions of fourth and fifth income quintiles increased over the 1971-1979 period from 31.1 to 31.5 and 24.5 to 27.2 respectively. In 1979 about 27 percent of Canadian families and unattached individuals earning more than $30,400 annually lived in nonmetropolitan areas, while 32.7 percent of total population lived there. These figures suggest nonmetropolitan areas had a substantial proportion of the affluent, though not as many as their share of the population warranted.

To assess the distribution of the poor we turn to Table 3.11, which provides a more sharply focused picture of the low-income families and individuals in Canada. While in 1971, 12 percent of Canadian families lived in small urban centers, about 13 percent of the low-income families were living in these places. By 1979 such centers had 10 percent of the low-income families, against 11 percent of the total population — less than their proportionate share. The concentration of poor households in towns and villages seems to have declined over this period. This finding contradicts the popular image that small places have large concentrations of the poor.

The trend regarding the distribution of unattached individuals parallels the distribution of low-income families. Between 1971 and 1979, the proportion of low-income individuals declined from 15.5 to 12.3 percent in small urban centers, yet in 1979, there was still a greater proportion of low-income individuals in towns and villages than their share of this population. The large increase in incomes in towns and villages seems to have reduced the overconcentration of the poor in towns and villages, despite a proportionately larger share of the low-income, unattached (and perhaps elderly) individuals in these places.

8. SUMMING UP: THE SOCIAL ECONOMY OF TOWNS AND VILLAGES

What are the sources of income for residents of towns and villages? This question, the *raison d'être* of the chapter, has been answered in general terms. We found that the opportunities for earning a livelihood in towns and villages are not radically different from those in other parts of Canada. Towns and villages, as an aggregate, manifest about the same mix of activities as can be found in contemporary cities. Manufacturing, mining, public services, and trade constitute bases of local economies, although there are noticable regional differences.

The labor-force participation and unemployment rates in towns and villages conform to national trends. The personal incomes in towns and villages are low compared with metropolitan centers, although the differences between the two were reduced during the 1970s. Even the concentration of poor households has been reduced in centers having 1,000 people or more. Hamlets may still have disproportionately large shares of the poor. However, our analysis gives a relatively reassuring account of the economic health of towns and villages. Their fortunes seem to swing with the provincial and national economies, at least at an aggregate level. Individual towns or some regional cluster of small communities may vary from these trends.

The above-described findings fall into an explicable pattern. Towns and villages are encased in national and regional economic organizations. They are locales for production, distribution, and consumption of goods and services commonly available to all Canadians. By being strung into vertically integrated Corporate Canada, towns and villages partake of provincial and national resources and modes of production. Post offices, schools, railway stations, weather offices, service stations, supermarkets, banks, and so on, meant to serve the resident population, become sources of employment and sustain small communities. What the economic-base theory categorizes as nonbasic activities turn out to be basic activities, although they are partially sustained by pooled national (or provincial) finances.

This is a manifestation of the modular society that has come to characterize industrial countries, where a standard set of institutions and services is available for a population cohort. There are indications that the spatial contexts of towns and villages have also undergone change. The lateral links between towns or villages and their surrounding countrysides are not necessarily centripetal in character. The centrality of individual towns and villages has been transformed into multichannelled interlinkages among local centers and the hinterland. A set of centers and the intervening countryside constitute the spatial unit for economic and social purposes. Such a set is the lower-level unit of the settlement hierarchy. It constitutes the labor market and its various elements operate like districts of a city, wherein each one has a distinct identity and function to complement the other. The towns and villages of the frontier regions are exceptions to this spatial framework. The cellular spatial framework has been prompted by increased mobility, which makes it possible for residents of towns and villages to live in one place, commute to work in another, and moonlight in the third, or to engage in part-time farming in the intervening countryside. These arrangements lend variety to small communities' economies and sustain them through national business cycles.

Although corporations, franchises, chains, and public bureaucracies have filtered down into towns and villages, it is the horizontal interlinking of these vertically organized institutions that lend uniqueness to individual localities. Such horizontal linkages are brought about through formal arrangements such as local Chambers of Commerce/Service Clubs or by the informality of personalized relationships engendered by smallness. Towns and villages tend to have a highly individualized economic climate. One place may be vigorous and community minded, while another may be frozen into inaction, yet both may have almost the same mix of activities. The point here is that merely identifying structural features of small-community economies does not tell the whole story. One has to look at the social relations of production and consumption and local power structures to fully understand the performance of town and village economies.

Town and village economies lack depth in the sense that they have neither the full spectrum of modern production activities nor numerous establishments carrying on the same activity. One business failure, or the layoff of a score or more workers, ripples through a local economy. It is not unusual to find an economically depressed town in the midst of a booming national economy and *vice versa*, the reason being that a small variation in the production schedule of a plant or a change in import policies in a distant country can precipitate a major downturn in a local economy. Similarly, the opening of a new school or an increase in the number of personnel at a nearby army base can raise the employment and business prospects in a small community. Yet the irregular economy that seemingly plays a greater role in towns and villages cushions the effect of business cycles to some extent.

Exchanging services, bartering goods, and producing for household consumption are more prevalent practices in small communities. They are the functional necessities of small-town living. In a place where a plumbing company does not exist, individuals who can do such work are called upon for help; where there is no bakery, exchanging desserts may be a necessity. These are manifestations of what has been called an irregular or informal economy. Many transactions of the irregular economy are carried on with cash, but usually go unreported, for example, buying meat from a farmer or paying for a ride (as there may not be any taxi service). The estimates of irregular economic activity in Canada range from 5 to 22 percent of the national product. It is a widespread phenomenom, some of it illegal, but it seems that in small communities the irregular economy is a functional necessity and a part of the local ethos. The irregular economy also serves as a source of jobs, in that unemployed or underemployed workers can make do with casual work, while those gainfully employed can supplement their earnings through barters, exchanges, and production for self-consumption.

NOTES

1. Jean Burnet, *Next-Year Country: A Study of Rural Social Organization in Alberta* (Toronto: University of Toronto Press, 1951), 53.
2. *Ibid.*, 59.
3. *Ibid.*, 89.
4. The "dispersed city hypothesis" as applied to small centers is expressed thus by Hart: "Today many villages are dominated by a single function, and their residents drive to other villages to obtain the other goods and sources they require." John Fraser Hart, *The Look of the Land* (Englewood Cliffs, N.J.: Prentice-Hall, 1975), 168.
5. *Ibid.*
6. Fred A. Dahms, "The Evolving Spatial Organization of Small Settlements in the Countryside — An Ontario Example," *TESG (Journal of Economic and Social Geography)* 71:5 (1980): 305.
7. *Ibid.*, 301, Table 2.

8. Rex A. Lucas, *Minetown, Milltown, Railtown* (Toronto: University of Toronto Press, 1971), 17.

9. Estimates derived from data in addendum of Government of Canada, Department of Regional Economic Expansion, *Single-Sector Communities* (Ottawa: Government of Canada, 1979), 62-78.

10. Location Quotients are coefficients of localization or specialization, and are compiled by the following formula:

$$\frac{L_i}{L_E} \Big/ \frac{N_i}{N_E}$$

Where L_i = Local employment in industry i; L_E = Total local employment; N_i = National (provincial) employment in industry i; N_E = National (provincial) total employment. Charles E. Tiebout, *The Community Economic Base Study* (New York: Committee for Economic Development, 1962), 47.

11. James W. Simmons, *Canada: Choices in a National Urban Strategy,* Research Paper No. 70 (Toronto: University of Toronto, Centre for Community Studies, 1975), 1.

12. Niles M. Hansen, "Preliminary Overview," in Niles M. Hansen, ed., *Human Settlement Systems* (Cambridge, Mass.: Ballinger, 1978), 7.

13. John Friedmann, "The Urban Field as Human Habitat," in L.S. Bourne and J.W. Simmons, eds., *Systems of Cities* (New York: Oxford University Press, 1978), 42.

14. "Percentages of Market Share of Chain Stores and Franchises" as reported in H.J. Adler and D.A. Brusegard, *Perspectives Canada III* (Ottawa: Statistics Canada, 1980), 716, Table 193.

15. The 202 million dollars were the total earnings of federal employees in nonmetropolitan Canada in 1981, as reported in Statistics Canada, *Federal Government Employment in Metropolitan Areas,* Cat. 72-205 (Ottawa: Ministry of Supply and Services Canada, 1981).

16. Queen's University School of Urban and Regional Planning, "Land and People of Wolfe Island" (Kingston: Queen's University, 1974, Mimeographed), 4.

17. Corporation of the Town of New Liskeard, "Town Profile" (New Liskeard, Ont.: Clerk-Administrator, 1975, Mimeographed), 2-7.

18. Saskatchewan Department of Industry and Commerce, *Community Profile, Weyburn* (Regina, 1974-75), 6-7, Employment Table.

19. Alberta, *Town of St. Paul* (Pamphlet) (St. Paul, 1973), 14-21.

TABLES/CHAPTER 3

TABLE 3.1

Single-Industry (SI) Towns and Villages by Dominant Type of Activity, Canada, 1971

	Manufacturing	Metal Mines and Refining	Non-metal Mines and Refining	Wood and Wood Products	Utilities and Transport	Food Processing	Fish Processing	Agriculture Service Centers	Construction and Tourism	Public Administration	Total
Canada	50	78	51	294	26	30	131	7	48	64	779*

*Numbers reported in this table exclude SI Communities of more than 10,000 population; therefore numbers in columns as well as the total do not match with the source.

SOURCE: Government of Canada, DREE, *Single Sector Communities*, 1979.

TABLE 3.2

Percentage of Labor Force 15 Years and Over by Industry Group in Different Settlement Types in Canada, 1971

Settlement Type	Agriculture, Forestry, Fishing, & Trapping	Mines, Quarries, Oil Wells	Manu- facturing	Construction	Transportation & Communications	Trade, Finance, Insurance, Real Estate	Community, Business, and Personal Services Industries	Public Administra- tion	Industry Unspecified	Total
					(percent)					
Rural Farm	63.1	0.9	6.9	3.9	3.0	5.2	8.9	2.4	5.8	100.0
Nonfarm and Village	9.3	2.6	17.7	9.3	8.3	15.6	20.0	7.0	10.3	100.0
Towns										
under 5,000	4.7	4.5	18.4	6.9	7.9	17.8	24.1	7.4	8.2	100.0
5,000-10,000	2.8	3.9	20.0	6.0	7.9	18.0	24.8	8.9	7.7	100.0
Cities										
10,001-30,000	2.8	3.6	21.6	5.7	7.8	18.5	24.8	7.8	7.4	100.0
30,001-100,000	1.0	1.7	24.1	5.8	7.6	18.9	26.3	7.2	7.4	100.0
Metropolises										
100,001-500,000	0.8	1.3	19.4	6.5	7.3	20.7	27.4	9.4	7.2	100.0
500,000+	0.5	0.3	22.1	5.6	8.8	22.1	25.2	7.5	7.9	100.0

SOURCE: *Census of Canada*

TABLE 3.3

Location Quotients (LQ) by Industry Type for Small Settlements, by Province, 1971

	Mines and Quarries	Manu-facturing	Trade, Finance, Insurance	Community, Business, and Personal Services	Public Administration
	(1)	(2)	(3)	(4)	(5)
Newfoundland					
Nonfarm and Hamlets	0.68	1.11	0.80	0.75	0.69
Villages and Towns					
under 5,000	1.50	1.41	0.91	0.85	0.68
5,001-10,000	Negligible Activity (N.A.)	0.91	1.04	1.09	1.75
Prince Edward Island					
Nonfarm and Hamlets	N.A.	1.36	1.01	0.85	0.68
Towns under 5,000	N.A.	1.76	1.21	1.08	0.75
Nova Scotia					
Nonfarm and Hamlets	0.80	1.22	0.87	0.80	0.66
Towns under 5,000	N.A.	1.36	0.97	1.03	0.94
5,001-10,000	N.A.	0.79	1.19	1.16	1.20
New Brunswick					
Nonfarm and Hamlets	1.43	1.26	0.77	0.79	0.71
Towns under 5,000	N.A.	1.10	1.01	1.10	0.83
5,001-10,000	N.A.	1.20	1.03	1.04	1.62
Quebec					
Nonfarm and Hamlets	1.70	0.93	0.78	0.84	0.89
Towns under 5,000	3.36	1.08	0.85	0.97	0.84
5,001-10,000	2.81	0.92	0.92	1.07	1.06
Ontario					
Nonfarm and Hamlets	2.02	0.90	0.86	0.86	0.95
Towns under 5,000	3.75	0.87	0.96	0.98	1.01
5,001-10,000	3.08	1.09	0.86	1.02	1.02
Manitoba					
Nonfarm and Hamlets	1.22	0.62	0.86	0.94	1.39
Towns under 5,000	2.16	0.68	1.00	1.15	1.84
5,001-10,000	N.A.	1.07	1.07	1.26	0.82
Saskatchewan					
Nonfarm and Hamlets	1.78	0.52	1.05	0.99	1.00
Towns under 5,000	2.26	2.47	1.34	1.29	1.11
5,001-10,000	2.84	3.36	1.27	1.36	0.87
Alberta					
Nonfarm and Hamlets	1.23	0.74	0.86	0.89	1.00
Towns under 5,000	1.86	0.73	1.11	1.18	1.02
5,001-10,000	1.68	0.95	1.03	1.04	2.08
British Columbia					
Nonfarm and Hamlets	2.0	1.01	0.73	0.82	0.90
Towns under 5,000	3.25	1.05	0.80	0.92	1.12
5,001-10,000	3.87	1.04	0.94	0.96	0.80

SOURCE: *Census of Canada*

TABLE 3.4

Number of Incorporated Towns and Villages by Type of Economic Specialization and Size, Canada 1971

| Population | Type of Economic Specialization | | | | | | | |
	I	II	III	IV	V	VI	Residual*	Total Centers
0-500	96	19	35	29	61	12	11	263
	36.5%	7.2%	13.3%	11.0%	23.2%	4.6%	4.2%	100.0%
501-1,000	53	51	47	36	44	11	9	251
	21.1%	20.3%	18.7%	14.3%	17.5%	4.4%	3.6%	100.0%
1,001-2,500	58	92	76	21	39	25	2	313
	18.5%	29.4%	24.3%	6.7%	12.5%	8.0%	0.6%	100.0%
2,501-5,000	38	60	43	17	15	14	0	187
	20.3%	32.1%	23.0%	9.1%	8.0%	7.5%	—	100.0%
5,001-10,000	11	43	27	5	5	18	0	109
	10.1%	39.4%	24.8%	4.6%	4.6%	16.5%	—	100.0%

*"Residual" includes centers that had a larger proportion of labor force in unspecified industries.
SOURCE: Census of Canada

TABLE 3.5
Labor Force as a Percentage of Population 15 Years and Over by Size of Place and Province, Canada, 1971

	Percentage of Population 15 Years or Over									
Size of Place	Newfoundland	Prince Edward Island	Nova Scotia	New Brunswick	Quebec	Ontario	Manitoba	Saskatchewan	Alberta	British Columbia
500,000 +	—	—	—	—	56.1	65.6	62.4	—	—	60.7
100,001-500,000	56.6	—	62.2	—	51.8	61.3	—	62.1	64.8	55.5
30,001-100,000	56.0	—	52.8	58.9	52.4	60.9	59.9	53.2	60.8	61.7
10,001-30,000	50.3	58.8	49.8	54.9	52.0	60.2	61.5	57.3	59.8	57.9
5,001-10,000	45.1	—	53.6	52.5	50.4	58.6	56.1	57.5	58.1	60.2
Under 5,000	—	52.0	52.5	50.3	49.1	56.6	54.1	51.6	57.8	57.3
Rural Nonfarm	38.7	53.3	48.3	47.8	45.4	55.2	48.1	49.0	52.4	55.6
Rural Farm	48.2	63.1	57.2	55.0	54.3	68.5	66.3	65.9	68.8	66.0

SOURCE: *Census of Canada*

TABLE 3.6
Unemployed Labor Force by Size of Place and Province, Canada, 1971

	Percentage of Labor Force, Unemployed									
Size of Place	Newfoundland	Prince Edward Island	Nova Scotia	New Brunswick	Quebec	Ontario	Manitoba	Saskatchewan	Alberta	British Columbia
500,000 +	—	—	—	—	9.3	6.9	7.4	—	—	9.6
100,001-500,000	7.8	—	7.0	—	9.4	7.7	—	8.1	7.5	8.7
30,001-100,000	7.7	—	11.4	7.3	11.8	7.9	6.7	8.5	7.1	9.3
10,001-30,000	8.9	6.9	10.6	8.8	10.8	6.7	9.2	7.8	7.4	9.0
5,001-10,000	8.6	—	8.1	9.1	11.5	6.5	6.1	6.2	6.4	8.2
Under 5,000	—	5.6	7.7	7.8	9.8	6.2	5.2	5.5	6.3	7.8
Rural Nonfarm	11.0	6.1	8.4	10.2	13.3	6.6	6.3	5.0	6.4	8.8
Rural Farm	8.7	2.7	3.5	3.9	6.0	2.0	1.6	1.5	1.6	3.9

SOURCE: *Census of Canada*

TABLE 3.7

Average Income of Individuals 15 Years and Over in Different Settlement Types, Canada, 1971

Settlement Type	Average Income ($)	Percent of the National Average
Rural:		
Farm	3,561	70
Nonfarm/Village	4,090	81
Town:		
Under 5,000	4,540	90
5,001-10,000	4,847	96
City:		
10,001-30,000	5,052	100
30,001-100,000	5,012	99
Metropolis:		
100,001-500,000	5,382	106
Over 500,000	5,641	112
Total Canada	5,033	100

SOURCE: *Census of Canada*

TABLE 3.8

Average Income of Individuals 15 Years and Over for Different Settlement Types in Canadian Provinces, 1971 (Dollars)

	Rural		Towns		Cities		Metropolises		Total
	Farm	Nonfarm & Villages	Under 5,000	5,001-10,000	10,001-30,000	30,001-100,000	100,001-500,000	500,000 +	
Newfoundland	2,942	2,955	3,676	4,435	5,872	4,517	—	—	3,816
Prince Edward Island	2,649	3,065	3,424	—	4,201	—	—	—	3,416
Nova Scotia	3,135	3,537	4,241	4,265	4,081	4,408	5,296	—	4,210
New Brunswick	2,907	3,270	3,919	4,275	4,539	4,601	—	—	3,946
Quebec	3,536	3,850	4,516	4,608	5,010	4,639	5,260	5,464	4,969
Ontario	4,067	4,671	4,870	5,063	5,248	5,376	5,507	6,009	5,459
Manitoba	2,887	3,616	4,267	4,314	5,639	4,407	—	4,901	4,452
Saskatchewan	2,949	3,342	3,860	4,341	4,354	4,264	4,800	—	3,926
Alberta	3,585	4,041	4,607	4,981	4,744	4,945	5,546	—	4,978
British Columbia	4,565	5,044	5,172	5,573	5,223	5,324	4,940	5,428	5,255
CANADA	3,561	4,090	4,540	4,847	5,052	5,012	5,382	5,641	5,033

SOURCE: *Census of Canada, 1971*

TABLE 3.9

Median Incomes of Families and Unattached Individuals by Areas of Residence, Canada and Its Regions, 1971 and 1979

	Canada ($)	Atlantic Provinces ($)	Quebec ($)	Ontario ($)	Prairie Provinces ($)	British Columbia ($)
1971						
Metropolitan Areas	8,665	7,604	8,154	9,477	8,143	8,329
Nonmetropolitan Areas	6,384	5,237	5,991	7,822	5,497	8,291
Small Urban Areas*	6,961	6,322	6,390	8,329	6,347	8,245
Ratio of Nonmetropolitan Median Income to the Metropolitan Income	0.73	0.69	0.73	0.83	0.68	0.99
Ratio of Small Urban Areas Median Income to the Metropolitan Income	0.80	0.83	0.78	0.88	0.8	0.99
1979						
Metropolitan Areas	18,479	16,084	18,027	19,695	17,151	18,274
Nonmetropolitan Areas	16,427	13,784	15,925	17,726	16,787	19,413
Small Urban Areas*	16,419	13,528	15,266	18,154	16,423	19,802
Ratio of Nonmetropolitan Median Income to the Metropolitan Income	0.89	0.86	0.88	0.90	0.98	1.06
Ratio of Small Urban Area Median Income to the Metropolitan Income	0.89	0.84	0.85	0.92	0.96	1.08

*Small Urban Areas include urban centers of less than 15,000 population (1,000-14,999)
SOURCE: Statistics Canada: *Income Distributions by Size in Canada,* 13-207, 1971 and 1979

TABLE 3.10

Distribution of Families and Unattached Individuals within Income Quintiles by Metropolitan and Nonmetropolitan Areas, Canada, 1971-1979

	Lowest Quintile		Second Quintile		Third Quintile		Fourth Quintile		Highest Quintile		Total Population	
	1971	1979	1971	1979	1971	1979	1971	1979	1971	1979	1971	1979
Metropolitan Areas	53.4	64.5	56.1	64.7	62.3	65.8	68.9	68.5	75.5	72.8	63.2	67.3
Nonmetropolitan Areas	46.6	35.5	43.9	35.3	37.7	34.2	31.1	31.5	24.5	27.2	36.8	32.7
Total	100.0	100.0	100.0	100.0	100.0	100.0	100.0	100.0	100.0	100.0	100.0	100.0

SOURCE: Statistics Canada — *Income Distributions by Size in Canada*, 13-207, 1971 and 1979

TABLE 3.11

Low-Income Families and Unattached Individuals by Place of Residence, Canada, 1971-1979

Place of Residence	Families		Unattached Individuals	
	Low Income Only	All	Low Income Only	All
1971				
Metropolitan Areas	41.5	61.6	57.4	68.0
Other Cities 15,000-30,000	5.8	5.9	8.5	7.5
Small Urban Centers 1,000-15,000	12.9	12.0	15.5	11.7
Rural Areas	39.8	20.5	18.6	12.7
	100.0	100.0	100.0	100.0
1979				
Metropolitan Areas				
500,000 +	32.2	33.0	38.8	38.9
100,001-500,000	22.8	24.0	25.2	26.4
30,001-100,000	9.1	7.6	9.5	8.3
Other Cities —				
15,001-30,000	6.1	5.5	6.3	5.8
Small Urban Centers	10.0	11.0	12.3	10.8
Rural Areas	19.8	18.8	7.9	9.7
	100.0	100.0	100.0	100.0

SOURCE: Statistics Canada, *Income Distributions by Size in Canada,* 13-207, 1971 and 1979

4 Regional Relations of Small Towns

Each small town exists within a larger national, provincial, or metropolitan region. Since it seldom dominates such a region, the small town is subject to the forces and factors that govern the larger region's economy, social development, and growth prospects. But the small town is, at the same time, the center of its own subregion. It may, depending on its size, supply shopping services and job opportunities and be an educational, religious, and social center for the population living in the area surrounding the town as well for its own residents.

The small town, thus, has two major roles to play: it serves to organize the economic and social activities of its local region, and it participates with other towns and cities in the ongoing development of the large region. The popular wisdom is that the fortunes of the small town are entirely dependent on the fortunes of the larger region, of its economy and its cities. Indeed, it is often contended that the population growth occurring in small towns that is discussed in previous chapters is due to the "spillover" of metropolitan centers. When one combines the latter with the view of farm depopulation and of town and village commercial decline, which has been current for several decades, the picture of small-town powerlessness is understandable.

But how true is this view of small-town dependency in Canada today? To what degree are the recent population tendencies in small towns due to the expansion of metropolitan areas? What kind of regional milieu do small towns actually participate in? These questions are probed in this chapter in order to provide a clearer perspective of the regional roles that small towns in Canada play in this last quarter of the twentieth century. It is clear from the discussion in the foregoing chapters that small towns today are different from their predecessors. We shall not, therefore, retrace the history of small town roles, but rather describe the contemporary regional setting and functioning of small centers.

1. THE INFLUENCE OF METROPOLITAN AREAS ON POPULATION GROWTH

It is rather generally assumed that the small-town growth described in earlier chapters is due to the inflow of people who have decided to move out of cities. For several decades settlement studies presumed that the proximity of a small center to a metropolis or large city was the major explanation of town and village growth. Yet the Canadian experience does not bear out such a broad generalization. Although the data for small towns, particularly regarding migration flows, do not permit conclusive answers, it does appear from several analyses that metropolitan influence on population growth of towns and villages is much less than presumed.

In order to determine more precisely the importance of proximity to a metropolitan area for small-town growth, a set of distance zones can be established around each of Canada's twenty-three Census Metropolitan Areas (CMAs). Several tests of metropolitan influence were conducted on this basis, the most comprehensive of which examines growth tendencies in all towns and villages from 1961 to 1971. A simple test of growth or no-growth in population is used for each small center, and the result attributed to the Census Division (CD) or county in which the small center is situated. The distance factor to the nearest metropolitan area is computed using the geographic centroid of the CD or county. The following general pattern emerges for the country as a whole using six distance zones. Comparable data for each major Canadian region are found in Table 4.1.*

Proportion of Canadian Towns and Villages Growing in Population Relative to Metropolitan Areas, 1961-1971

Distance to Nearest Metropolitan Area (Miles)					
0-30	31-60	61-100	101-150	151-200	Over 200
71.9%	52.8%	47.9%	45.8%	49.5%	56.0%

SOURCE: Table 4.1

Almost 72 percent of the small centers located within thirty miles of a metropolitan area experienced some degree of population growth in the 1961-1971 period. There is then a sharp drop in this growth experience beyond thirty miles. In all successive zones, the proportion of growing towns and villages fluctuates in a small range around 50 percent; it will be remembered that about 51 percent of all small centers were found to be experiencing some growth in this same period. Although the proportions of growing towns and villages in the six zones differ from region to region in Canada, the general shape of the gradient is similar for all regions (Table 4.1).

---

*All numbered tables appear at the end of this chapter.

Looking behind the proportions at the absolute number of small centers reveals other facets of metropolitan influence. In the first zone, for example, there are just over 1,100 towns and villages situated within a thirty-mile radius of the twenty-three metropolitan centers of Canada. Thus, the population growth experienced by about 800 small centers seems definitely associated with metropolitan spillover. In the remaining zones there are over 3,800 small centers experiencing growth, and here proximity to the metropolis seems not to play a significant role. Further, one-quarter of the small centers located near a metropolis declined in population. Even when a more detailed look is taken at towns within specific metropolitan regions, it will usually be found that neither the size of the town nor its previous population growth rate has much part in its recent growth or lack of it. Again, the best that can be said is that up to thirty miles from a metropolitan center there is a strong probability of growth for a town or village.

The substantial change in population growth tendencies of small centers that occurs at about thirty miles is also worth commenting on. This distance represents the limit for most people living in the countryside who might need to commute to a job in the city. Metropolitan transportation studies have consistently noted that 85 percent or more of commuters seek to limit their trips to 25-30 minutes. Given less-congested traffic conditions in the countryside, the city-bound commuter could travel 20-25 miles in this time period. Later in this chapter it will be shown that even those who live and work in countryside locations tend to limit their daily commuting trip to a similar level.

Two tests of metropolitan influence, using more recent population data, sharpens the perspective somewhat. In one instance the growth experience from 1971 to 1976 of towns and villages located in a representative quadrant adjacent to a metropolitan center was examined. In ten such situations (one in each province), it was again found that over two-thirds of the small centers experienced some population growth when located within thirty miles of a large city. Beyond this distance the proportion of growing towns drops off. Moreover, those situated within thirty miles had average growth rates three and four times higher than the average growth rate of 6 percent for all towns and villages in this period. Thus, when small towns in the metropolitan orbit do grow, their growth is bound to be very vigorous.

The second test of metropolitan influence draws upon data compiled by Canadian demographer Leroy Stone to describe recent metropolitan expansion in Canada.[1] For successive rings of municipalities surrounding each of the twenty-three metropolitan central cities, data are provided for 1971 to 1976 on the rates of population growth, natural increase (births minus deaths), and migration (the difference between population growth and natural increase). Translating the data for the rings of municipalities into distance zones results in the following pattern for metropolitan regions.

Components of Population Growth for Municipalities in Different Distance Zones around Metropolitan Centers, 1971-1976

	Distance to Metropolitan Center in Miles			
	0-15	16-30	31-45	46-60
Population Growth Rate (%)	9.5	10.4	2.7	3.1
Natural Increase Rate (%)	6.1	6.8	4.9	5.8
Net Migration Rate (%)	2.2	3.6	-2.2	-2.7

SOURCE: Stone, 1981

Although these data are for municipalities, rather than being directly for small towns,[2] they do provide a good picture of the population dynamics in the regions surrounding metropolitan centers. Three facets of the pattern are illuminating. The first is that population growth is substantially higher for those municipalities within thirty miles of metropolises. The second is that natural-increase rates are uniformly high in all zones. A comparison with natural-increase rates for the central city would show the latter seldom reach 60 percent of the level of the fringe municipalities. The third facet is that up to thirty miles, municipalities gain more population from those moving in than they lose by people leaving to live elsewhere; beyond this distance the reverse is true.

The net result of these several probes is that proximity to a metropolis is a limited influence on the growth of small towns. In spatial terms, that influence drops off very sharply beyond thirty miles from a metropolitan center. Even within thirty miles of a metropolitan center, not all towns and villages can count on growing, but those that do will experience dramatic growth. Indeed, town and village growth seems mostly attributable to their higher-than-average rates of natural increase and their ability to keep a sizable proportion of this growth from moving away. Implicitly, there seems to be little difference between small towns located near or far away from a metropolis. That issue is examined in greater detail in the following section.

2. METROPOLITAN INFLUENCE ON SOCIAL AND ECONOMIC CHARACTERISTICS

Although metropolitan proximity has a limited effect on town and village population growth, is it possible that other characteristics of small centers might be influenced? All of the incorporated small towns, about 1,600 in all in 1971, provide a helpful perspective through which to probe for influences on such things as income, household size, labor-force composition, household rent, and unemployment rates. Towns and villages situated within a Census Division that contains a Census Metropolitan Area would comprise a metropolitan set, and the remainder of small towns a nonmetropolitan set. Further, with these data it is possible to distinguish differences in the population size of centers and thereby examine whether smaller or larger towns are influenced more.

The accompanying set of graphs illustrate the results of these probes. They reveal similar tendencies between small centers in metropolitan regions and those in nonmetropolitan regions on eight indicators. Although there is not a perfect correspondence of the two curves, they resemble each other in form and, often, in slope. The main features of each graph are described below.

Average Household Income (1971): People in smaller places fare worse than those in larger towns in regard to household income in both metropolitan and nonmetropolitan regions. Although the curve for centers in metropolitan regions shows them with slightly higher incomes in all sizes of centers, only at the level of 2,500 population is the difference as much as 7 percent (Figure 4.1).

FIGURE 4.1
**Average Household Income in Centers in Metropolitan
and Nonmetropolitan Regions, 1971**

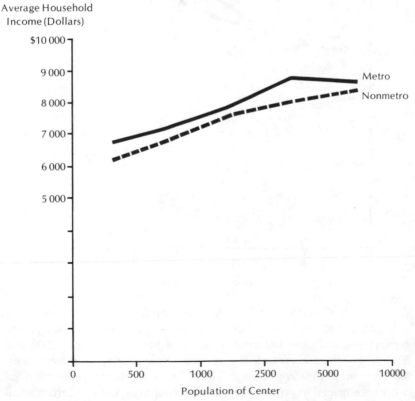

Average Household Rent (1971): At up to 2,500 population, the average household rent is within 6 percent for metropolitan and nonmetropolitan centers of different sizes. Thereafter, towns in metropolitan regions have increasingly higher rents so that at 10,000 population the difference is 15 percent. This is a reflection of urban housing conditions — higher land values, greater variety in housing types, and more higher-cost housing — starting to affect small centers within the metropolitan orbit (Figure 4.2).

FIGURE 4.2
Average Rent in Centers in Metropolitan and Nonmetropolitan Regions, 1971

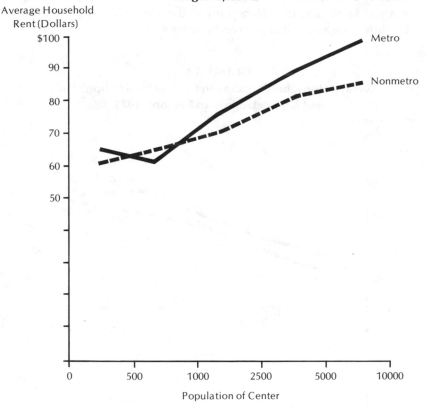

Average Household
Rent (Dollars)

Population of Center

Labor-Force Composition (1971): The proportion of the labor force engaged in each of three main categories — primary, secondary, and tertiary — is similar for small centers of both regions of 1,000 and under. For larger centers the curves show distinctive differences. Centers in nonmetropolitan regions have a higher proportion of workers engaged in *primary* activities, as might be expected from small centers located in agricultural and natural resource base regions. *Secondary* (mostly manufacturing and processing) industries are more prominent in larger metropolitan-region centers, probably as a result of the suburbanization of factories. Both metropolitan- and nonmetropolitan-region small centers show a remarkably similar proportion of their labor forces engaged in *tertiary* (mostly commercial) activities, reflecting a similarity in commercial roles of small centers regardless of location (Figures 4.3, 4.4, 4.5).

FIGURE 4.3
Labor Force in Primary Industry in Centers in Metropolitan and Nonmetropolitan Regions, 1971

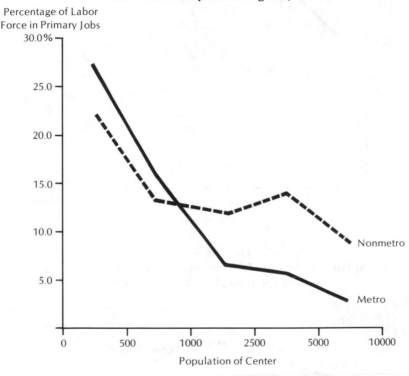

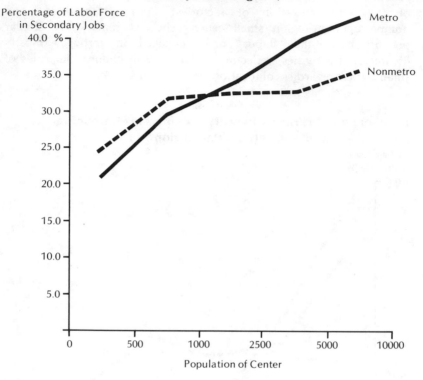

FIGURE 4.4
Labor Force in Secondary Industry in Centers in Metropolitan and Nonmetropolitan Regions, 1971

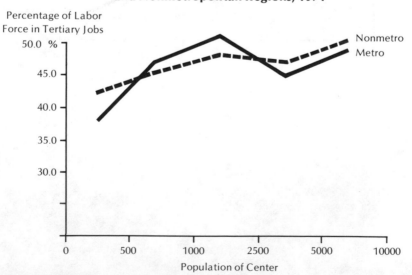

FIGURE 4.5
Labor Force in Tertiary Industry in Centers in Metropolitan and Nonmetropolitan Regions, 1971

Unemployment Rate (1971): Neither metropolitan- nor nonmetropolitan-region small centers show substantially different unemployment conditions. One noticeable tendency, however, is for the smallest centers, hamlets and small villages, to have significantly lower rates of unemployment than larger villages and towns (Figure 4.6).

FIGURE 4.6
Unemployment Rates in Centers in Metropolitan and Nonmetropolitan Regions, 1971

One overall conclusion that may be drawn from these graphs is that small centers within the orbit of metropolitan areas show very few differences from those situated well beyond the metropolis. This seems to be true regardless of the population size of a center. However, in both metropolitan and nonmetropolitan settings, those places with populations of 1,000 or less tended to be structurally and functionally different from small and large towns in the same regional situation. Thus, the size of a small center is a more distinctive characteristic than is proximity to a metropolis, when seeking to compare the performance of towns and villages.

A second conclusion may be drawn from the similar tendencies among centers. Since the various indicators used here reflect the degree of urbanization of a center's population, the close similarities may more likely have their source in the diffusion of national and societal norms than in simple proximity to an urban center. The results, thus, affirm the existence of homogenizing tendencies throughout the Canadian settlement system as discussed in Chapters 3 and 5.

3. CONTEMPORARY TOWNS AND VILLAGES AS TRADE CENTERS

Almost all of Canada's towns and villages were founded to service the needs of farmers, fishermen, trappers, miners, and loggers when the various regions of the country were being broadly settled. Thus, a persistent image of small centers is the role they play as trade centers for surrounding rural areas and for the people who live and work in the countryside. As a result of changes that began as early as the 1920s in the way in which the above occupations were conducted, and as a result of the increased mobility and accessibility of rural residents, the image of the rural trade center became tarnished. Indeed, reports in the popular media and in academic circles began to promote the notion of the dying rural trade center. Well into the 1960s it was not uncommon to find reports concluding with the gloomy prospect, "The handwriting is on the wall for most small towns." But is this still the case?

Trends in Trade Center Relations to 1960

Small-town businesses were, undoubtedly, hard hit by the technological advances in rural industries especially since the 1930s. These led to an outflow of rural people who were no longer needed in the forests or on the farms and fishing grounds. Results from studies of three Canadian regions in the 1950s — Saskatchewan, Prince Edward Island, and Eastern Ontario — showed trade center decline to be very prevalent, as illustrated in the accompanying table.[3]

Aggregate Changes in the Trade Center Systems of Three Canadian Regions, 1951-1961

Number of Centers	Saskatchewan Number	%	Eastern Ontario Number	%	Prince Edward Island Number	%
At start of period	892	100.0	441	100.0	108	100.0
Emerging in period	16	1.8	28	6.4	10	9.3
Expiring in period	129	14.5	77	17.4	32	29.6
Declining in period	148	16.6	52	11.8	7	6.5
At end of period	779	—	392	—	86	—

SOURCE: Hodge, 1966

Looked at in historical perspective, the 1950s represent the low point in a long period of decline for small centers generally, throughout North America. Not long after 1900, cars and trucks started to come into common use in rural areas, thus initiating the decline of population and economic functions of towns and villages.[4] Motor vehicles were a "double-edged sword" for small places at this time, for not only could rural customers shop more widely but wholesale suppliers to rural stores also could choose their distribution patterns more freely. Dahms encapsulates the process of change in trade centers in Ontario in the passage that follows, a process probably not much different from that occurring at about the same time in other Canadian regions.

> After 1911, major changes occurred. Cars and trucks became increasingly popular in Ontario, and by the 1930s, both rural roads and Provincial highways had been greatly extended and improved. Centralization of goods and services into larger, older, urban places began in earnest. Those that had already outstripped their rivals and attracted the railway in the 1850s became dominant manufacturing centers. Others at strategic route junctions provided high-order shopping for customers now able to travel far beyond their local settlement to shop. During this process, many of the widespread towns and villages of the 1880s became bypassed and entered economic decline. Innovations such as prohibition, rural mail delivery and catalogue shopping speeded this process — why bother going to the local general store when the wonders of Eaton's and Simpson's were as close as your mail box? Many combined general store-post offices closed for good after 1911. Dozens of local taverns suffered the same fate. Between 1911 and the 1960s, the number of settlements functioning as central places decreased dramatically with many "disappearing" in terms of the provision of goods and services.[5]

While the specter of commercial decline hovered around many small centers through the first sixty years of this century, it must also be seen as a period of "sorting out" the functions that towns and villages could perform. It was an era that featured increased mobility and accessibility for people and firms, increased consolidation and specialization in commerce, and the increased centralization of social facilities such as schools and hospitals. And, it should not be overlooked, the automotive mechanization that made the latter changes possible also had counterparts in all the natural resource industries of the countryside — farming, fishing, forestry, mining — which led to an outflow of rural population.

Trade Center Revitalization Since 1960

Renewed research interest in the 1970s into the prospects of towns and villages began to reveal distinctive changes in the prospects for trade centers as compared to previous decades. Both the work of Stabler in Saskatchewan and that of Dahms in Ontario shows the 1960s to be a period when the precipitous decline in the number of commercial establishments in small centers ceased for many, if not most, places. The data for

Saskatchewan from 1961 to 1976, gathered by Stabler, are indicative of similar trade center trends in other regions.[6]

Changes in the Number of Business Outlets in Saskatchewan Trade Centers, 1961-1976

Population Class (1961)	Average Number of Business Outlets		
	1961	1972	1976
under 200	6	3	4
201-500	14	10	12
501-1,000	25	23	29
1,001-2,500	47	46	58
2,501-5,000	95	115	152
5,001-15,000	201	215	260

SOURCE: Stabler, 1978

One can see from these data a considerable amount of stability in the local commercial sectors beginning to set in during the 1960s. Small places, especially those with fewer than 500 residents, did continue to experience sharp declines through to the early 1970s, but by 1976 were recording gains in the numbers of their commercial establishments. For all the 473 Saskatchewan trade centers studied by Stabler, the period 1972-1976 saw a 22 percent increase in the total number of business outlets. If it is also remembered that rural portions of the Prairie Provinces, and Saskatchewan in particular, suffered substantial population outflows as a result of adjustments in farm size due to mechanization in the period since 1941, then the decline and sorting out of trade center businesses is more readily understandable. What accounts for the apparent recent turnaround in trade center fortunes?

Before considering that question it will be helpful to examine comparable data for a sample of trade centers from across Canada for the period of the 1970s. Using the representative one-hundred-center sample (see Appendix A), data were obtained for the number of business establishments in retail, services, wholesale, and manufacturing endeavors for both 1971 and 1981. Again, we see from the accompanying table that the Saskatchewan experience in recent trade center growth was occurring throughout the country. Over 81 percent of these centers added some retail establishments in the 1971-1981 period and nearly 60 percent saw their retail base grow by more than one-fifth. Even more striking is the fact that 85 percent of the centers experienced an increase in the total of all commercial establishments. The difference is made up, most noticeably, of expansions in wholesale and manufacturing enterprises.

Change in the Commercial Base of Canadian Towns and Villages, 1971-1981

	Proportion of Towns Experiencing					
	Decline			**Growth**		
Firms	**Over -20%**	**From -10% To - 20%**	**From -1% To - 10%**	**From 0% To + 10%**	**From + 11% To + 20%**	**Over + 20%**
Retail	8.8	5.5	4.4	9.9	13.2	58.2
			mean = 32.6%			
Commercial	5.5	5.5	4.4	9.9	9.9	64.8
			mean = 40.5%			

SOURCE: Tables 4.2, 4.3

If we break these figures down, there are differences between the trade centers of the various regions of Canada and between sizes of centers (see Tables 4.2 and 4.3). For example, the smallest centers in the sample did not fare as well as the larger ones, especially those under 1,000 in population. Even so, 76 percent of them did see an increase in retail establishments, and 80 percent saw their total number of business enterprises grow. Looked at by region, the Prairies and British Columbia, not surprisingly, had growth in both retail and total establishments in over 90 percent of their centers. Somewhat unexpectedly, 88 percent of the Atlantic Region centers expanded their commercial base, while Ontario small centers were the most subject to decline.

When the above analysis was conducted, an opportunity was taken to examine changes in the commercial base of small centers in relation to the changes they had experienced in population numbers from 1971 to 1981. Correlation coefficients were found to be quite low between population and both retail growth ($r = 0.28$) and total commercial growth ($r = 0.33$). Only for those centers between 2,500 and 5,000, and for the centers in Quebec, did the correlation coefficients exceed 0.5. In the Atlantic Region, for example, the average population growth of its sample centers for 1971-1981 was negative (-0.16%) while the growth in retail establishments was very high ($+31.3\%$). Generally during this period, in all regions and sizes of centers, growth in numbers of firms far exceeded population growth in small centers. This then leads back to the question posed earlier: why the renewed vigor in the commercial base of small centers in Canada?

Factors in Trade Center Resurgence

Towns and villages will continue to play the role of service centers for people who live in rural regions, probably in a more vigorous way than in previous decades. The already obvious revitalization of trade centers is, however, coming about under new circumstances in the nation as a whole and in the countryside in particular. Some centers will continue to see their commercial base contract, and in some, it will cease entirely. Both the decline and the more likely situation of growth for trade centers in the future are a continuation of the longer-term trends of "sorting out" the functions among centers within regions. But the "sorting out" is now subject to new terms of reference.

Several new conditions have come to prevail in regard to rural regions in Canada, especially since the 1960s, that shape the current trends and future prospects for towns and villages as trade centers. These new conditions involve the population, the income and tastes of people, and the cultural and institutional milieux in rural areas.

Recent Rural Population Growth. The 1981 census reveals that, for the first time in many decades, the 1976-1981 period saw the rural population in Canada grow faster than the population as a whole. Rural population has been growing steadily for nearly twenty years. Since 1966, despite the decline in farm population, more people have come to live in the countryside and in small towns than have left. The net result, which can only be crudely estimated due to data inconsistencies, would seem to be well over one million more people living in rural Canada than fifteen years ago. Thus, for the trade centers in many rural regions the number of potential customers is expanding. This must be counted as the central factor in trade center recovery.

Changes in Purchasing Power. The incomes of rural people have grown steadily over the past three decades, although not nearly as fast as their urban counterparts. Further, the fastest-growing segment of the rural population is the "nonfarm" group whose occupations are more likely to be in urban-type jobs, in many cases in cities and towns. This further raises the average level of disposable income of rural residents. In addition, more and more rural households have two principal wage earners. If these aspects are coupled with the increase in the numbers of people living in rural areas and small towns, it can reasonably be surmised that, compared with the 1960s, trade center business establishments now have a dramatically increased purchasing power of customers in their trade area.

The growth in the number and purchasing power of rural consumers does not always translate into an increase in the number of retail outlets in a small town, but it does affect the "mix" of businesses. In his studies of Ontario centers, Dahms notes the increase in the number and importance of services whose purpose is to accommodate the automobile — service stations, garages, and auto-parts stores.[7] The very phenomenon that was predicted to assure the demise of small commercial centers is now part of its salvation in many regions.

Also evident since 1971 is an increasing diversity in the kind of commercial establishments found in small trade centers, regardless of whether they gained or lost businesses. A review of the composition of establishments in the Canada-wide sample of small towns shows that in the 1970s there emerged many new businesses catering to the increased "discretionary" incomes of rural and small-town residents. There is a noticeable increase in such businesses as sporting goods stores, restaurants, music stores, taverns, jewelry shops, bakeries, and nurseries. The changes in retail composition differ from one community to another due to differences in taste, market area size, entrepreneurship, and so on, but the tendency toward diversification is clear-cut.

Changes in Infrastructure. In the two decades following World War II, major changes occurred in the infrastructure of rural regions in Canada. On the one hand, this period saw the concept of "consolidation" of public services being vigorously implemented. Dispersed country schools and hospitals, in particular, were each combined in fewer, more central locations. Thus, some centers were favored over others; travel and activity patterns of rural and small-town dwellers changed as a result. On the other hand, this period saw great improvement in roads and highways throughout rural Canada. Better roads were considered necessary to allow rural people to get to the new centralized public services. But better roads, in the age of the automobile, also meant much greater personal mobility and, thus, greater choice in shopping and residence.

Both these changes in infrastructure — consolidation and better roads — were certainly responsible for much upheaval among trade centers. However, by about 1970, both these revisions in rural infrastructure had been largely achieved in most regions. In other words, the rural cultural milieu has settled down. It is, of course, more centralized in its activities and has a more mobile population, but it is also more stable within this context. Add to this the new ubiquitous social policy measures available to rural people, referred to in earlier chapters, as well as improved rural electrification and communications, and one must conclude that small towns and rural areas are reasonable, and possibly apt, places in which to live. This is, undoubtedly, why many rural people have stayed and many more new residents have come to live in rural regions. It has meant stability and even growth for commercial enterprises in trade centers. The data and trends of recent years indicate a generally viable future for towns and villages that function as trade centers. There will, of course, continue to be differences between centers within regions as well as between the centers of the various regions in the nation. Ontario trade centers, for example, appear less buoyant, perhaps because many of the processes of rural rationalization and urbanization of the countryside began earlier there than in other regions. Trade centers in British Columbia and Alberta are not only buoyed by fast population growth and prosperity; their trade center systems are maturing. The characteristics of the other regions will also give a special context for the performance of their small commercial centers.

Trade Center Patterns in the 1980s

Accompanying the resurgence in the commercial life of rural trade centers in Canada is a significant new trend in the spatial patterns of shopping and in the locations of rural businesses. For some time now, it has been noticed that rural residents conduct their shopping activities in ways that do not correspond to the regular hierarchical arrangements envisioned by central-place theory. That is, instead of adhering to the principle of traveling the minimum distance to obtain particular goods or services, rural residents turn to a variety of small and large centers at various distances from their homes. Residents of one community may, for example, shop for groceries in one nearby village, patronize a restaurant in another, and buy building materials in yet another. The much greater mobility and flexibility in the lives of rural people, along with their greater incomes, allow them to exercise their preferences in what they buy and where they buy it.[8]

Rural residents of Wellington County, Ontario, interviewed by Dahms in 1977, indicated that convenience shopping (bread, milk, cigarettes) is almost always done locally, as is the use of a bank or drug store if the latter are available.[9] But for major purchases of groceries, clothing, furniture, and appliances, and for recreation and entertainment, rural residents are prepared to travel far afield and in diverse directions to suit their personal tastes. The following one-way travel times for various purchases in rural Ontario are probably close to the norm for residents in much of rural Canada. (They also may not be far off the times taken by city dwellers for the same sorts of purchases.)

Median One-Way Travel Time (Minutes) for Selected Purchases by Rural Residents of Wellington County, Ontario, 1977

Destination	Median Travel Time
Convenience Grocery Shopping	5
Major Grocery Shopping	20
Furniture Purchase	25
Appliance Purchase	30
Clothing Purchase	35

SOURCE: Dahms, 1977

The tendency of rural consumers to "shop around" is very influential both in sustaining many rural businesses and in encouraging changes in the spatial patterns of trade centers. As noted earlier, one of the most obvious changes is in the "mix" of stores and services in small centers. Quite noticeable in many small towns has been the addition of business establishments that cater to people's leisure-time needs or their desire for extra convenience. Among these new businesses one is likely to find fast-food outlets, "jug milk" stores, taverns, sporting goods and furniture stores, as well as auto parts dealers and shops for fabrics, crafts, gifts, books, and music.

Characteristically, the new businesses are more specialized, and many are associated with regional or national franchises. But most are spun off the efforts of long-lived businesses in the town or are the inventions of new residents. Often, one or a few town businesses develop a reputation for the quality of their service or product, and may draw people from as far as thirty to forty miles away.

Although the mix of businesses has changed in most town and village trade centers in recent years, the particular mix differs from town to town. Thus, the pattern of trade centers for the 1980s is one in which a number of small places collectively provide the needed goods and services to the residents of a rural district. It is a pattern already much in evidence.

This more amorphous rural trading pattern has generated some theorizing that the various service centers in a rural district are much like the neighborhood or community shopping and service areas of a big city, but simply "dispersed over the countryside [and] separated by open country farms."[10] "Dispersed city" is a term often applied when describing contemporary trade center systems.[11] Whether it is apt to use the analogy of a city in rural contexts is still the subject of research. Nevertheless, one commonly finds in rural districts that it is a *complex* of towns and villages that provides for the commercial, social, and institutional needs of people. It almost goes without saying that these trade center complexes will overlap and not be subject to easy delineation. They are, after all, the result of rural consumer behavior, which changes as the rural population changes and as rural people are affected by changes of taste and income. But whatever the shifts might be in shopping patterns, it is safe to say that trade centers can no longer be usefully categorized according to central-place theory.

4. JOB COMMUTING PATTERNS IN SMALL-TOWN REGIONS

Although towns and villages are obviously the shopping and cultural centers in rural regions, very little consideration is given to them as employment centers. The single-industry town, the place that grows up around a mine or pulp mill, for example, is subject to much scrutiny.[12] This latter attention, however, tends to focus on those towns created to exploit a single resource in an isolated wilderness situation. But most towns and villages are not resource development enclaves. For that matter, most single-industry towns are not isolated, but are part of a functioning region along with other towns.

Often overlooked are the employment opportunities, both in commerce and in public agencies, in small towns in the tertiary sector. Just the jobs in the thirty to forty stores, garages, restaurants, and other service establishments, plus those in the school, post office, and local government in a typical Canadian small town of about 1,000 people, will often provide close to 300 jobs. These jobs along with others in manufacturing, natural resource development, or public institutions will, thus, constitute a broad job market not only for town residents but also for the residents of the countryside and other small towns in the vicinity. And, not uncommonly, there is an interchange of workers who live in one town but work in another. The net result is likely to be a considerable amount of home-to-work commuting occurring among the communities within a rural region. If there happens to be a city nearby, its job opportunities will contribute to more job commuting, both with rural residents traveling to the city and city dwellers commuting to jobs in the small towns and countryside.

With the release of the 1971 census came the first opportunity to study the patterns of home-to-work commuting for small Canadian centers. For all those towns and villages that were incorporated municipalities, a total of nearly 1,600 of all sizes, it is possible to determine (1) the proportion of a town's labor force who commute to jobs outside the community; (2) how far they travel; and (3) the proportion of in-commuters who share the job opportunities in the town. No more recent data on commuting are available on a Canada-wide basis, but commuting information from two regional studies in 1981 confirm the picture provided by the previous census.

The Incidence of Out-Commuting from Small Centers

Given the generally held opinion that few job opportunities exist in towns and villages, one would expect to find considerable out-commuting by residents. However, in the towns and villages throughout Canada in 1971, only 28.9 percent of the resident labor force were out-commuters. Very near the same proportion prevailed in centers of all sizes, as the summary table shows.

Proportion of Resident Labor Force in Canadian Towns and Villages Who were Commuting to Outside Jobs, 1971

	Population Size of Center				
Under 500	501-1,000	1,001-2,500	2,501-5,000	5,001-10,000	All Small Centers
25.7%	29.8%	32.9%	30.1%	29.3%	28.9%

SOURCE: *Census of Canada*

The smallest centers have the lowest rate of out-commuting, but there is no regular increase in the proportion of out-commuters with increasing population size. Indeed, there is only a modest variation in the degree of commuting, and the raw data show very small standard deviations. There are some small differences between regions with small-town residents in Prince Edward Island, Ontario, and Quebec doing more commuting than the national average, while out-commuting is below average in all other provinces' small centers (Table 4.4).

There is no acknowledged standard against which to compare the rate of out-commuting by town and village residents. However, the fact that nearly three-quarters of the labor force are able to find work in their home community indicates not only the existence of a substantial pool of jobs in small communities, but also a great deal of self-sufficiency in employment in rural regions.

Commuting Distances for Small-Town Residents

Of the 25 to 30 percent of town and village workers who commute, one might wonder how far they must travel to their jobs. Among all small centers in 1971 the average distance traveled by out-commuters was 22.4 miles. As the accompanying table shows, the variation is barely two miles among the different sizes of centers.

Average Distance Traveled by Out-Commuters from Canadian Towns and Villages, 1971

		Population Size of Center			All Small
Under 500	501-1,000	1,001-2,500	2,501-5,000	5,001-10,000	Centers
23.3 miles	22.0 miles	21.6 miles	22.5 miles	22.1 miles	22.4 miles

SOURCE: *Census of Canada*

Differences in the settlement geography of the various regions of Canada affect the commuting distance in rural areas. For example, commuters from towns and villages in the three westernmost provinces and Newfoundland travel slightly more than the average distance. Commuters in the Maritimes, Quebec, and Ontario travel substantially shorter-than-average distances to their jobs. In New Brunswick, the average commuter from a small center travels about 16 miles; in Quebec, it is about 18 miles. In Saskatchewan and Alberta, commuters travel the greatest distances on the average, 26 and 29 miles respectively (Table 4.4).

If one now translates these commuting distances into travel times, even considering regional differences, the average journey takes probably thirty minutes or less. Many transportation studies have shown that a commuting journey of this duration is very similar to that of suburban commuters in Canadian metropolitan areas. This finding has two interesting implications. First, it shows not only that small-town commuters have travel behavior similar to that of city commuters, but also that most of those who cannot or choose not to work in their own town are able to find jobs within a half-hour's drive of home. Second, when one considers, as we have noted, that 80 percent of the towns and villages of Canada lie well beyond a half-hour drive of our metropolitan areas, it is apparent that rural regions themselves provide the bulk of employment opportunities for small-town residents.

Towns and Villages as Employment Centers

We have alluded a number of times to the substantial role played by towns and villages in providing jobs to their own residents and the inhabitants of the surrounding countryside and other nearby towns. A simple test of this argument is to determine the number of people involved in a small town's employed labor force who commute to the town for work. It turns out that, in 1971, nearly 35 percent of those employed in small centers were in-commuters. Those centers with fewer than 500 residents had the lowest proportion of in-commuters, while in those with between 500 and 2,500 residents, almost 40 percent of the jobs were held by people living in other communities.

If one then compares the proportion of in-commuters with the proportion of residents who worked outside their own towns, it is possible to measure the importance of small-town jobs in rural regions. Thus, in the accompanying table an index of the difference between out-commuters and in-commuters is provided. An index of over 100 shows that a community has more job opportunities than its own population could fill.

Canadian Towns and Villages as Suppliers of Jobs to Other Communities, 1971

	Population Size of Center					
	Under 500	501- 1,000	1,001- 2,500	2,501- 5,000	5,001- 10,000	All Small Centers
In-commuters in Employed Labor Force (%)	30.9	39.9	38.6	34.7	33.2	34.9
Index of Nonlocal Job Provision	105.2	110.1	105.7	104.6	102.9	106.0

SOURCE: *Census of Canada*

One interpretation of this index is the degree of "job self-sufficiency" of a town or village. The average index value for all sizes of center throughout the nation is 106.0, which is a clear indication of the substantial way in which towns and villages act as employment centers in rural regions. Towns and villages in four provinces — Saskatchewan, Quebec, Prince Edward Island, and Newfoundland — have, on the average, fewer jobs than required by their own residents. Five provinces' small centers are well above the national norm in local job provision.

The results of studies of two rural regions in 1981 in quite different parts of Canada, the east coast of Vancouver Island and Frontenac County in

Eastern Ontario, confirm several facets of the picture of commuting that emerged from the 1971 data. The median commuting distance for residents both of small communities and of the countryside in rural Frontenac County was 15.6 miles in 1981.[13] On Vancouver Island, in a region between 15 and 35 miles north of Nanaimo, 85 percent of the residents found work within 15 miles of their homes.[14] In both areas there are cities within reasonable driving range, Kingston (pop. 60,000) and Nanaimo (pop. 47,000), yet they are not the destinations of most rural commuters. About 30 percent in both regions have jobs located within 5 miles of home and another 30 percent have jobs in small towns within 10-20 miles (such as Parksville, Qualicum Beach, and Lantzville on Vancouver Island; and Sharbot Lake, Verona, and Perth in Eastern Ontario).

In summary, the main features of town and village commuting patterns are that there is considerable commuting both in and out of small communities; the commuters find jobs usually within a driving time of one-half hour or less of their homes; and towns and villages provide enough jobs to cover the needs of their residents as well as those of many outsiders. Another aspect also emerges: the area of interchange of people and jobs is quite *compact* in rural regions, and does not show a great deal of dependence on the presence of a nearby city. Again, as with trade center relations, there are complex *local interdependencies* between place of residence and jobs in the regions of small towns. That people can find jobs locally is a major factor in the persistence of towns and villages.

5. TRANSPORTATION DEPENDENCIES IN RURAL AREAS

The previous two sections have described how small-town and countryside residents are involved in an extensive system of shopping, obtaining services, and working — in short, they have to contend with large distances. Possibly more important is that all of this is held together primarily by one mode of transportation: the private automobile. The 1971 census, the latest overall data available, showed that 83 percent of rural households owned two cars, as compared with 76 percent of urban households. A sample of four hundred countryside and small-town households surveyed in Huron County, Ontario in 1979 showed that 93 percent owned and were able to operate a licensed motor vehicle.[15] These figures are not surprising, since collective transportation serving general local needs is almost nonexistent in rural regions of Canada. They simply point up a vital fact of rural life: rural people are extremely dependent on the ownership or availability of an automobile (or small truck) in order to participate in normal activities.

Personal mobility is bound to be constrained no matter where one lives, and especially for some groups of people. The aged, the young, the poor, and the handicapped are highly dependent on others to provide transportation. When they are unable to obtain access to a means of transportation, public or private, they become "transportation disadvantaged," as some studies call them.[16] But the issue of transportation dependency is more acute for these groups and others in rural areas, for there are few, if any, alternative forms of transportation to the private motor vehicle. As Todd notes in his study of a rural area in Ontario,

> the potentially disadvantaged may also include the housewife who cannot visit friends or see a doctor because her husband has the automobile at work all day, the teenager who cannot participate in after school activities because he/she has no way of getting home, and the unemployed worker who has to turn down a job in another town because he does not have a car to travel to the employment.[17]

We are only beginning to become aware of the extent of this problem. The two Ontario studies both show a significant number of rural households that do not own a car: 7 percent in Huron County and 4 percent in Frontenac County. But transportation dependency in rural areas is more than just a question of automobile ownership. On the one hand, those not owning a car may have access to a friend or relative with a car. On the other hand, those households owning a vehicle may not have it available at all times; some household members may not be able to drive and/or the car may be away for long periods during the day.

When one structures the rural transportation situation around the various conditions of access to transportation, something of the true extent of rural transportation disadvantage becomes clear. About one-third of the rural Ontario households studied have a significant lack of access to transportation at some times. As well, a small percentage apparently have no vehicle in the household and no one available on a regular basis to provide transportation either in or outside the household.

Level of Transportation Access for Rural Households in Two Ontario Counties

| | Percent of Households | | |
	Zero Mobility	Partial Mobility	Complete Mobility
Huron County (1978)	1.7	38.2	60.1
Frontenac County (1981)	3.6	28.6	67.8

SOURCES: Armstrong & Fuller, 1979; Todd, 1981

It is not possible to be any more definitive about rural transportation dependency in other parts of rural Canada; suffice to say that the problem is recognized and a wide array of formal and informal solutions are being tried. In some areas intercity bus service is being instituted on a limited basis, such as a once-a-day service along a main highway to a nearby city to accommodate work commuters or a once-a-week "shopping bus" from different towns each day. Experiments are being carried out in the use of vans, mini-buses, and even school buses in the middle of the day. One of the most popular and most appropriate of the new forms of rural transportation is the "mobility club" concept. It consists of organizing the services of volunteer drivers with access to private automobiles and matching them with the needs of those residents of the community who have zero or partial mobility. Such services may be organized by voluntary community organizations, public social service agencies, or rural municipalities. Often a modest ridership fee is charged. A less formal type of ride-sharing, prevalent in rural areas, is the car pool. The cluster of parked cars one frequently sees at the junction of some major rural road and the Trans-Canada Highway is clear evidence not only of a problem but also of the willingness of rural people to find a viable solution.

The large distances rural residents must travel for most goods, services, and jobs, and the low population density in rural areas, allows for few viable alternative forms of transportation. The convenience and flexibility of the private vehicle is eminently suited to life in rural regions. And, as one American study concluded, any alternative system of rural transportation will probably closely resemble the characteristics of the private vehicle if it is to be successful.[18]

6. REPRISE ON SMALL-CENTER REGIONAL RELATIONS

At the outset of this chapter several questions were posed regarding the influence of large cities on small towns in Canada, and about the local milieux within which towns and villages currently find themselves. What emerges rather strikingly from the discussion in this chapter is that small centers today do not function according to the concepts of metropolitan dominance and central-place theory. That is, these conventional organizing principles do not apply in any regular way and do not capture the existing relations of the majority of towns and villages.

How then would one characterize the regional setting of small centers today in Canada? A review of the trade center relationships and the work commuting patterns suggests that many basic needs are provided by *regional complexes* of towns and villages. In each rural locality a number of small centers collectively provide from their own distinctive arrays of stores, services, jobs, and social and cultural activities for the residents of small towns and the countryside. Hierarchical arrangements within these complexes are difficult to discern, as are regional boundaries between complexes. In any case, they are probably irrelevant to the new spatial patterns of rural life.

The new rural spatial format implies a great deal of autonomy or independence for small-town and rural residents. But autonomy must not be construed as self-sufficiency and self-containment. It seems more likely that this greater autonomy for small towns is the spatial manifestation of the social, economic, and cultural integration of Canadian society discussed in earlier chapters. It is as if the national complex of support services and values provides a tableau on which the unique geographical entities, cultures, and initiatives of rural Canada can be rendered, each in its distinctive way.

NOTES

1. Leroy O. Stone, "Small-Community Aspects of Demographic Processes in a Steady-State Economy," in *Proceedings of the Conference on Approaches to Rural Development* (Guelph: University of Guelph, 1981), 110-29.
2. Town and village data are enmeshed in the municipal data in two ways: some small centers are incorporated muncipalities; and those that are not are included with township or other such rural municipality data.
3. Gerald Hodge, "Do Villages Grow? Some Perspectives and Predictions," *Rural Sociology* 31:2 (June 1966): 183-96.
4. *Cf.*, Norman T. Moline, *Mobility and the Small Town*, Research Paper No. 132 (Chicago: University of Chicago Department of Geography, 1971); and Richard Lamb, *Metropolitan Impacts on Rural America*, Research Paper No. 162 (Chicago: University of Chicago Department of Geography, 1975).
5. Fred Dahms, "Small Town and Village Ontario," *Ontario Geography* 16 (1980): 19-32.
6. Jack C. Stabler, "Regional Economic Change and Regional Spatial Structure: The Evolving Form of the Urban Hierarchy in the Prairie Region," in B. Wellar, ed., *The Future of Small and Medium-Sized Communities in the Prairie Region* (Ottawa: Ministry of State for Urban Affairs, 1978), 1-26.
7. Dahms, *op. cit.*
8. One of the earliest observations of this tendency was Glenn V. Fuguitt, "The City and the Countryside," *Rural Sociology* 28 (1963): 246-61; a perceptive account of the same phenomenon in Canada is in M.L. Meredith, "The Prairie Community System," *Canadian Farm Economics* 10 (1975): 19-27.
9. Fred Dahms, "Declining Villages?" in T.A. Crowley, ed., *Proceedings: Second Annual Agricultural History of Ontario Seminar*, University School of Part-Times Studies and Continuing Education, University of Guelph, (1977), 50-65.
10. Meredith, *op. cit.*
11. The earliest analogy is I. Burton, "Retain Trade in a Dispersed City," *Transactions of the Illinois State Academy of Science* 52 (1959): 149-50; an evocative reformulation is found in J.F. Hart *et al.*, "The Dying Village and Some Notions About Urban Growth," *Economic Geography* 44 (1968): 343-49.
12. Among the best studies of this genre are Ira M. Robinson, *New Industrial Towns on Canada's Resource Frontier*, Research Paper No. 73 (Chicago: University of Chicago Department of Geography, 1962); and Rex A. Lucas, *Minetown, Milltown, Railtown* (Toronto: University of Toronto Press, 1971).
13. Gerald Hodge, *Domestic Energy Use in Rural Ontario: Some Findings from Frontenac County* (Kingston: Queen's University School of Urban and Regional Planning, 1982).
14. Regional District of Nanaimo Planning Department studies: "Nanoose Bay: Local Residents and Interest Group Viewpoints," and "Lighthouse Country: Local Residents and Interest Group Viewpoints," Nanaimo, B.C., 1981.
15. Marcia B. Armstrong and Anthony M. Fuller, *Profile of the Transportation*

Disadvantaged in a Rural Area of Southwestern Ontario (A Report to the Urban Transportation Research Branch, Transport Canada, Montreal, 1979), 20.

16. John C. Falcocchio and Edmund J. Cantelli, *Transportation and the Disadvantaged* (Lexington, Mass.: Lexington Books, 1974).

17. Kenneth R. Todd, "Transportation in Rural Areas: A Case Study of North Frontenac County" (Unpublished Master's Report, Queen's University School of Urban and Regional Planning, 1981), 2-3.

18. Vary Coates and Ernest Weiss, *Revitalization of Small Communities: Transportation Options*, vol. 1 (Washington, D.C.: United States Department of Transportation, 1975).

TABLES/CHAPTER 4

TABLE 4.1

Proportion of Towns and Villages Experiencing Population Growth in Relation to Distance to Nearest Metropolitan Area in Canada, 1961-1971

Region	Miles from Nearest Metropolitan Area					
	0-30	31-60	61-100	101-150	151-200	Over 200
	Percentage of Towns Growing					
British Columbia	63.2	64.2	55.0	72.7	62.1	54.7
Prairie Region	60.7	34.9	34.5	37.9	27.8	54.1
Ontario	75.5	66.5	55.6	46.8	55.1	54.8
Quebec	82.8	54.1	50.3	38.2	33.3	56.9
Atlantic Region	69.2	50.7	47.4	47.8	56.2	58.0
CANADA	71.9	52.8	47.9	45.8	49.5	56.0

SOURCE: *Census of Canada*

TABLE 4.2

Rate of Change in Number of Retail Establishments in Towns and Villages by Population Size and Region, Canada, 1971-1981

	Proportion Declining			Proportion Growing		
	Over −20%	−10% to −20%	−1% to −10%	0% to +10%	+10 to +20%	Over +20%
Population of Center						
Under 1,000	20.0	4.0	0.0	8.0	8.0	60.0
1,001-2,500	10.3	6.9	10.3	10.3	6.9	55.2
2,501-5,000	0.0	4.5	4.5	18.2	31.8	40.9
5,001-10,000	0.0	6.7	0.0	0.0	6.7	86.7
Region						
Atlantic	0.0	8.0	4.0	12.0	16.0	60.0
Quebec	12.5	6.3	0.0	25.0	18.8	37.5
Ontario	26.3	5.3	15.8	0.0	15.8	36.8
Prairie	5.0	0.0	0.0	5.0	10.0	80.0
British Columbia	0.0	9.1	0.0	9.1	0.0	81.8
CANADA	8.8	5.5	4.4	9.9	13.2	58.2

SOURCE: Dun and Bradstreet, *Reference Book*, for May 1971 and May 1981, as applied to a sample of 100 centers (see Appendix A)

TABLE 4.3

Rate of Change in Total Commercial Establishments in Towns and Villages by Population Size and Region, Canada, 1971-1981

	Proportion Declining			Proportion Growing		
	Over -20%	-10% to -20%	-1% to -10%	0% to +10%	+10 to +20%	Over +20%
Population of Center						
Under 1,000	16.0	4.0	0.0	8.0	12.0	60.0
1,001-2,500	3.4	10.3	6.9	6.9	10.3	62.1
2,501-5,000	0.0	0.0	9.1	22.7	13.6	54.5
5,001-10,000	0.0	6.7	0.0	0.0	0.0	93.3
Region						
Atlantic	4.0	8.0	0.0	8.0	8.0	72.0
Quebec	0.0	12.5	12.5	12.5	18.8	43.8
Ontario	21.1	0.0	10.5	21.1	10.5	36.8
Prairie	0.0	5.0	0.0	5.0	10.0	80.0
British Columbia	0.0	0.0	0.0	0.0	0.0	100.0
CANADA	5.5	5.5	4.4	9.9	9.9	64.8

SOURCE: Dun and Bradstreet, *Reference Book*, for May 1971 and May 1981, as applied to a sample of 100 centers (see Appendix A)

TABLE 4.4

Characteristics of Commuting Patterns for Incorporated Towns and Villages by Province, Canada, 1971

	Commuters to Other Communities (Percent)	Average Commuting Distance (miles)	Job Self-Sufficiency* (ELF/RLF)
Newfoundland	22.1	23.9	95.6
Prince Edward Island	32.7	17.0	98.3
Nova Scotia	28.1	16.5	125.4
New Brunswick	24.3	16.1	127.5
Quebec	42.8	17.6	88.3
Ontario	35.8	19.8	109.4
Manitoba	20.1	21.8	100.5
Saskatchewan	19.1	25.5	94.2
Alberta	21.0	29.3	112.9
British Columbia	26.4	24.9	111.6
CANADA	28.9	22.4	106.0

*A ratio of Employed Labor Force (total employed persons) and Resident Labor Force (those residing in the community)

SOURCE: *Census of Canada*

5 The Social Structure of Towns and Villages

Having examined the phenomenon of town and village growth and explored its economic underpinnings, we now turn to the investigation of the social characteristics of these communities. Who lives in these places? Are there any sociological features that distinguish residents of towns and villages? Answers to such questions will have to be sought in order to delineate the social contours of small communities. Underlying these broad questions are numerous theoretical and empirical matters which will surface on probing into the social characteristics of towns and villages. For example, any examination of the age distribution in small communities will not remain merely a matter of measuring relative proportions of various age groups, but become a test of the "Rural-Urban Continuum" hypothesis[1] or for instance, of the present notion that small towns are becoming communities of the elderly, with the in-migration of retirees and the departure of the youth. Whether examining age profiles or charting household trends, or observing any other social indicator, in each case our probes are guided by the theories, mental images, or popular beliefs about towns and villages. Inevitably, the results of such probes would test and elaborate upon these notions.

Social structure is one of those sociological terms whose meanings can seldom be pinned down. It refers to the "patterns discernible in social life," but what one sees as a pattern depends on one's perspective.[2] Whereas students of small-group dynamics view social structure as the organizational chart of a group, that is, an arrangement of statuses and roles, for macrosociologists it is a matter of historical continuities and abiding organizational features of a society. We are primarily interested in describing those features of the populations of towns and villages that reflect their organizations, define individual roles, and generally "represent an initial ordering of the facts about a large scale social system,"[3] as Porter calls them. Broadly, these are parameters of social structure or, as Blau says, bases of "social distinctions people make in their social interaction. Age, sex, race, socio-economic status illustrate parameters, assuming that such differences actually affect people's role relations."[4]

Before proceeding further, a minor clarification is necessary. The term "social structure" is not meant to imply that about 9,500 Canadian towns and villages are so linked together that they constitute a unified system. They are an aggregate, a universe, or a conceptual category. The question, then, is to what does the term social structure refer in this case? It refers to parallel but similar features found in a cross-section of such communities. Its point of reference is the average "social" structure of a town or village, and as a concept it is similar to terms such as family size, which could take a value in fractions (for example, 2.6), yet there could not be any family with half or 0.6 members. The common central tendencies of various structural indices are this chapter's object of investigation.

1. HOUSEHOLD SIZE

Whether a population is divided into large numbers of small households or organized into fewer units of a large size is a significant indicator of underlying demographic and social processes. Large households are characteristic of familistic social structures wherein birth rates are high; successive generations are strongly tied together through economic and social interdependencies and mobility is low, while small households are indicative of highly differentiated, occupationally graded, or individualistic social structures.

The rural-urban continuum model postulates that differences between rural and urban societies measured along nine dimensions such as size (of community), occupation, density, social stratification, and type of social interaction are manifest in relative terms suggesting degrees of ruralness or urbanness.[5] Though somewhat dated, this model continues to undergird many of the contemporary notions and images of cities as well as villages. A logical deduction from this postulate is that large households indicate a relatively greater degree of ruralness, whereas small households reflect urbanness. In recent times a greater economic independence of individuals through scholarships, unemployment and welfare allowance, and old age pensions combined with increasing life expectancy and a sharply rising divorce rate, have resulted in an absolute reduction of family size and have brought about a splitting up of households into small units. The question, then, is how far have these trends swept through towns and villages?

Number of Persons Per Household in Different Types of Settlement, 1981

Farm	Nonfarm Village	Under 5,000	5,001-10,000
3.7	3.2	2.9	2.9

10,001-30,000	30,001-100,000	100,001-500,000	Over 500,000
2.9	2.8	2.8	2.7

SOURCE: Census of Canada

The distribution of average household size across the Canadian settlement system shows two tendencies. Longitudinally, the averages have been falling in all types of settlements. Even the average for farm households has declined by about 20 percent since 1961 (from 4.6 persons per household to 3.7) (Table 5.1).* Cross-sectionally, the farm sector is the only one whose household size was significantly (37%) higher than the corresponding figure for metropolises in 1981. Towns had an average household size of 2.9 persons, which was higher than the metropolitan average by only 6 percentage points. A certain degree of convergence of household sizes toward common societal norms has taken place in Canada. Individually, provinces broadly show a similar pattern of household-size distribution across their respective settlement spectrums, although there are noticeable differences among them (Table 5.2).

Newfoundland stands out as the province of large households. The average household size of its towns and villages ranges from 4.0 for places of 1,001-2,500 inhabitants, to 3.8 for communities with populations of 5,001-10,000. New Brunswick and Quebec similarly show higher household sizes for almost each type of settlement. These provinces are relatively underdeveloped and manifest strong influences of historical social structures. Contrastingly, household sizes in Ontario, Manitoba, Saskatchewan, and British Columbia are both low and relatively invariant within the urban segment of the settlement system. For example, Manitoba's metropolitan household size (2.6) is only about 4 percent higher than the corresponding average for villages and small towns. Ontario reveals a constant (2.8) household size all across the nonrural segment of its settlement system.

Thus, a three-step (level) structure is discernible from household size data of the individual provinces as well as of Canada as a whole. The farm sector has relatively large households, followed by rural nonfarm areas, suggesting that agrarian and ex-urban populations constitute one social segment. Small towns and villages constitute an intermediate level, although they are closer to the metropolitan norm in household size than to the rural average. Cities and metropolises comprise the third level, with the smallest households. This structure is observable over time as well as across provinces. The Atlantic Provinces have generally larger households for almost every type of settlement. Overall, a general tendency of convergence towards societal norms is manifest, as is the trend of sharply decreasing household sizes over time.

2. TOWNS VS. VILLAGES: DIFFERENCES IN HOUSEHOLD COMPOSITION

Although for the settlement system as a whole, household size is mildly but

---

*All numbered tables appear at the end of this chapter.

inversely related to the size of a community, a closer look at towns and villages seems to suggest a significant departure from this theme. The 1971 census data for incorporated towns and villages of less than 10,000 population (Census Subdivisions) were analyzed to uncover social structural differences among these communities. In Chapter 3, the procedures used in abstracting these data have been outlined and their limitations noted. Presently we will discuss ways in which household compositions vary among towns and villages.

Table 5.3 shows a direct correlation between the size of a center and average household size. (The product-moment correlation coefficient (r) for this table is 0.89, but the t value is 1.282, which is not significant at the 95 percent level; this in turn suggests a high degree of correlation that can occur randomly, and does not necessarily indicate any statistical causality between the two variables.) It can be observed that the average household size for hamlets and villages in less than that for towns (5,001-10,000 population) by about 19 percent. Relatively larger centers had bigger households on the average. This, apparently, is the converse of the pattern observed for the national settlement system. It can be surmised that small households in villages may have resulted from a concentration of elderly households in small centers. To test this proposition, we turn to an analysis of the age of the heads of households in small centers.

Among 1,378 centers whose household distribution by the age of the head is presented in Table 5.4, the proportion of younger household heads (0-24, 25-44) is lower in hamlets and villages (population 0-1,000) than in towns (population 5,001-10,000). The reverse also holds, that is, households headed by the elderly (65+) are proportionately greater in the smaller centers than in the larger. (To test the association between the age of the head of the household and the center size, the Chi-Square for this table was computed. It equals 12,999 at a .99 percent significance level. As the frequencies formulas of cells are very high, it is inevitable that the Chi-Square would be high. Correcting for this distortion, it was found that Cramer's V equals 0.07. This indicates a weak association between the two variables. Essentially it means that there is a bipoplar association; hamlets and villages have higher proportions of older households, and towns of 1,000 or more have lower proportions with little significant variation among the towns themselves.)

Having observed proportionately greater concentrations of the elderly in hamlets and villages, the question arises whether this trend is affected by proximity to urban centers, that is, are there any differences between small places near metropolitan areas as opposed to those located in rural settings? To answer this question, the Census Subdivision data file was split into two sets: (1) one set is comprised of towns and villages located within a Census Division that contained a metropolitan area; and (2) the second set consists of towns and villages not falling within the Census Division of a metropolis.

These two sets of data were then separately cross-tabulated for selected variables. The graphs in Figures 5.1 and 5.2 present the results of plotting the sizes of towns and villages against household size and percentage of one-person households respectively.

FIGURE 5.1
Percentage of One-Person Households in Centers in Metropolitan and Nonmetropolitan Regions, 1971

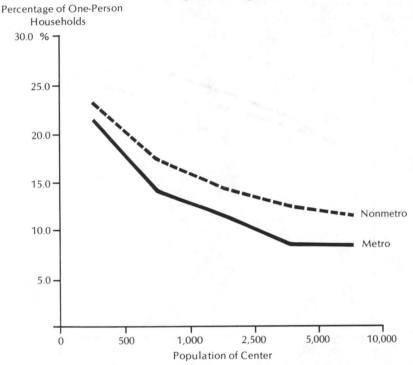

From Figure 5.1, it appears that towns and villages within the metropolitan orbit had, in 1971, slightly larger households, particularly in places of 2,501-5,000 population, than nonmetropolitan small communities. It may be noted that the two curves have the same point of origin, and then diverge only to converge again for towns of 5,001-10,000 population. In Figure 5.2, towns and villages located in metropolitan Census Divisions had about 1-3 percentage points fewer one-person households than the nonmetropolitan small communities, although the slope of the two curves is almost the same. Together these two graphs suggest that proximity to metropolitan areas reduces the attraction of small places as centres of one-person, small households — usually of elderly persons. It seems that hamlets and villages in nonmetropolitan settings were becoming retirement centers. This finding not only illuminates the role of small villages and hamlets in the countryside, but also implies that if these trends continue, then with the aging of the Canadian population there might be a further acceleration in the growth of small places.

FIGURE 5.2
Average Household Size in Centers in Metropolitan and Nonmetropolitan Regions, 1971

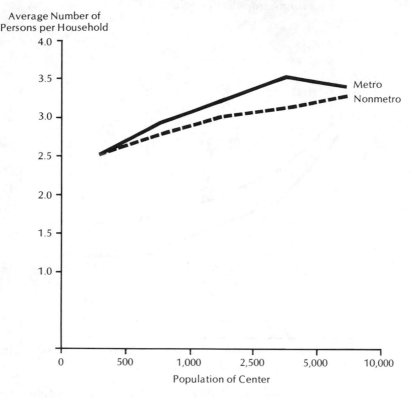

3. SEX RATIOS

The number of males per one hundred females is a succinct index of the sociodemographic structure of a community. To understand its potential as an indicator, one has to be aware of historical trends. In western industrialized societies, out-migration from rural areas generally has been heavy among females. This means that rural communities have been left with proportionately more males than females — thus, high sex ratios — and cities have reflected inverse proportions. Over time, these empirical norms have come to serve as indicators of a community's social structure. We also make use of sex ratios to assess the degree of urbanism of settlements of various sizes.

Sex Ratio (Number of Males/100 Females) in Different Types of Settlement, 1981

Farm	Nonfarm Village	1,001-2,500	2,501-5,000	5,001-10,000
117	105	98	98	98

10,001-30,000	30,001-100,000	100,001-500,000	Over 500,000	
97	95	94	95	

SOURCE: *Census of Canada*

The Canadian settlement system conforms to the expectations about sex ratios. A mild continuum-like distribution of values, sex ratios being highest for farm areas and lowest for metropolises, is evident for each of the four time periods indicated in Table 5.5. This pattern has remained undisturbed over successive decades. Further, the sex ratios for farm areas and metropolises have remained almost the same, 117 and 94 respectively, over this thirty-year period. The only noticeable change has been the steadily declining sex ratios (fewer males) of nonfarm areas, towns, and medium-size cities. These ratios have come close to the corresponding values for metropolises. To the extent that this indicator is valid, it suggests that small towns and cities are becoming more urban in character, while farm areas stand apart almost as a separate sector. Convergence of sex ratios to common values among towns, cities, and metropolises suggests the permeation of the mass society throughout the settlement hierarchy. Although small towns have higher sex ratios (98), they are only about 4 percentage points above the corresponding value for metropolises, a difference that is not only small but has also become smaller in each decennial census since 1951.

The natural longevity of females shows up in the form of a greater number of females in the population (206,605 in 1981). But on close examination of the census data, it can be observed that the number of males was greater for all age categories below 55 years of age, and it steadily fell behind the count for females for each successive age group, so much so that in the 90+ age group, females outnumbered males by more than two to one. This information suggests a future scenario. As the Canadian population matures, the sex ratio will fall, and the small settlements may increasingly become centers of elderly women.

Provinces generally conform to the national pattern of sex ratios. Rural areas have high sex ratios, while towns and cities have more women. Provinces specializing in primary production, Newfoundland, Saskatchewan, and Alberta show a wider spread among sex ratios for rural areas, small towns, and cities respectively, whereas the larger and more heavily urbanized as well as industrialized provinces, Ontario and Quebec, show smaller variations in sex ratios (Table 5.6).

All in all, it can be concluded that towns and villages could be categorized as urban in character by the criterion of sex ratios.

4. DEPENDENCY RATIOS

Although there are a number of ways to describe the age structure of a population, the dependency ratios are perhaps one of the most succinct measures. A dependency ratio is an index of the proportion of the "dependent" (normally not eligible to work or capable of work) segment of a population to its adult workforce. As children and the elderly are the two "dependent" groups, dependency ratios therefore measure the number of children and/or elderly per one hundred adults in a population. We have computed separate dependency ratios for persons less than 20 years of age (most of whom are children or school-going young adults), and for the elderly, defined as 70 years of age or older.[6] Tables 5.7 and 5.8 present the results of these computations.

Children

Table 5.7 reveals a few systematic and consistent patterns of population composition both over time and across settlements of various sizes. First, there has been a decline in the ratio of dependent children (less than 20 years of age) to the adult and work-eligible segment of populations (20 to 69 years of age) since 1961. This decline became very sharp in the decade 1971-1981, as the postwar "baby boom" worked its way into adulthood. The decline is observable in every type of settlement, including the farm sector, where the dependency ratio fell from 99 in 1961 to 69 children per 100 adults in 1981.

Dependent Population Under 20 Years of Age per 100 Aged 20-69 in Different Types of Settlement, 1981

Farm	Nonfarm Village	1,001-2,500	2,501-5,000	5,001-10,000
69	63	59	57	58

10,001-30,000	30,001-100,000	100,001-500,000	Over 500,000
56	52	50	45

SOURCE: Census of Canada

On the other end of the settlement spectrum, metropolises experienced an increase in the dependency ratio up to 1971; however, the 1981 census registered a remarkable drop in the ratio of children to adults, that is, dependency ratios of 45 or 50 in 1981, compared to 70 in 1971. A second notable pattern is a continuum-like spread of the dependency ratio across the settlement system. Farms have retained the highest dependency ratios and metropolises the lowest, with other settlements falling in between. Dependency ratios of towns and villages are almost at the midpoint in the range of values for lows of metropolises to highs of farms. This pattern is visible for all of the four periods reported in Table 5.7, and means that towns and villages remain homes to relatively large families (by national norms) of more children, though over time there has been a general decline in the proportions of children to adult populations. In 1981, towns and villages had 57-63 children per 100 adults. By itself this ratio has declined by almost one-third since 1961, yet it was 14 percent higher than the dependency ratio for metropolises.

Table 5.9 presents 1981 dependency ratios for the provinces. Overall, the provinces conform to the national patterns described above, though there are some regional variations from the national theme. Newfoundland and Alberta had relatively higher proportions of children, as indicated by high dependency ratios, while British Columbia's dependency ratios were generally below the national averages for each type of settlement.

Dependent Population Over 70 Years of Age Per 100 Aged 20-69 in Different Types of Settlement, 1981

Farm	Nonfarm Village	1,001-2,500	2,501-5,000	5,001-10,000
5	11	17	15	13

10,001-30,000	30,001-100,000	100,001-500,000	Over 500,000	
11	11	11	10	

SOURCE: Census of Canada

The Elderly

The number of elderly persons (70 years or over) per 100 adults (20-69 years of age) is indicated by the dependency ratios reported in Table 5.8. From the table it appears that the ratio of elderly persons has been steadily increasing since 1951, except in the farm sector. This is a manifestation of, by now, the well-documented phenomenon of the maturing population in Canada. The proportion of the elderly in local populations is increasing, and in villages and small centers it had reached a level in 1981 where there were 17 elderly for every 100 working-age adults. Cross-sectionally, the dependency ratios for the elderly do not manifest a continuum of value across the settlement spectrum. Metropolises and small cities have similar dependency ratios. The farm sector stands apart with substantially lower values. The notable exceptions to a generally flat terrain of dependency ratio are towns and villages. Dependency ratios of the elderly in these places have not only been high, but also are becoming higher. Evidently the elderly from farms and the countryside retire in hamlets and villages. Similarly there may be some movement of the elderly from cities to towns and villages to retire in an environment of peace and tranquillity — at least, this is what the folklore about "retiring in the country" promises. It appears that a concentration of the elderly is becoming a distinguishing feature of the town and village social mix. When this observation is combined with the finding from Table 5.7, a clear picture of the social structure of towns and villages emerges. They have households with greater numbers of children on the one hand, and one- or two-person households of the elderly on the other; the former reflects the traditional familistic influences, and the latter indicates the results of the new urbanism.

Table 5.10 provides a cross-sectional (1981) view of the elderly's dependency ratios for the provinces. Once again, the national pattern is evident across the settlement spectrum of almost every province. Towns and villages stand out as locales of elderly concentrations. Towns in Ontario, Manitoba, and Saskatchewan particularly manifest dependency ratios that are much higher than the corresponding national values, suggesting that the elderly constitute significant proportions of local populations. It may be noted that the smaller of the small towns (places of 1,001-5,000 population) have much higher dependency ratios in these three provinces. British Columbia measures low on this index, which indicates that in this province there is a concentration of youthful and working-age population.

5. EDUCATIONAL ATTAINMENT

Educational levels attained by a group are indicative of its economic prospects, relative standing in the social hierarchy, and its overall openness to new values. From our point of view, measuring the educational attainments of town and village populations would provide insights into the present social situation and future prospects. This objective has prompted us to cross-tabulate percentage distributions of the educational attainment of individuals who were 5 years of age or over with settlement type and size (Table 5.11).

As 1981 census data on educational attainment have not been released at this point, 1971 data is relied upon. On examining the cross-sectional profiles of educational attainments for various settlements, a number of patterns become evident (Table 5.11). First, a mild continuum-like distribution of educational attainments from small-to-large communities can be observed. Farm populations had the lowest educational attainments (individuals with elementary-school education only predominate, and there are relatively few university/vocationally trained persons), whereas metropolitan populations had the highest educational attainments; small cities and towns fell in between. Second, small towns were relatively closer to cities than to rural areas by the criterion of educational attainments. For example, the percentage of persons with secondary school and vocational diplomas in towns of 5,001-10,000 population was 14.6, while the corresponding metropolitan value was 15.4. Similarly, the proportion of university graduates in town populations was closer to the corresponding index for big cities than to that of the countryside. The third notable pattern is that formal education has permeated all segments of Canadian society. Almost every sector of Canadian society has been affected by higher education and formal training, to the extent that 3 percent of the individuals living on farms were university graduates; this represents one-third of the proportion of graduates in metropolises. Thus in contemporary Canada the rural-urban dichotomy does not lie along the lines of "country hicks" *vs.* "city sophisticates." A high degree of convergence to common norms has occurred in gross socioeconomic indices.

Provinces manifest almost the same patterns as those described in the preceding paragraph. (Table 5.12 bears out this conclusion.) A mild continuum of low to high educational attainments is observable across the settlement spectrum, ranging from the farm sector to the metropolises. Towns are closer to cities in the educational attainments of their populations, but rural areas are not bereft of the educated. Provinces differ in terms of the amplitude of the distribution of educational attainments, and economically peripheral provinces such as Newfuoundland, New Brunswick, Prince Edward Island, and Manitoba had small proportions of university graduates and lower median values of educational attainment. Ontario, Quebec, Saskatchewan, Alberta, and British Columbia were similar to each other and conformed to the national patterns. There were some anomalies, however, such as a noticeably low percentage of university graduates in the Quebec farm population, and strikingly high proportions (15.2 percent) of university graduates in Manitoba's towns of 5,001-10,000 population. Why these departures from established patterns? This question requires a closer examination of the corresponding communities, a task beyond the scope of this study. Yet the fact that these exceptions stand out is indicative of the pervasiveness of general patterns.

6. UNIFORMITY OF SOCIAL INSTITUTIONS AND THE PROCESSES OF CONVERGENCE

The preceding discussions and the findings of earlier chapters, particularly those of Chapter 3, suggest that a process of social convergence has been underway in the Canadian settlement system for almost twenty years. Canada now is not only physically an urbanized society with about 75 percent of its population living in urban areas, but also almost all its social institutions have incorporated urban values and outlooks. It is no longer an agrarian society comprised of relatively self-contained communities and localized economies. Its mode of production, economic organization, and ways of life have been profoundly reorganized by modern technology and urban values. Whether one lives in a Newfoundland outport or in Vancouver, one is subject to the same bank rate, monetary policy, tariffs, and taxes; one relies on essentially the same technology though producing different goods; one is governed by similar civil or criminal jurisprudence, and follows similar marriage practices. Without stretching the argument of institutional uniformity too far, it is self-evident that Canada has become a modern industrial nation whose institutional framework has not only been vertically integrated, but has also spread out horizontally. This statement is not meant to underplay regional differences and the deeply rooted cultural duality, English and French, of Canada. It only suggests that a high degree of structural uniformity has come to characterize broad social and economic institutions. And it is this uniformity that underlies the social convergence observed in this chapter.

On every parameter of social structure analyzed so far, towns and villages have been shown to be similar to cities. Average household sizes of towns and cities are only 6 percentage points apart; sex ratios of towns are only 2 percentage points higher than those of cities; and educational attainments have a mild continuum-like distribution, ranging from low in rural areas to high in metropolises. Chapter 3 revealed a resemblance in the distribution of the resident labor force's industrial activities among villages, towns, and cities, and also indicated a progressive narrowing of the income gap across the settlement spectrum. These are essentially manifestations of the pervasiveness and uniformity of social institutions. They suggest that conventional rural-versus-urban distinctions have ceased to be significant in contemporary mass society. Undoubtedly, farms still stand slightly apart from the rest of the settlements on many parameters, but it is as much the outcome of the farm population being a distinct industrial-occupational group as it is a reflection of a peculiar community structure. In any event, even the farm sector, despite its uniqueness, manifests the same social trends as the society as a whole: households becoming smaller, male-to-female ratios declining, educational attainments rising, and so forth. Overall, the social-structural homogenization of the Canadian settlement system documented here was also borne out by other observers. Elkin concluded in the early 1960s that the Canadian rural family is no longer very different in its material and social life from the urban.[7] Tremblay found an increasing homogeneity of family structures and consumption patterns among wage-earning urban, as well as rural, French Canadians.[8] As a differentiating criterion, social status may be more significant than the type of community one lives in.

Our analysis suggests that Canadian settlements can be arrayed in two or three clusters by social characteristics. On the one end are rural areas, farm and nonfarm, which manifest some residual conventional social features, for example, relatively larger households and more males. Towns and villages can be differentiated from cities on some criteria, but only slightly. However, on various social indices, they do not lie midway between rural areas and cities; rather, they fall closer to cities. Cities and metropolises, of course, have consistently reflected social characteristics associated with urban ways of life, and thus constitute a distinct cluster of values of various parameters. Despite these two or three differentiable tiers of social attributes, it is striking that these variations appear in narrow bands around national norms. If households are becoming smaller, it happens all across the settlement system; if sex ratios fall, they fall noticeably in rural areas as well as urban. It seems that the overall national social system sets the trends and lays the ground for local social structures.

Settlements of various types and sizes reflect the national features to various degrees. As the material, technological, and institutional bases of a society become uniform and cohesive, it is inevitable that its constituent elements manifest tendencies toward convergence. This has become evident in most of the industrialized world, particularly North America and Western Europe. Fuguitt and Voss warn that to consider American nonmetropolitan areas as uniform — as sleepy small towns closely tied to basic resource industries such as farming, forestry, and mining — is suspect and can lead to a near-total misunderstanding of what is actually occurring in these areas.[9] They further say that when clerks, salesmen, craftsmen, and professionals move to nonmetropolitan areas, the emerging situation could appropriately be called "countryfied cities," but it is not so much a rural renaissance as dispersal of urban America.[10] Although the recent demographic trends of accelerating decentralization,[11] to use Drewett *et al.*'s apt phrase, have been widely documented as the prevailing urbanization trends in Western Europe, it is implicit in such studies that the counterurbanization movement is a creation of nothing less than an urban civilization without cities in the physical sense of the term. These are manifestations of convergence trends.

Urbanism as a way of life has spread beyond urban areas. It has become the national lifestyle, and towns and villages are immersed in it. The nuclear family, the technology of mass production, unemployment insurance and compulsory public education, motor cars and banks, and so on, are no longer urban artifacts only. They are items of Canadian culture which have permeated all settlements, large and small. These institutions underlie all settlements and define the range of their variations.

7. UNIQUENESS AMIDST UNIFORMITY: THE PARADOX OF TOWN AND VILLAGE LIFE

On gross social indices, towns and villages bear a close resemblance to cities. This conclusion raises some questions. Are villages and cities indistinguishable? Are there not any differences in quality of life? Why is there a preference for living in small towns and the countryside, as expressed through numerous national polls and attitude surveys?[12] These questions articulate intuitive feelings that there must be some distinguishing social features of towns and villages, even though conventional indices may no longer be relevant measures to register them. Undoubtedly this is the case, and we must qualify the foregoing conclusions.

The convergence trends observed earlier not only affirm the hypothesis of the parallelism of urban and rural social structures, but also contradict the conventional images of town and village life. They show that small towns and villages are not "little houses on the prairies," where community life is organized around the agrarian economy and familistic values. They have moved along with the rest of the country on the path of modernization and urbanism.

Social convergence has been observed at the level of statistical aggregates; however, it does not reflect the structural features of individual communities, which can vary considerably within given parameters. On closer examination we find a great deal of diversity and a high degree of individuality among towns and villages. One is a minetown, another is an historical seat of the farm gentry, a third may be a retirees' village, and yet another may be a service center, and so on. This is the social paradox of modern towns and villages. They retain a high degree of uniqueness individually, while remaining within the Canadian mainstream. The question, then, is how does this uniqueness arise?

The uniqueness of towns and villages arises from some readily identifiable factors. Perhaps the single most significant factor is their small size. The smallness of a locality means that it cannot sustain numerous activities or serve a multiplicity of functions. Also, the activities drawn to it are limited in scope. The institutional base of small communities is shallow, and a relatively limited number of actors unavoidably must have personalized dealings. One community may be a friendly or harmonious place where people take care of each other on account of the harmonious relationship among local leaders, while another may be stultifying and racked with factional conflicts between the old guard and the newcomers. These are examples of how the personalized dealings necessitated by smallness affect social relations and foster uniqueness.

Another factor that contributes to the uniqueness is the mix and relative influence of locally represented societal institutions. In a small community not all institutions (for example, business, military, religion, and government) may be represented to the same degree, and each of them may not have proportionate influence. One community may be dominated by governmental institutions (for example, a military base), while another may be a businessmen's town, and a third may be a college town. Such variations in the mix of institutions is the basis of a small community's individuality.

Environmental and historical factors also lend uniqueness to small communities. The land, the sky, streams, and flora and fauna are not only more evident but also more visibly affect the layout and organization of towns and villages. A river, a waterfall, a hill, or a promontory are far more evident determinants of the physical form of a place and provide bases of local identity and pride. Over time, legends grow around such natural features and the historical events associated with them. These legends, enacted through parades and fairs, affect the social organization of a community, and thus contribute to its individuality.

A substantial proportion of Canadian towns and villages have a peculiar basis for being different from each other. Almost 25 percent of the population of towns and villages in Canada live in Single-Industry (SI) communities. Many of these SI communities are also company towns. A single-industry town is essentially a dormitory community for workers, and thus the home of a young mobile and working-class population. When it is controlled by a company, its social structure tilts all the more towards the corporate interests. As Plaskin describes Churchill Falls, Labrador: "It is . . . a place where the company is not only the main employer, but also the only employer; a place where the company owns the house you live in, the street you drive on, the restaurant you eat in . . . and everything else for miles around, including the cars, the airports, the school, the hospital."[13]

Not only are minetowns and milltowns different from each other; each minetown differs from the others by virtue of who controls it. The rhythm of life in a SI community is determined by the exigencies of corporate decisions and the business cycles of the industry. Tourist villages, leisure towns, and retirement communities, though not industrial communities in the strict sense of the term, also manifest similar trends. Altogether, it seems that the peculiarities of economic base and power structure contribute significantly to sociological divergences among towns and villages.

Before concluding this section, it is worth noting that the summation of unique characteristics of small communities adds up to a social profile that resembles the national averages. The peculiarities of one town complement the uniqueness of another, thereby resulting in a rounded whole. It should, therefore, not be a surprise that Canadian towns and villages, as an aggregate, conform closely to national norms, but individually they are noticeably different from each other.

8. TOWNS AND VILLAGES AS TRUNCATED COMMUNITIES

Despite the relative uniformity of the Canadian settlement system, there is one dimension along which towns and villages can be unmistakably differentiated from metropolises. This is the dimension of social power and economic standing. By and large, small communities lack managerial functions and the social strata that dominates national or provincial decision-making processes, for example, a bureaucratic elite, corporate executives, or political leadership. They lack the full cast of actors required to make a community both a microcosm of the society and give it control of its own destiny. Towns and villages have increasingly become dependent on metropolitan centers for decisions, activities, grants, and even information. The autonomy characterizing an agrarian community has been lost, and towns and villages have been absorbed into the national institutional fabric.

Although major institutions have filtered down, only their lower echelons have actually permeated towns and villages. A town may have a bank, but the significant investment decisions are made at the head office. Similarly, there may be a Canada Manpower office in a nonmetropolitan center, but it is manned by young professionals who merely execute policies made at provincial and national capitals. Not only do the higher-order activities of each institution remain beyond the influence of small communities, but the upper strata that perform such functions is not to be found in these places. As Forcese observes: "Wealth, power, and prestige are concentrated in the cities, especially in those with major industrial and financial institutions."[14] This does not mean that a majority in the city enjoy such prerogatives, but that small communities have come to be predominantly the abodes of the working and lower-middle classes. These features make towns and villages truncated communities.

A disquieting trend observed in this chapter is the increasing concentration of the elderly in hamlets and villages. This suggests that a process of demographic truncation is underway for small communities. Similarly, we have already pointed out the working-class, youthful, and transitory nature of Single-Industry communities. All these conditions detract from the wholesomeness of small places, making them truncated communities. Many current problems of small communities can be attributed to their truncated social structures — the absence of vigorous leadership, a sense of powerlessness, lack of entrepreneurship, narrow economic base, vulnerability to business cycles, and unfavorable public policies, and so on. This is not to suggest that every little village should be socially and economically self-contained and wholesome, but whatever the role of a community in the national setting it should have the full cast of actors to be self-sustaining. Vertically integrated socioeconomic institutions preempt such possibilities for small communities. Perhaps this is the price of modernism. The thesis that towns and villages are truncated communities essentially refers to their position in the national system of social stratification. *How* they are internally stratified remains to be discussed.

9. SOCIAL STRATIFICATION IN TOWNS AND VILLAGES

Within towns and villages, distinctions of social class are masked by an aura of familiarity. With few exceptions, such as the traditional gentry, the underclass, and native Indians, almost everyone lives in similar houses, buys from the same stores, and drinks at the same bars. This apparent similarity of lifestyles creates the myth of small-town equality. Yet almost every sociological study of a small community has uncovered a fairly rigid and sharply divided social hierarchy. Undoubtedly the composition and character of the dominant classes have changed with the evolution from agrarian to industrial, and now service, economies, and in this sense there is not a monolithic upper class, but inherited wealth and family name are still important.

The primary cleavage in the social structure of a small community runs along the "old" versus "new" residents' line. "One has to have about three generations buried in the town cemetery before one will be locally accepted." This is a common refrain heard from newcomers to small towns. Burnet describes the class structure of Hanna, Alberta, circa 1946, in the following terms: "The most important division is between those who are and those who are not considered townspeople."[15] Among the former were professionals, merchants, clerks, and laborers "who live in Hanna and supply goods and services." The latter group included railroaders who came to live in the town on a round of duty, retired farmers, and other transients.[16] The social situation in Fringetown, a village of about 2,000 near Guelph, Ontario, in the early 1970s was not much different from Hanna's in 1946. Sinclair and Westhues, in investigating the local conflict over the proposal to build the first apartment building in the village, found that Fringetown was divided into two camps, which the *Globe and Mail* termed "materialists" versus "intellectuals." They were comprised, on the one hand, of the old residents controlling the village council, and on the other, of newcomers who had formed a Citizens' Action Committee.[17] The fissure dividing the old and the new, and the ensuing struggle for power, now takes the form of conflicts over civic priorities, local development proposals, and environmental issues. In a sociological sense, it is a symptom of the interjection of new interests in an existing social order. Yet it is largely a division along the horizontal axis of the social structure.

Along the vertical axis, towns and villages are divided into social strata arranged in a trapezoidal form — having a wide base and a narrow, but flat, top. As Forcese notes, "From early community studies, we know that people make fine distinctions among themselves," and he designates such differentiations as microstratifications, meaning the class structure of a locality.[18] In the agrarian phase of the Canadian economy, ranchers, big farmers, and bankers constituted the upper strata but, as Canada has evolved into a modern industrial services economy, local social stratification has also undergone change. Gold has vividly documented the enduring social pyramid in St. Pascal, a small town in rural Kamouraska County, Quebec, and he shows how the mercantile elite of an agrarian service center has been replaced by an industrial capitalist elite.[19] He identifies four main social strata in the currently industrial St. Pascal: (1) the entrepreneurial group, consisting of several dozen administrators, businessmen, professionals, and other members of the C.D.E. group (Le Centre des Dirigeants d'Entreprise); (2) merchants and tradesmen, and those who run family enterprises; (3) white-collar workers; and (4) blue-collar workers.[20] He also documents four evolutionary phases of the power structure, beginning with the rule of the seigneurial group, to the domination by the clergy, to the ascendency of merchants, leading to the present entrepreneurial class, which is not to be identified with owners and proprietors alone, but includes administrators, corporate managers, and other key personnel of industrial and service establishments.[21] He points out that "the entrepreneurial group is linked to a myriad of both regional and national networks, and successfully espouses what once were locally unorthodox values."[22]

The Single-Industry communities of corporate sponsorship present a slightly variant form of social stratification. Here the industrial hierarchy is fully reflected in residential community. The managers and administrators who form the sponsoring corporation constitute the elite and dominate community life.

From the foregoing description, it should be obvious that the character of the dominant elite has changed with broader social changes. Those who can operate successfully in the modern mode, and those who are affiliated with Corporate Canada and are knit into the provincial or national decision-making bodies, have come to be dominant. Not infrequently the old families have adapted to the new demands of power and status. As Forcese says, a "small town provides a stratification system in microcosm. The small town businessman, lawyer and doctor are ultimately subordinate to or dependent upon the corporate owners and managers, but they probably do not rank very highly in terms of status in Canadian society as a whole. . . . But within their communities they are top rank, because of their influence with other townspeople."[23] This brief examination of the social stratification in small communities indicates that the process of "embourgeification" (becoming bourgeois in character) has engulfed them.

10. OVERVIEW

Our probing into the social structure of towns and villages has revealed as much an account of its broad contour as evidence of its evolutionary change. The thesis emerging from this chapter is that the broader social system and economy are the primary determinants of the social systems of small communities. They set the stage and define the range of characteristics within which a local community acquires its individuality. As the national economy and polity change, towns and villages, or any other elements of the settlement system, follow suit. Canada has become an industrial and services-based economy. It has evolved into a corporate society where vertically integrated social institutions pervade the landscape. A fair degree of universalization of essential facilities and services has taken place across the nation. These conditions have promoted what we earlier called the modular society. Towns and villages are encased in this society and they partake of the modern milieu. These findings suggest the new reality of contemporary Canadian towns and villages, and calls into question social images that personify them in the agrarian idiom. It might be noted that the present upsurge in the demographic fortunes and the counterurbanization trends have become possible because of the standardization and universalization of basic facilities, services, and institutions.

Towns and villages are part of the national urban milieu, but individually they are not miniature cities. They manifest a high degree of individuality and uniqueness within the range of modernism. Individually they are unique due to the variations in: (1) the mix of activities and institutions; (2) the variety of the modes of local integration of national institutions; (3) small size; and (4) the truncation of social structures. While the conventional rural-urban differences have eroded, new factors have come into play to distinguish small and large communities. Thus the problems, expectations, and needs of small communities are most similar to those of urban areas; small communities require prosperity, jobs, viability, stability, equity, and a sense of control over their destinies. Yet there are qualitative and threshold distinctions to be observed in dealing with them. Towns and villages may not be a separate universe, but they certainly are a distinct genre of the contemporary urban species.

NOTES

1. The rural-urban continuum hypothesis emerged to soften the polarity inherent in folk *vs.* urban typology. Though holding that urban social organization contrasts with that of the rural, it postulated a continuum of values between the two ideal types on nine criteria. Thus a typical community could have varying degrees of ruralness or urbanness without being consigned to one or the other category.

2. Peter M. Blau, "Introduction: Parallels and Contrasts in Structural Inquiries," in Peter M. Blau, ed., *Approaches to the Study of Social Structure* (New York: Free Press, 1975), 3.

3. John Porter, *Canadian Social Structure* (Toronto: McClelland and Stewart, 1967), 1.

4. Peter M. Blau, "Parameters of Social Structure," in Blau, ed., *op. cit.*, 221.

5. Sorokin and Zimmerman formalized the rural-urban continuum hypothesis and postulated nine dimensions along which the two social structures could be differentiated. Pitrim Sorokin and C.G. Zimmerman, *Principles of Rural-Urban Sociology* (New York: Kraus Reprint Co., 1969).

6. We have used 20 and 70 years as the cut-off points to define children and the elderly as dependent groups. Many studies use 15 and 65 years as their respective limits. Yet, in many provinces, children are required to attend school

until 16 years of age, and many workers in the private sector do not retire at 65. So no matter what cut-off points are used, some overlap and vagueness of estimates are inevitable. We have taken the view that in postindustrial Canada, people are attending school longer and retiring later. On this assumption, we have used 20- and 70-year age points as the upper and lower limits of children and elderly populations respectively. We have followed the convention set by Marc-Adelard Tremblay and W.J. Anderson, *Rural Canada in Transition* (Ottawa: Agricultural Council of Canada, 1966), 19.

7. Frederick Elkin, *The Family in Canada* (Ottawa: Vanier Institute, 1968), 70.

8. Marc-Adelard Tremblay, "Authority Models in the French Canadian Family," in Gerald L. Gold and Marc-Adelard Tremblay, eds., *Communities and Cultures in French Canada* (Toronto: Holt Rinehart, 1973), 15.

9. Glenn V. Fuguitt, Paul R. Voss, and J.C. Doherty, *Growth and Change in Rural America* (Washington, D.C.: Urban Land Institute, 1979), 54.

10. Citation from a paper of the Commission on Intergovernmental Relations, "The Role of Metropolitan Organization in Natural Growth and Development," in Fuguitt *et al., ibid.*, 56.

11. The phrase "accelerating decentralization" has been taken from Roy Drewett, John Bodelard, and Nigel Spence, "Urban Britain: Beyond Containment," in Brian J.L. Berry, ed., *Urbanization and Counterurbanization* (Beverly Hills: Sage, 1976), 51; the rest of the idea in this sentence paraphrases R. Drewett and A. Rossi, "General Urbanization Trends in Western Europe," in L.H. Klaassen *et al.*, eds., *Dynamics of Urban Development* (Aldershot: Gower, 1981), 120.

12. In recent times, small communities have become very popular places to live. Gallup polls taken in Canada have shown that consistently high (31-32%) proportions of national samples express a preference for living in small towns. Similar trends have been observed in the United States.

13. Robert Plaskin, "A Stake in the Future," *Globe and Mail*, Toronto, 9 October 1978, 11.

14. Dennis Forcese, *The Canadian Class Structure*, 2nd ed. (Toronto: McGraw-Hill Ryerson, 1980), 34.

15. Jean Burnet, *Next-Year Country: A Study of Rural Social Organizaton in Alberta* (Toronto: University of Toronto Press, 1951), 96.

16. *Ibid.*, 96-97.

17. Peter R. Sinclair and Kenneth Westhues, *Village in Crisis* (Toronto: Holt Rinehart, 1974), 53.

18. Dennis Forcese, *op. cit.*, 28.

19. Gerald L. Gold, *St. Pascal* (Toronto: Holt Rinehart, 1975).

20. *Ibid.*, 74-82.

21. *Ibid.*, 83.

22. *Ibid.*, 125.

23. Forcese, *op. cit.*, 32.

TABLES/CHAPTER 5

TABLE 5.1

Average Household Size in Different Types of Settlement, Canada, 1951-1981

Settlement Type	Number of Persons Per Household			
	1951	1961	1971	1981
Rural				
Farm	4.5	4.6	4.3	3.7
Nonfarm/Village	4.1	4.0	3.8	3.2
Town				
Under 5,000	} 4.1	3.9	3.6	2.9
5,001-10,000		3.9	3.6	2.9
City				
10,001-30,000	4.0	3.8	3.6	2.9
30,001-100,000	3.9	3.8	3.5	2.8
Metropolis				
100,001-500,000	} 4.0	3.7	3.3	2.8
over 500,000			3.2	2.7

SOURCE: *Census of Canada*

TABLE 5.2

Average Number of Persons Per Household by Size of Center and Province, Canada, 1981

Province	Size of Place								
	Farm	Non-farm	1,001-2,500	2,501-5,000	5,001-10,000	10,001-30,000	30,001-100,000	100,001-500,000	500,000 +
Newfoundland	4.4	4.0	4.0	3.7	3.8	3.6	—	3.4	—
Prince Edward Island	4.1	3.3	3.1	—	—	2.8	—	—	—
Nova Scotia	3.8	3.2	2.9	2.8	2.8	3.2	3.1	2.8	—
New Brunswick	4.0	3.4	3.2	2.8	3.2	3.1	2.9	—	—
Quebec	4.3	3.3	3.1	3.0	3.0	3.0	2.8	2.9	2.7
Ontario	3.7	3.1	2.8	2.8	2.8	2.8	2.8	2.8	2.8
Manitoba	3.6	3.1	2.7	2.5	2.8	2.9	2.6	—	2.6
Saskatchewan	3.5	2.8	2.6	2.6	2.6	2.7	2.7	2.7	—
Alberta	3.6	3.1	2.9	2.9	2.9	3.0	2.8	—	2.7
British Columbia	3.6	3.0	2.9	2.7	2.8	2.8	2.7	2.4	2.6

SOURCE: *Census of Canada*

TABLE 5.3

Average Number of Persons Per Household in Incorporated Towns and Villages by Size of Population, Canada, 1971

	Population of Center				
	0-500	501-1,000	1,001-2,500	2,501-5,000	5,001-10,000
Average Household Size (persons)	2.6	2.8	3.0	3.0	3.2
Number of Centers	298	261	318	190	113

SOURCE: *Census of Canada*

TABLE 5.4

Number of Households by Age of the Head and Size of Center for
Incorporated Towns and Villages, Canada, 1971

Population of Center	Age of Household Head				Total Number of Households	Number of Centers
	Less than 25	25-44	45-64	65+		
0-500	1,483	10,052	13,925	13,390	38,850	412
	3.8%	25.8%	35.8%	34.5%	100.0	
501-1,000	2,878	19,816	22,906	20,755	66,355	303
	4.3%	29.8%	34.6%	31.3%	100.0	
1,001-2,500	8,480	53,780	52,908	37,377	152,545	349
	5.6%	35.5%	34.6%	24.5%	100.0	
2,501-5,000	12,940	75,600	68,180	41,060	197,780	200
	6.5%	38.2%	34.5%	20.8%	100.0	
5,001-10,000	15,549	85,947	75,844	38,235	219,175	114
	7.1%	40.8%	34.6%	17.4%	100.0	

Chi-Square = 12,999.1   Degrees of Freedom = 12   Cramer's V = 0.07
SOURCE: *Census of Canada*

TABLE 5.5

Sex Ratio in Different Types of Settlement, Canada, 1951-1981

Settlement Type	Number of Males/100 Females			
	1951	1961	1971	1981
Rural				
Farm	117	116	116	117
Nonfarm/Village	110	109	107	105
Town				
1,001-2,500	⎫	101	101	98
2,501-5,000	⎬ 99	100	99	98
5,001-10,000	⎭	99	100	98
City				
10,001-30,000	96	99	99	97
30,001-100,000	96	98	98	95
Metropolis				
100,001-500,000	⎫ 94	⎫ 98	⎫ 97	94
500,000 +	⎭	⎭	⎭	95
CANADA	102	102	102	99

SOURCE: *Census of Canada*

TABLE 5.6

Sex Ratio by Type of Settlement and Province, Canada, 1981 (Number of Males Per 100 Females)

Settlement Type	Newfoundland	Prince Edward Island	Nova Scotia	New Brunswick	Quebec	Ontario	Manitoba	Saskatchewan	Alberta	British Columbia
Rural										
Farm	119	119	117	116	119	114	117	120	119	111
Nonfarm/Village	106	104	103	104	105	104	104	103	108	108
Town										
1,001-2,500	103	92	96	99	98	96	97	95	102	103
2,501-5,000	100	–	94	91	97	95	91	95	102	102
5,001-10,000	100	–	92	100	97	97	95	97	103	101
City										
10,001-30,000	101	87	95	93	97	95	101	94	104	100
30,001-100,000	–	–	93	92	95	95	91	94	100	97
Metropolis										
100,001-500,000	93	–	94	–	94	96	–	94	–	90
500,000 +	–	–	–	–	94	95	93	–	103	96

SOURCE: *Census of Canada*

TABLE 5.7

Dependent Population Under 20 Years of Age in Different Types of Settlement, Canada, 1951-1981

Settlement Type	Number Under 20/100 Aged 20-69			
	1951	1961	1971	1981
Rural				
Farm	89	99	92	69
Nonfarm/Village	80	97	87	63
Town				
1,001-2,500	} 71	86	80	59
2,501-5,000		84	78	57
5,001-10,000		83	79	58
City				
10,001-30,000	63	81	76	56
30,001-100,000	55	77	70	52
Metropolis				
100,001-500,000	} 52	} 66	} 70	50
500,000 +				45
CANADA	66	79	75	52

SOURCE: Census of Canada

TABLE 5.8

Dependent Population Over 70 Years of Age in Different Types of Settlement, Canada, 1951-1981

Settlement Type	Number Over 70/100 Aged 20-69			
	1951	1961	1971	1981
Rural				
Farm	8	8	7	5
Nonfarm/Village	10	12	12	11
Town				
1,001-2,500	} 9	13	13	17
2,501-5,000		11	12	15
5,001-10,000		11	10	13
City				
10,001-30,000	7	9	10	11
30,001-100,000	7	8	9	11
Metropolis				
100,001-500,000	} 9	} 9	} 9	11
500,000 +				10
CANADA	8	9	9	10

SOURCE: Census of Canada

TABLE 5.9

Dependent Population Under 20 Years of Age by Type of Settlement and Province, Canada, 1981

Settlement Type	Newfoundland	Prince Edward Island	Nova Scotia	New Brunswick	Quebec	Ontario	Manitoba	Saskatchewan	Alberta	British Columbia
					Number of Persons under 20 Years of Age per 100 Aged 20-69 Years					
Rural										
Farm	72	67	63	67	73	64	70	68	71	66
Nonfarm/Village	82	68	62	68	60	59	70	67	69	57
Town										
1,001-2,500	81	66	57	60	53	56	57	56	68	59
2,501-5,000	76	—	55	52	53	55	50	57	61	54
5,001-10,000	84	—	54	63	53	70	57	59	62	55
City										
10,001-30,000	69	51	59	54	56	54	65	56	64	56
30,001-100,000	—	—	54	52	48	52	50	57	55	52
Metropolis										
100,001-500,000	59	—	48	—	49	51	—	54	—	39
500,000 +	—	—	—	—	44	45	47	—	47	41

SOURCE: *Census of Canada*

TABLE 5.10

Dependent Population Over 70 Years of Age by Type of Settlement and Province, Canada, 1981

Settlement Type	Number of Persons over 70 Years of Age per 100 Adults Aged 20-69 Years									
	Newfoundland	Prince Edward Island	Nova Scotia	New Brunswick	Quebec	Ontario	Manitoba	Saskatchewan	Alberta	British Columbia
Rural										
Farm	6	9	9	8	4	6	5	5	4	4
Nonfarm/Village	9	13	12	10	8	10	16	20	10	7
Town										
1,001-2,500	9	19	18	14	13	20	19	27	16	10
2,501-5,000	10	—	21	19	11	16	30	24	13	12
5,001-10,000	7	—	15	11	10	14	18	21	10	11
City										
10,001-30,000	7	18	14	12	9	13	11	17	8	10
30,001-100,000	—	—	14	12	9	11	16	15	9	13
Metropolis										
100,001-500,000	10	—	8	—	8	11	—	10	—	19
500,000 +	—	—	—	—	9	9	12	—	6	11

SOURCE: *Census of Canada*

TABLE 5.11

Educational Attainment of Population (5 Years of Age and Over, Not Attending School Full-Time) in Different Types of Settlement, Canada, 1971

Settlement Type	Elementary School	Elementary School & Vocational Training	Secondary School	Secondary School & Vocational & Post-Secondary	University	University & Vocational	Total
				(percent)			
Rural							
Farm	51.2	1.9	34.1	8.9	3.0	1.0	100.0
Nonfarm & Village	49.4	2.2	32.5	10.7	3.8	1.4	100.0
Town							
Under 5,000	43.2	2.3	34.5	12.9	5.3	1.9	100.0
5,001-10,000	37.7	2.3	37.6	14.6	5.6	2.3	100.0
City							
10,001-30,000	36.1	2.3	38.3	15.3	5.8	2.2	100.0
30,001-100,000	36.5	2.3	37.5	14.9	6.4	2.4	100.0
Metropolis							
100,001-500,000	29.6	2.4	39.6	17.2	8.3	2.9	100.0
500,000 +	32.7	2.5	36.8	15.4	9.3	3.3	100.0

SOURCE: *Census of Canada*

TABLE 5.12

Educational Attainment of Population (5 Years of Age and Over, Not Attending School Full-Time) by Different Types of Settlement and Province, Canada, 1971

Settlement Type	Elementary School	Elementary School & Vocational Training	Secondary School	Secondary School & Vocational & Post-Secondary	University	University & Vocational
		(percent)				
Newfoundland						
Rural Farm	60.5	0.5	31.5	3.9	2.9	0.7
Nonfarm & Villages	63.5	0.8	27.5	4.9	2.9	0.4
Under 5,000	53.3	0.9	33.0	7.9	4.2	0.8
5,001-10,000	40.7	1.2	37.3	12.9	6.4	1.5
10,001-30,000	31.5	0.9	44.0	14.9	7.1	1.6
30,001-100,000	32.1	1.2	40.4	15.3	8.7	2.3
Prince Edward Island						
Rural Farm	49.2	1.2	36.1	8.2	4.4	0.9
Nonfarm & Villages	51.0	2.3	30.8	9.8	4.9	1.2
1,001-2,500	42.9	1.5	34.8	11.9	7.8	0.8
10,001-50,000	30.6	1.8	37.9	16.9	9.7	3.1
Nova Scotia						
Rural Farm	38.2	0.8	44.6	10.9	4.4	1.1
Nonfarm & Villages	44.9	1.6	37.5	11.3	3.5	1.2
Under 5,000	34.0	1.6	39.9	15.1	7.4	2.0
5,001-10,000	33.0	2.0	37.3	18.1	7.2	2.4
10,001-30,000	37.4	2.1	39.0	14.2	5.8	1.5
30,001-100,000	34.0	2.3	41.5	13.6	6.9	1.7
100,001-500,000	24.8	1.5	38.7	20.7	11.1	3.2

New Brunswick

Rural Farm	58.1	2.2	26.1	9.2	2.8	1.6
Nonfarm & Villages	60.8	2.1	24.4	8.6	2.9	1.1
Under 5,000	48.6	2.6	27.9	12.7	6.1	2.0
5,001-10,000	37.5	2.0	36.0	16.5	5.7	2.3
10,001-30,000	41.3	2.3	33.9	13.4	7.0	2.1
30,001-100,000	34.5	2.4	35.6	17.0	8.0	2.5

Quebec

Rural Farm	66.1	2.6	21.9	7.2	1.6	0.6
Nonfarm & Villages	62.2	2.9	22.8	8.4	2.6	1.1
Under 5,000	53.0	2.8	27.4	11.1	4.0	1.6
5,001-10,000	50.6	2.9	28.9	11.8	3.9	1.9
10,001-30,000	46.3	2.8	30.9	13.1	4.9	2.0
30,001-100,000	46.9	3.0	29.8	12.8	5.4	2.1
100,001-500,000	39.2	2.6	33.7	14.4	7.7	2.7
500,000 +	41.0	2.8	31.5	13.2	8.5	3.0

Ontario

Rural Farm	47.5	2.0	36.5	10.2	2.6	1.8
Nonfarm & Villages	41.6	2.4	38.0	12.8	3.4	1.8
Under 5,000	37.2	2.2	39.4	14.2	4.7	2.3
5,001-10,000	33.7	2.1	41.7	14.7	5.3	2.5
10,001-30,000	32.0	2.3	42.0	16.0	5.3	2.4
30,001-100,000	33.0	2.1	41.1	15.1	6.2	2.5
100,001-500,000	31.5	2.6	40.7	15.9	6.5	2.8
500,000 +	28.4	2.3	39.3	16.4	10.0	3.6

Manitoba

Rural Farm	54.4	1.5	33.2	7.5	2.5	0.9
Nonfarm & Villages	53.4	1.9	30.1	9.5	3.7	1.4
Under 5,000	39.9	2.1	35.3	13.7	6.4	2.6
5,001-10,000	43.4	2.1	33.5	13.4	15.2	2.4
10,001-30,000	31.9	2.0	41.6	16.9	5.4	2.2
30,001-100,000	31.1	2.0	40.4	16.6	7.0	2.0
500,000 +	29.0	2.2	40.6	16.5	8.7	3.0

(Table cont'd on next page)

TABLE 5.12 — Continued

Settlement Type	Elementary School	Elementary School & Vocational Training	Secondary School	Secondary School & Vocational & Post-Secondary	University	University & Vocational
Saskatchewan						
Rural Farm	50.1	1.2	36.8	7.3	3.5	1.1
Nonfarm & Villages	52.8	1.6	30.8	8.4	5.0	1.4
Under 5,000	44.9	2.0	33.5	11.3	6.2	2.1
5,001-10,000	37.8	2.2	38.4	13.6	5.9	2.1
10,001-30,000	39.3	1.9	35.4	14.4	7.0	2.0
30,001-100,000	37.2	1.8	38.2	14.5	6.2	2.1
100,001-500,000	29.1	2.1	37.9	17.3	10.4	3.2
Alberta						
Rural Farm	42.7	1.6	41.2	10.0	3.7	0.8
Nonfarm & Villages	43.5	2.0	36.7	11.1	5.3	1.4
Under 5,000	33.7	2.1	39.8	15.4	7.1	1.0
5,001-10,000	30.8	2.2	40.6	17.3	6.9	2.2
10,001-30,00	32.7	2.2	38.8	16.8	7.4	2.1
30,001-100,000	28.2	2.5	39.5	18.6	8.9	2.3
100,001-500,000	23.6	2.3	40.8	20.1	10.3	2.9
British Columbia						
Rural Farm	38.2	2.5	39.4	12.2	5.7	2.0
Nonfarm & Villages	32.4	2.5	41.7	18.8	6.4	2.2
Under 5,000	29.9	2.4	42.3	16.1	7.9	2.3
5,001-10,000	26.6	2.1	42.8	17.4	8.4	2.7
10,001-30,000	28.4	2.3	42.7	17.2	7.0	2.4
30,001-100,000	29.3	2.3	41.2	17.3	7.5	2.4
100,001-500,000	20.8	2.6	45.4	18.7	9.3	3.2
500,000 +	23.6	2.4	42.3	18.1	10.1	3.5

SOURCE: *Census of Canada*

6 Life in Towns and Villages

This chapter is addressed to a seemingly simple question, although as we will soon discover, it is a rather difficult one to answer: what is it like to live in contemporary Canadian towns and villages? We will attempt to compose a generalized picture of the "way of life," as Louis Wirth called it,[1] of small communities, and will compare the social relations observable in cities with those in Canadian society at large. We will also examine the quality of life in towns and villages. All that can be promised is a brief exploration of these topics, and some theorizing about them. The information about them is scarce, and their inherent intractability forbidding.

The 1970s witnessed a renaissance of rural values in Canada, the United States, and the rest of the western world. The "peace, friendliness, and simplicity" of life in the countryside beckoned city-weary, ecology-conscious, and independent-spirited urbanites. Even if they could not move to such places they viewed them longingly. Gallup polls taken in Canada in 1974 and in 1981 showed consistent preferences for farm and small-community living. In answer to a question about the "preferred" place of living, on both occasions 21 percent opted for the city, while 31 to 32 percent expressed a desire to live in a small town. In 1981, while 21 percent of city dwellers (residents of centers with more than 100,000 people) expressed a preference for small towns, only 4 percent of small-town residents wanted to live in a city. The majority (41%) of small-town residents preferred to continue living in small towns, and the second-largest group (35%) wanted to move to still-sparser settlements, that is, to farms.[2] The 1981 Gallup report concludes that "while fewer Canadians today (20%) than in June, 1974, indulge in daydreams about farm living, still the number who would choose this lifestyle is about four times the proportion who actually do live on a farm."[3] Similar preferences have been reported through Gallup polls in the United States.[4] These expressions of residential preferences indicate that in the public mind, towns, villages, and countryside have come to be associated with intimate social relations, and with a healthful way of life. The belief is in itself a social fact, regardless of the objective reality. It raises the theoretical question, is there a relationship between the type of place and the nature of the social order? For the current thinking on this topic, we briefly turn to the sociological literature.

1. PLACE AND SOCIAL ORDER

Although Robert Redfield is generally credited with the formulation of the urban-versus-folk dichotomy, the tradition of associating varying degrees of social solidarity, community feelings, and intimacy of mutual relationships with particular types of settlements goes far back in the history of western sociological thought.[5] For example, Toennies described the social order of a town or village as *Gemeinschaft* (local orientation and kin solidarity), and attributed to a city a *Gessellschaft* type of social relations, which is individualistic and cosmospolitan in character.[6] Louis Wirth, in moving away from such dichotomies, spelled out the "social action and organization" that typically characterize a city. Defining a city as a relatively permanent, compact settlement of a large number of heterogeneous individuals, he deduced that it is a crucible for specialization and differentiation of social roles, a community of secondary relations and impersonalized dealings.[7] The identification of the city with impersonal and segmentalized social relations implicitly affirmed the conventional image of village life.

In the second half of the twentieth century, cities have become the primary locales of North American populations, and thus obvious objects of social discontent. Mounting urban problems and the burdens of day-to-day living in cities provided a concrete ground for popular disenchantment. In comparison with cities, towns and villages began to appear as havens of untroubled and friendly lifestyles. Not only had small become beautiful, but the visible absence of congestion, noise, and blight made small communities attractive places to live. The above-cited Gallup polls essentially document such popular assumptions. But the evidence about the assumed relationship between the type of pattern of social organizations and the size or nature of settlement is inconclusive. It seems that broad societal and cultural forces shape the patterns of human relations and define role-sets, and they may vary slightly from one place to another in a country, but it is unlikely that they will be radically different among cities and villages in the same country.

As Pahl says, "Today I think we would all be extremely cautious in attributing a particular style or pattern of social relations to particular categories of people and places. . . . Hence the *size* of settlement may not be a significant variable when people listen to the same radio and television programmes, read the same newspapers and consume the same goods, no matter where they live."[8] Our probes of the social structure and the economic bases of Canadian towns and villages bear out Pahl's thesis. The observed convergence suggests the unlikelihood of wide divergences in patterns of social life among settlements of various sizes in Canada. Instead of looking only for the elusive "order, warmth, and peacefulness" of small-community life, we should direct our attention toward the concrete experiences of life in towns and villages, and the forces that shape them.

The experiences would vary by social class and economic status of individuals, as well as by the peculiarities of the size and location of a settlement.[9]

Contemporary sociological theory suggests that there is no inherent basis for assuming that towns and villages of contemporary Canada are places of extraordinarily harmonious relations and community-mindedness, although such sentiments might prevail in some such settlements. There is as much variety of social relations among small communities as between them and the larger settlements. For example, a company town may be a regimented place where everyone knows where he or she belongs, while a tourist village of comparable size might be a community of fun and frolic. The point is that in contemporary urbanized Canadian society, a locality's culture and social relations reflect the peculiarities of what Warren has called the "horizontal" integration of national institutions.[10] The quality of horizontal integration depends not only upon the size of a community, but upon the mix of institutions and the degree of truncation. Our attention, therefore, should be focused as much on the social institutional features of towns and villages as on their smallness, in attempting to observe and explain patterns of interpersonal relations.

2. EXPERIENCE OF LIVING IN TOWNS AND VILLAGES

Not only do towns and villages differ from each other in their social environments; they offer divergent life experiences to persons of varying backgrounds. How a town is experienced or felt by a Metis is not the same as it appears to White merchants. Obvious though this point may be, it needs to be reiterated to underscore the often-overlooked variety of lifestyles sustained in towns and villages. A meaningful way to comprehend this is to examine the life experiences of various social classes.

As described earlier, a noticeable fissure in the social structure of a town or village runs along the line of old-versus-new residents. Those who have lived in an area for generations are surrounded by kin, and enmeshed in cohesive social networks. Often they constitute a clan, and operate with some degree of self-containedness and exclusivity. It is difficult for newcomers to penetrate such networks; they remain isolated and, not infrequently, lonely. Among newcomers, social relations proceed primarily along interest lines. As a result, newcomers are not as much of a community as the old clans are, unless a political or social controversy necessitates their banding together. Thus, behind the facade of mutual familiarity and acquaintance, small communities are no more models of conviviality and sociability than are other settlements.

Most social interaction in towns and villages flows along either kinship or shared-interest channels. If one does not find friends among cousins, then one's "community" is comprised of persons one works, plays, or politicks with — a familiar contemporary social pattern. Within each group, namely the old and new residents, life experiences and circles of friends and acquaintances are organized by classes and social statuses. A social class in a town or village is not merely a broad stratum (for example, upper, middle or lower), but a delineated group of distinct lifestyles and economic stakes.[11] Class distinctions take the form of microstratifications,[12] such as "landed genry" versus "movers and shakers," commuters versus local employees, and members of service clubs versus stay-at-homers.

Racial and ethnic minorities stand almost outside these social hierarchies. For them, small communities are difficult places in which to live. They are tolerated and sympathized with, but seldom accepted. The treatment meted out to the Hutterites and Doukhobors in Alberta, the Japanese and East Indians in British Columbia, the Chinese and French in the Prairie Provinces, and to native Indians across Canada are historical reminders of the harsh treatment of visible minorities by small towns. Recent immigrants have not fared much better.

As John Irving says, "The code of small towns is simple but encompassing. If many forms of craziness are allowed, many forms of cruelty are ignored."[13] Almost everywhere it is signalled to individuals where they belong, and with whom they should associate. The point to note is that small communities are not "populist republics" as the rural myth makes them out to be. They are like the rest of society, where social standing, lifestyle, and shared interests constitute the bases of community life.

On the top of a typical social hierarchy are old families, prominent local merchants, and elected office holders who hold sway over decision-making. Professionals and managers, brought into a locality by their organizations, in combination with transplanted urbanites such as community organizers, teachers, and what has come to be called the "Harrowsmith Crowd" (named after the Canadian magazine that promotes values such as self-sufficiency and back-to-the-land), make a parallel social network. They coalesce around environmental or social causes, and find companionship through such organized interests. What would be the working class in a city (namely, farmers, miners, mechanics, self-employed craftsmen, hydro-linesmen, and so on), constitute the middle strata of various hierarchies. They constitute the silent majority who to a large extent stay out of political controversies and have little involvement in community causes. Minor hockey leagues, curling, volunteer fire departments, church socials, and euchre or bingo nights are the anchors of their life routines. Through these activities they form friendships and develop social networks. Their kinship, friendship, and work networks overlap and define the boundaries of their social world. Lucas says, in the case of railway workers, that they "associate with those who share the same work, the same vocabulary and problems."[14] Shift work cuts into their activities and further limits their social circle.

The lower social strata of towns and villages is comprised of the working poor, the unemployed, and racial minorities; and still below them is, usually, a small underclass of the down and out — the handicapped, widows, the destitute. The working poor are the inhabitants of tar-paper houses and shacks that line dusty back alleys, or are away from the main road on rocky lands. Their social world is insulated from the mainstream of the village or town life. They are often isolated and friendless. Who are they? In most communities they are landless farmers or their descendants,[15] whose marginal holdings were rendered uneconomical by corporate agriculture, and who could not climb aboard the train to jobs in the city. In Winkler, a town of 3,200 people eighty miles southwest of Winnipeg, the poorest people are called "Mexicans." Heather Robertson explains that they are descendants of Mennonites "who migrated to Mexico in the twenties" but have drifted back destitute.[16] "Virtually illiterate, fluent only in Low German, the Mexicans are treated with loathing and contempt. . . . Everything that goes wrong in Winkler is usually blamed on the 'Mexies.' Their greatest sin is going on welfare."[17]

In the short story, "Thanks for the Ride," Alice Munro gives a glimpse of the life of the poor in a resort village: "The smell, the slovenly, confiding voice — something about this life I had not known, something about these people. . . ."[18]

3. DYNAMICS OF SMALLNESS

The smallness of towns and villages is the catalyst that triggers social patterns normally associated with such communities. Even Pahl, who convincingly argues against attributing primacy to geographic milieux as a determinant of social relations, concedes that low population densities, as well as the intensity of role relations characteristic of small settings, affect local living patterns.[19] Many distinguishing features of interpersonal relations observed in towns and villages are essentially reflections of their small size.

Visibility

Small communities are supposed to be gossipy places where one's affairs are grist for the village's rumor mill. True as this description may be, being acquainted with and talking about each other does not necessarily suggest a close relationship. In towns and villages, almost everybody can be seen on the main street or in the supermarket; similarly, in a somnolent village street the few comings and goings cannot help being observed, even if no special effort is made to peek from behind lace curtains. Mutual acquaintances, familiar faces, and the visibility of daily routines are staples of living in small communities. This feature has been described by a correspondent to the "Letters to the Editor" column in *Maclean's* magazine: "In Trail (B.C.), which has a population of about 10,000 — we can walk down the street and say 'Hi' to practically every person we meet along the way. These people care about us, and we care about them. To me, that is living."[20] Town newspapers, and church or supermarket noticeboards, also help sustain familiarity by disseminating information about births, marriages, visits, and deaths of residents. Almost everyone is a somebody in a small community, in that one's activities are local news. But the visibility and familiarity should not necessarily lead to the presumption of friendliness and sociability. In a later section of this chapter we will present some data indicating that there is not much more mutual visiting and spending time together in rural areas than in the urban setting. Currently it may be noted that beyond the circles of kin or friends, the level and intensity of mutual relations among small-community residents are not unusually high, despite familiarity and mutual visibility.

An old-timer in an Eastern Ontario village, on the mention of another resident's name, indicated that she knew him as he had lived on her street, although they had not been inside each other's houses in the ten years that he had lived there. This is an illustration of the visibility without sociability that characterizes contemporary Canadian towns and villages. One American observer reports that "Social Psychologists . . . surveyed several rural communities and large metropolises, and found no less loneliness in the small friendly towns than in the big unfriendly cities."[21]

Mutual Help

There is an ethos of mutual help in small communities. It is a functional necessity. In a community where services are elemental, resources limited, and social structure truncated, coming to each other's help in emergencies or situations of necessity is a matter of enlightened self-interest. "If today I help my neighbour to get his sick child to the hospital, tomorrow I can expect the same," is the operational rule. In cities, the professionalization of help and availability of services reduces this mutual dependence and dissipates such expectations, whereas in the country the residents' survival depends on mutual assistance. This is not limited to exchanges among individuals. The modern organized voluntary sector has also fully permeated towns and villages. The Rotary and Kiwanis clubs, the Canadian Legion, the Jaycees, and the United Way have filtered down into small villages. Westport, an Eastern Ontario village of about 600 people, has six service clubs. A community of about 1,500 people in British Columbia was reported to have 30 to 40 voluntary organizations. Lucas cites examples of communities of 1,500 to 3,000 having 125 to 150 associations.[22]

The ethos of mutual help is an asset of small communities in times of natural disaster or external threat, for example, in the case of a proposed highway or dam not desired by the locality. Stories of towns and villages mobilizing to fight floods or resist governmental intrusions are legion.[23] In such unusual times, smallness and residents knowing each other promote unity and community-mindedness.

Personalized Decision-Making

Small communities have a sense of powerlessness in relation to national institutions and provincial bureaucracies. The proverbial "they" (referring to city institutions and corporations) may be blamed for almost every problem in a town or village. This attitude is not limited to the common citizen; it is shared equally by local power wielders. Internally, small communities tend to have a pyramidal power structure. Usually, a coalition of old families and local businessmen run civic affairs. But the visibility and accessibility of the power wielders give an aura of democracy and accessibility to the decision-making processes. Local representatives of federal and provincial departments and business corporations constitute another power bloc whose influence is pervasive. By administering and interpreting the policies of higher levels of government, this group commands substantial resources, which makes them very influential in local affairs.

The dependence of small communities on national and regional institutions affects local power structures in another way. Access to "outside" resources and influence in supracommunity organizations become sources of power in local affairs. Lawyers, land developers, former civil servants, and businessmen dominate local power structures as much for their local status as for their association with larger institutions. They can get things done at provincial and national levels, and that legitimizes their power.

In small communities, the decision-making process is highly personalized. Important functionaries are personally known to residents, and they are approached on that basis even for routine matters. Reeves and mayors of towns and villages receive personal calls for snow removal or bylaw enforcement. Almost everywhere, informal networks evolve around formal decision-making structures, but in small communities they become very dominant. Who receives welfare payments? When should one be cut off the welfare rolls? Such decisions are based on the personal dispositions of the persons in power. This tendency toward the personalization of the decision-making process is also a manifestation of smallness.

4. PATTERNS OF DAILY LIFE

How people use time is an indicator of their personal needs and preferences, as well as of their social situations. From studies of the use of time, social analysts have been able not only to compose pictures of the patterns of life in a society or community, but also to suggest policies that may help improve living conditions. Our interest lies in observing the daily routines of residents of towns and villages in contemporary Canada. But no sooner does one begin to think about these routines than questions about their comparability to the mainstream of Canada, which is metropolitan in character, come to the fore. Furthermore, popular beliefs about the leisureliness and friendliness of small communities beckon to be tested. Thus the task of observing patterns of daily life becomes an inquiry into the bases and meanings of these routines.

Time-budgets are a neat concept to parsimoniously measure the daily routines of a group. By asking members of a group to describe through questionnaires and to make available records (diaries) of their daily activities, data are generated to compose profiles of daily time-budgets. Surveying of time-budgets has become a common analytical procedure in many countries of the world, in both the Eastern and Western blocs.[24] The first national time-use survey in Canada was carried out in September, 1981. It was sponsored jointly by three federal ministries, including Statistics Canada.[25] A multistage cluster sample of national populations was drawn by first selecting specific communities, and then selecting individual respondents. Among the communities sampled were twelve metropolitan areas and three nonmetropolitan counties (Census Divisions). These procedures have resulted in the data set that can be differentiated into rural-versus-metropolitan time-budgets. As towns and villages have been included in the rural set, we will analyze rural time-budgets and assume that they reflect patterns of daily routines in small communities.

At this juncture, a brief description of the way in which time-budget data have been averaged-out needs to be given. Data from individual questionnaires and diaries were aggregated separately for the whole sample and by single activities. In the latter case only the data from individuals who engaged in an activity were aggregated. For example, regarding "time spent on work," in the second case only the data from those who reported having worked were taken into account, and children or housewives with no work time to report were not included. As the reporting group was different for each activity, averages of time spent on an activity by those engaging in it do not add up to twenty-four hours.

5. TIME-BUDGETS

A Canadian residing in a rural area (including towns and villages) who engaged in a pertinent activity, spent about 7 hours a day on work; about 11 hours on sleep and other personal needs; about 5-6 hours on leisure, both active and passive; another 2.1 hours on entertainment — almost as much time on entertainment and leisure as on work; and 2.8 hours on housework, in addition to an average of 1.5 hours on child care (Table 6.1).* Travel for work, shopping, and all other activities took about 1.5 hours every day (Table 6.1). With the inclusion of those who reported no time spent in respective activities, namely the whole sample, average times are reduced (Table 6.1, column 7).

Comparing rural daily routines with metropolitan patterns, (column 3 versus column 5; column 5 versus column 9 of Table 6.1), the striking fact is that there are very small differences in time-budgets, if any. The work takes about one-third of an hour more in metropolitan areas (7.29 for those who work), and housework takes a little less time (2.18 hours compared with 2.84 hours in rural areas). Child care has almost the same average, and time spent in sleep and other personal needs in metropolitan settings is not much different from that required in rural areas. There is slightly more time spent (about eight minutes) on entertainment by those engaged in such activities in metropolitan areas, while slightly less time is invested in active leisure. What is surprising and contrary to popular belief is that the overall time spent in travel to and from various activities, including work, in metropolitan areas is slightly more (about ten minutes on the average) than in rural areas. The evidence is unmistakable that the social convergence observed throughout this book has swept through every corner of Canadian society and structured life patterns. All in all, rural and metropolitan settings make little difference in the time-budgets and daily routines of Canadians.

On comparing Canadians with residents of other countries in terms of time-budgets, national cultural differences can be observed. Although incompatibilities of definitions and data categories make comparisons both difficult and a bit dubious, one can observe some broad features of the respective societies. It appears that Canadians on the whole spend relatively less time on work (about 3.2 hours a day) than Russians (6.2 hours in Pakov), Americans (8.3 hours), and the residents of Reading, England (5.1 hours).[26] Rural Canadians work slightly less. Time spent on sleep and personal care seems to be a constant in industrialized societies, averaging about ten hours everywhere, with small variations around this mean.

Incomes and education as indices of socioeconomic status would also have an influence on time-budgets. To standardize time-budgets by those variables, and thus reduce their effect in comparing rural and metropolitan patterns, Tables 6.2 and 6.3 have been drawn up. In these tables, the time categories pertain to some of those activities believed to be more prevalent in rural areas. Reading across the rows of these tables would allow holding income or education constant.

Table 6.2 shows that the rural poor spend more time working (6.6 hours) than the metropolitan poor (5.5 hours), to earn similar incomes. This may

---

*All numbered tables appear at the end of this chapter.

be due to the effect of low wages and the relative absence of unionization in rural areas. Generally, as incomes increase, the rural-metropolitan differences in time spent working decreases to the point where the situation is reversed. It takes slightly less time in rural areas to earn incomes of $35,000 or more. This may be the result of the leisurely pace of executive and managerial roles in settings distant from corporate head offices. Time spent on entertaining (visiting, partying) in rural areas is generally less than it is in metropolises, with the exception of the working class ($8,000-$16,000 annual income) and high-income households ($35,000 +). Similarly, time spent on phoning is consistently less for each income class in rural than in metropolitan areas. These observations contradict intuitive judgments about the patterns of rural life — there is no higher degree of sociability, getting together, visiting, or phoning. Almost the same conclusions are suggested by Table 6.3, which accounts for educational variations in rural and metropolitan populations.

6. QUALITY OF LIFE

Before concluding this chapter, it may be worthwhile to review some quality-of-life indicators of towns and villages. Our objective is to present an overview of health, housing, and crime conditions in these places. We are not attempting to formulate a systematic index or indices and then measure these conditions; we are merely interested in describing some broad social indicators that reflect pertinent conditions in these places.

Life Expectancy at Birth by Size of Settlement, Canada, 1970-1972

Size of Settlement	Years Expected to Live, 1970-1972	
	Male	Female
Less than 2,500	69.3	76.1
2,501-5,000	68.0	75.7
5,001-10,000	68.9	76.7
10,001-30,000	68.6	76.1
30,001-100,000	68.8	76.4
100,000 and over	69.5	76.8

SOURCE: K.G. Basavarajappa and J. Lindsay, *Mortality Differences in Canada, 1960-62 — 1970-72* (Ottawa: Statistics Canada, 1976)

From the above table it can readily be observed that one index of the state of health, life expectancy, varied little in rural areas, villages, towns, and metropolises. The longest life expectancy for males in 1970-1972 was in metropolises of 100,000 or more population, and the lowest was in towns of 2,501-5,000, with a range of 1.5 years. The female life expectancies ranged from 75.7 to 76.8 years — a range of 1.1 years, with the lowest and highest values coinciding with places of 2,501-5,000 and 100,000 and over respectively. The range of variation had narrowed over the previous decade, that is, since 1960-1962.[27] This crude indicator suggests that livability, from the health point of view, is highly comparable across the Canadian settlement system. Towns and villages neither offer any special advantages nor disadvantages by this indicator. What small communities may lack in health facilities and services they evidently make up with life-style advantages.

As the age and sex characteristics of residents of various settlements are different and tend to affect death rates as well as life expectancies, Basavarajappa and Lindsay have standardized age-sex distributions to compare mortality rates. Such age-sex specific standardized rates are presented in the table below.

Standardized Death Rates by Size of Settlement, Canada, 1970-1972

	Standardized Death Rate*	
Size of Settlement	Male	Female
Under 2,500	817	555
2,501-5,000	897	577
5,001-10,000	873	539
10,001-30,000	905	562
30,001-100,000	903	552
100,000 and over	863	535

*Number of deaths per 100,000 population

SOURCE: K.G. Basavarajappa and J. Lindsay, *Mortality Differences in Canada, 1960-62 — 1970-72* (Ottawa: Statistics Canada, 1976)

This table further confirms that no consistent livability characteristics can be attributed to small communities and, for that matter, there are no systematic differences between metropolises and towns and villages. While the lowest death rates for females are in cities of 100,000 or more population, the corresponding situation for males is to be found in rural areas of less than 2,500 population. Conversely, the highest death rates for females are in small towns of 2,501-5,000 population, while similar rates for males occur in small cities of 10,001-30,000 population. All in all, it is evident that health and livability situations were fairly similar across the Canadian settlement system.

Given that stress-induced diseases are associated with urban living, it may be appropriate to cite Basavarajappa and Lindsay's conclusions about mortality rates by such diseases. They suggest that standardized death rates for these diseases generally increased with the size of settlement, though places of 10,001-30,000 population showed the highest rates for 1970-1972. They surmised that the "presumed effect of better hospital and medical care facilities in the large size group of residence may have been more than compensated for by other natural advantages such as higher level of physical activity, different food habits, more leisurely life, more space, fresh air, etc. in the smallest size group of residence."[28] However, they found that the rates for hypertensive diseases were higher in the smallest-size groups. All in all, it appears that small communities have life-style advantages, particularly in and near the open country, which help keep the death rates from cardiovascular and renal diseases low, though the evidence is not unambiguous for all groups of diseases in this category.[29]

Death rates from accidents — motor vehicle as well as others — are inversely related to the size of settlement.[30] It appears that small communities have higher accidental death rates than large settlements.

Indicators of Housing Conditions in Small and Large Urban Centers, Canada, 1976

Indicator	Urban Places of less than 15,000	Metropolises
Percentage of Home Owners	74.8	55.7
Percentage of Housing Stock Predating 1940	34.1	23.2
Percentage of Housing Stock without Bath Facilities	4.1	0.7
Percentage of Housing Stock without Flush Toilets	2.4	0.5
Persons Per Room	0.6	0.6
Percentage of Households without Automobiles	18.2	22.5
Percentage of Households without Telephones	4.7	2.6

SOURCE: Census of Canada

The above table presents an overview of the living conditions in towns and villages of 1,000-15,000 population. Generally, towns and villages do not suffer from a noticeable deficiency of living facilities; the housing stock, though old, is livable; toilets and baths are available in more than 95 percent of dwellings; housing densities are low; and home ownership is widespread. But these indices also point toward a hard core of inadequate housing (perhaps of the under-class) which lack baths (4 percent) and toilets (2 percent). Almost one-fifth of households in towns and villages do not have an automobile, which, in a place where there is no public transport or taxi service, can be a great inconvenience.

Crime Rates by Size of Settlement, Canada, 1978

Settlement Size	Number of Offences Per 1,000 Population/Year
750-2,500	141
2,501-5,000	115
5,001-10,000	90
100,000 and over	98

SOURCE: Statistics Canada, Crime and Traffic Enforcement (Ottawa: Justice Statistics Division, 1978)

Towns and villages are not necessarily safer places as far as the overall crime situation is concerned. In fact, very small municipalities have the highest rate, but towns of 5,001-10,000 have the lowest. It appears that in small villages, conventional family feuds and an ethos of settling disputes through physical action have a bearing on the crime situation. For example, the rate of crimes of violence was the highest in such places, whereas the rate of property crimes was one of the lowest.[31] Perhaps minimum size and compactness are reached in places of 5,001-10,000 population to trigger thresholds of impersonalization necessary to curb crimes of passion, and promote effective law enforcement. All in all towns are relatively safe places; villages may be less so.

7. OVERVIEW

In this chapter we have attempted to portray the ways of life of towns and villages. The picture emerging from numerous sources of evidence is both pleasant and quite human. Towns and villages are harmonious and friendly places, but not without their own forms of exploitation and indifference. They offer a life of consistent routines and conformity, but of limited choices. Towns and villages *per se* are territorial groups and the territory is not the basis of social order in contemporary Canada. Any discussion of social life in small communities is inevitably faced with the issue of the physical determinability of social relations. It seems that in contemporary Canada, territory is only one of many interests around which communities are organized. Social class, ethnicity, occupation, life-style, and family life-cycle are equal if not stronger determinants of social life. Thus towns and villages, like the rest of Canada, are communities of interacting interests. But in small communities, the territory is both comprehensible and imaginable; therefore it becomes an integrating interest by itself, engendering sentiments of "we" versus "they." To the outside world, towns and villages present a face of serenity, but internally they are communities with a fair degree of individualism and social division. This conclusion is borne out by data on the daily routines and experiences of life in small communities.

The smallness of towns and villages results in the visibility of individuals, personalization of dealings, and an ethos of mutual help. But familiarity should not be taken as evidence of sociability and friendliness. Our exploration reveals a fairly consistent understructure of hard-core poverty, indifference (toward it), and prejudice in towns and villages. It takes the form of one-fifth of households lacking transport (automobiles), the relatively high incidence of violent crimes in hamlets, and in the whims of reeves and mayors determining who does or does not receive welfare payments. Racial and ethnic minorities are perhaps tolerated, but made to feel unwelcome in many ways. The upper social circuit of towns and villages itself is merely "middle class" in the national setting, and has little power to influence major events. These features generate a feeling of powerlessness in towns and villages, a feeling countered by recounting the blessings of country living, which are, of course, numerous.

NOTES

1. Louis Wirth, "Urbanism as a Way of Life," *American Journal of Sociology* 44:1 (July 1938): 8-20.
2. Canadian Institute of Public Opinion, *The Gallup Report* (Toronto, 23 December 1981, Mimeographed), 2.
3. *Ibid.*, 1.
4. Swanson *et al.* cite a Gallup poll of 1977 wherein it was found that there was a high degree of satisfaction with small towns: only 15 percent of residents of small towns expressed a desire to move, while 30 percent of city residents expressed a similar desire. Bert E. Swanson and Richard Cohen *et al.*, *Small Towns and Small Towners* (Beverly Hills: Sage, 1979), 20.
5. Robert Redfield, *The Primitive World and Its Transformation* (Ithaca, N.Y.: Cornell University Press, 1953), 20-21.
6. For an explanation of the terms *Gemeinschaft* and *Gesselschaft* see Ferdinand Toennies, "From Community to Society," excerpted in Amitai Etzioni and Eva Etzioni-Halevy, eds., *Social Change* (New York: Basic Books, 1973), 54-62.
7. Wirth, *op. cit.*
8. R.E. Pahl, *Whose City?* (Harmondsworth: Penguin, 1975), 84-85.
9. John D. Jackson, "Community Studies: The Traditional Approach Contrasted with a Class Approach," *International Journal of Urban and Regional Research* 4: 4 (1980): 578-79.
10. Roland L. Warren, "Towards a Reformulation of Community Theory," in Roland L. Warren, ed., *Perspectives on the American Community* (Chicago: Rand McNally, 1966), 70.
11. For example, see Pahl, *op. cit.*, 42.
12. Dennis Forcese, *The Canadian Class Structure*, 2nd ed. (Toronto: McGraw-Hill Ryerson, 1980), 28.
13. John Irving, "Trying to Save Peggy Sneed," *New York Times* Book Review section, 20 August 1982, 20.
14. Rex A. Lucas, *Minetown, Milltown, Railtown* (Toronto: University of Toronto Press, 1971), 160.
15. John Harp, "Canada's Rural Poor," in John Harp and John R. Hofley, eds., *Poverty in Canada* (Scarborough: Prentice-Hall, 1971), 180.
16. Heather Robertson, *Grass Roots* (Toronto: James Lewis & Samuel, 1973), 229.
17. *Ibid.*
18. Alice Munro, "Thanks for the Ride," in Wayne Grady, ed., *The Penguin Book of Modern Canadian Short Stories* (Harmondsworth: Penguin, 1982), 76.
19. Low population density in rural areas affects availability of facilities, and the density of role relationships is such that the upper strata must interact with the poor. For elaboration of these ideas, see Pahl, *op. cit.*, 91.
20. H.M. Keys, "Letter to the Editor," *Maclean's*, 13 September 1982, 6.
21. Louise Bernikow, " 'Alone' Yearning for Companionship in America," *New York Times, Sunday Magazine*, 15 August 1982, 25.
22. Lucas, *op. cit.*, 195-96.
23. For examples of towns and villages that were roused to fight and act as unified

communities, see James and Carolyn Robertson, *The Small Towns Book* (New York: Anchor, 1978).

24. John P. Robinson, Philip E. Converse, and Alexander Szalai, "Everyday Life in Twelve Countries," in Alexander Szalai, ed., *The Use of Time* (The Hague: Mouton, 1972).

25. The Canadian National Time Use Survey was sponsored jointly by Statistics Canada, the Ministry of Manpower and Immigration, and Communications Canada; it was carried out by Policy Research Inc. in September-October 1981.

26. For Russian and American figures, the source is Robinson *et al., op. cit.,* 114, Table 1. For British data, see Nicholas Bullock *et al.,* "Time Budgets and Models of Urban Activity Patterns," *Social Trends* 5 (1975): 13, Table 1.

27. K.G. Basavarajappa and J. Lindsay, *Mortality Differences in Canada, 1960-62 – 1970-72* (Ottawa: Statistics Canada, 1976), 21.

28. *Ibid.*, 25.

29. *Ibid.*, 26.

30. *Ibid.*, 27.

31. Rates of violent and property crimes, separately, by size of settlement are given in Statistics Canada, *Crime and Traffic Enforcement Statistics, 1978* (Ottawa: Statistics Canada, 1978), Table 3.

TABLES/CHAPTER 6

TABLE 6.1

Average Time Per Day Spent on Various Activities by Metropolitan and Rural Populations, Canada, 1981

	Mean Daily Hours Spent by							
	Metropolitan				Rural			
	Total Sample		Those who engaged in the activity*		Total Sample		Those who engaged in the activity*	
Activity	Number of Cases	Hours	Number of Cases	Hours	Number of Cases	Hours	Number of Cases	Hours
(1)	(2)	(3)	(4)	(5)	(6)	(7)	(8)	(9)
Work	2,201	3.23	978	7.29	481	3.09	213	6.98
Housework and home maintenance	2,201	1.90	1926	2.18	481	2.46	418	2.84
Child care	2,201	0.43	605	1.59	481	0.42	131	1.53
Personal care & needs (dressing, eating, sleep, etc.)	2,201	10.46	2201	10.46	481	10.99	481	10.99
Participation in organizations	2,201	0.20	236	1.89	481	0.22	56	1.92
Entertainment, including visiting friends	2,201	1.01	985	2.28	481	0.81	182	2.14
Active leisure	2,201	0.81	875	2.02	481	0.95	214	2.14
Passive leisure	2,201	3.32	2108	3.46	481	3.08	432	3.42
Shopping	2,201	0.47	1052	0.98	481	0.40	183	1.06
Education and studies	2,201	0.71	575	2.72	481	0.38	84	2.19
Travel for all activities	2,201	1.29	1941	1.46	481	1.07	396	1.29

*Only respondents who recorded some time spent on an activity were included in these counts. Those reporting zero time for an activity were excluded.

SOURCE: *National Time Use Project*, 1981

TABLE 6.2

Average Time Per Day Spent on Selected Activities by Income, Canada, 1981

| | Average Number of Hours Per Day Spent by Those Engaged in Activity | | | | | |
| | Metropolitan | | | Rural | | |
Income	Work	Entertaining	Phoning	Work	Entertaining	Phoning
Under $8,000	5.47	1.96	0.38	6.61	1.33	0.22
$8,001-16,000	7.73	1.62	0.35	5.16	2.14	0.33
$16,001-24,000	7.62	1.88	0.42	7.36	1.52	0.21
$24,001-35,000	7.09	1.76	0.35	7.34	1.28	0.24
Over $35,000	7.25	1.97	0.35	6.69	2.11	0.28

SOURCE: *National Time Use Project, 1981*

TABLE 6.3

Average Time Per Day Spent on Selected Activities by Educational Attainment, Canada, 1981

| | Average Number of Hours per day Spent by those Engaged in Activity | | | | | |
| | Metropolitan | | | Rural | | |
Education Level	Work	Entertaining	Phoning	Work	Entertaining	Phoning
Secondary or less	7.43	1.83	0.44	7.42	2.02	0.30
Some postsecondary	7.03	1.65	0.35	5.80	1.70	0.58
Postsecondary diploma	7.47	1.75	0.46	6.37	1.32	0.25
University degree	6.86	1.90	0.35	6.95	1.38	0.34

SOURCE: *National Time Use Project, 1981*

7 Housing and Land Use Patterns

The physical appearance of a small town is often one of contrasts. Within close proximity, because *small* towns are *small in area*, one may find a little-changed main street and several brand-new houses. Old houses that would qualify for "heritage" status may be found next door to a service station or a new fast-food outlet. A compact modern subdivision, with curbs and paved roads, may exist on the edge of a town that has many vacant lots. There is hardly a small town that can be called stagnant in terms of its physical development. In many ways, the persistence of the population patterns one sees for towns and villages is reflected in their housing trends and land use.

Growth and change occur in the physical development of today's towns and villages, just as they do in cities. But, due as much as anything to their small size, the changes often seem anomalous and unconnected to trends in population, job creation, or existing land use. Except for noting that most small towns do not constitute self-contained job and housing markets, little can be said about the reasons for their growth and change. However, knowledge about the nature and extent of physical development trends in small centers in Canada is increasing. From this, some general dimensions may be discerned not only of the prospects for their physical development, but also of some of the problems they face in housing and land use planning.

1. HOUSING DEVELOPMENT IN TOWNS AND VILLAGES

Housing development in Canadian towns and villages over the past two decades has been vigorous and impressive, if somewhat unexpected. A group of new houses often greet one's first view of towns that one knows have neither increased in population nor been the site of a new factory. This is the case for Beiseker, Alberta, for Lansdowne, Ontario, and for many other, if not most, small centers.

In order to determine how prevalent new housing development is in towns and villages, a study of the trends in the building statistics of small centers was undertaken. Data covering the period from 1962 to 1981 were gathered and analyzed. Since housing statistics are not available for all of Canada's towns and villages, a sample of one hundred centers was selected to represent the total. The sample centers were drawn from all the regions in about the same proportions as they are found in the entire array of 9,500 centers. They were also stratified to reflect both different sizes of centers and different growth rates. Although somewhat skewed toward places over 500 in population, in tests the sample has shown to be much like the total group of towns and villages.[1]

The regularly published building-permit data collected by Statistics Canada was the basic source of information.[2] These data are derived from regular reports obtained from municipal offices. Experience with such data sources suggests there may be some "unevenness" in the information forwarded to Statistics Canada, but probably not sufficient to reduce its reliability below 95 percent. A possibly more important caveat on the data is that they reflect only intended housing starts, not completed houses. Field checks to ascertain housing completions indicate that three-quarters of the permits result in completed houses within a year and well over 90 percent within three years.

New Housing, 1962-1972[3]

The one hundred small centers, selected from all provinces, added nearly 18,000 dwellings to their housing stock in the 1960s. This represents a growth rate of 27.1 percent in new housing.[4] If it is remembered that town and village populations were growing by 13.4 percent in the 1961-1971 decade, then this increase is indeed impressive (Table 7.1).*

The same strong tendencies in housing growth are found in the small centers of all regions of Canada and among all sizes of centers. Growth rates in housing are greatest in the Prairie Provinces' and British Columbia's small centers in this period. Regarding center size, larger towns added new housing faster than did small towns and villages. If we extrapolate the rate of new housing additions to all 9,500 towns and villages, it means that at least 275,000 new dwellings were built in small centers in Canada from 1962 to 1972.

Change in Housing Stock in Various Sizes of Canadian Towns and Villages, 1962-1972

Under 1,000	1,001-2,500	2,501-5,000	5,001-10,000	All Centers
18.2%	17.6%	26.4%	32.9%	27.1%

SOURCE: Table 7.1

*All numbered tables appear at the end of this chapter.

When one considers that close to one-half of the small centers in the country were either stable or declined in population in the same period, this increase in housing stock is even more dramatic. The sample of towns and villages used in the survey included such centers. Two of those places were Murray River, Prince Edward Island, which lost 26 residents and yet added 24 new single-family houses, and Oliver, British Columbia, which lost 159 residents and gained 100 new residences. In nine villages studied in detail in Eastern Ontario, 219 new dwelling units were added over fifteen years, from 1961 to 1976, despite a 4 percent loss in their combined population in the same period.

Of the new dwellings constructed in towns and villages, the single-family residence is the most popular, accounting for 58 percent of the total in the country from 1962 to 1972. Apartments accounted for 33 percent, and the remainder in two-family units and conversions. The proportion of apartments is close to half in larger towns of over 5,000 population, as one might expect. Single-family houses are much more prevalent in the towns and villages of the Atlantic and Prairie Provinces; in British Columbia and Ontario about half of the new residences were in the form of apartments (Table 7.2).

Finally, concerning the value of new dwellings, the average was about $12,000, and relatively stable for units built in towns and villages from 1962 to 1972. This value is similar for all regions — 10 percent less in the Atlantic region, 10 percent greater in the Prairies. The $12,000 construction cost was also similar in different sizes of centers. Extrapolating this value for the entire group of small centers in Canada means that almost $3.3 billion was invested in new housing in towns and villages in the 1960s.

New Housing, 1971-1981

The vigorous picture of housing development in towns and villages in the previous decade is found again in the 1970s, and even exceeded. The same sample of one hundred centers added over 27,500 dwellings to their housing stock between 1971 and 1981.[5] This represents a growth rate of 41.3 percent. Population growth in the same period for these centers was 16.7 percent. The latter figure closely parallels the growth for all small centers (Table 7.1).

The Prairie Provinces' and British Columbia's small centers continue to have the highest change in growth rates in housing among the regions. Although the second half of the 1970s saw a dampening of the country's economy, and is reflected in a diminished growth in housing from 1976 to 1981 in small centers, rates for the Prairies and British Columbia remained very strong. All sizes of towns and villages experienced similar and strong growth rates in housing in this decade. A simple extrapolation of the growth tendencies of the sample centers indicates that upwards of 450,000 new dwellings were built in towns and villages throughout Canada in the 1970s.

Change in Housing Stock in Various Sizes of Canadian Towns and Villages, 1971-1981

Under 1,000	1,001-2,500	2,501-5,000	5,001-10,000	All Centers
40.4%	37.9%	45.0%	40.3%	41.3%

SOURCE: Table 7.1

Single-family dwellings continued to dominate the new housing in all sizes of center, and comprised nearly two-thirds of the overall total. Medium-size small towns, those between 1,000 and 5,000 population, showed marked increases in apartments in the 1971-1981 period. Apartment construction in both the Prairie and Atlantic regions sharply increased in this period and declined in the other regions. The latter, British Columbia, Ontario, and Quebec, all increased in single-family dwelling construction (Table 7.2).

An estimate of the total value of housing added in the 1971-1981 decade is difficult to make because of the volatility of house prices in this period. Conservatively, if one assumes an increase in average construction costs of 50 percent between the two decades, close to $8 billion was invested in small town housing in the 1970s. However, more important than the total volume of house building is the fact of continuing confidence in small communities that is reflected in this investment.

Age of Housing Stock

The spate of new housing over the past two decades has dramatically changed the age and quality of the housing stock in small centers. In 1961, 61 percent of town and village housing in Canada was more than thirty years old; by 1981, this proportion had dropped to 34 percent. At the other end of the scale, the proportion of housing less than ten years old also increased substantially.

Change in the Age of Housing Stock in Canadian Towns and Villages, 1961-1981

	over 30 years	10-30 years	0-10 years
1961	61.1%	20.0%	18.9%
1981	34.0%	36.7%	29.3%

SOURCE: Census of Canada

There are two broad and important implications of these data. First, since condition of housing is directly related to age of housing, one can surmise that housing quality has also dramatically improved in recent decades in towns and villages. Second, the amount and quality of new housing that has been added in small centers greatly increases the likelihood of their continued persistence. In case it should be inferred that these tendencies started only in 1961, other data indicate considerable new house-building occurring in the 1950s.

2. DEVELOPMENT IN COMMERCIAL AND PUBLIC SECTORS

In addition to the expansion of housing, towns and villages have experienced growth in commercial, industrial, and public buildings in the past two decades. Using the same data source as for new housing both the composition and the value of this investment can be determined for the 1962-1972 period.

Nonresidential construction in small centers constituted 55 percent of the value of all new construction.[6] Not quite half of this investment was in institutional and government buildings; another one-third was in commercial facilities. In terms of values, the construction in the commercial and public sectors amounted to about $4 billion of investment from 1962 to 1972 in all Canadian small centers. This vigorous picture has continued into the 1970s (Table 7.3).

Types of New Construction in Canadian Towns and Villages, 1962-1972

Residential	Industrial	Commercial	Institutions and Government
44.8%	11.4%	17.9%	25.9%

SOURCE: Table 7.3

Commercial and public construction does not affect all small centers in the same way, of course. When looked at by population size, larger places, especially those over 5,000, receive significantly more of this type of development. But centers in two smaller classes, under 1,000 and 2,501-5,000, have been receiving above-average amounts of new commercial development. The least active places were those with populations between 1,001 and 2,500. By region, small centers experienced progressively higher levels of new nonresidential development as one moved from east to west. In part, this is due to differences in the costs of construction between region, with the West being regularly higher.

The actual kinds of new commercial and public buildings being constructed in towns and villages are quite diverse. A detailed study of nine centers in Eastern Ontario between 200 and 800 in population, for fifteen years prior to 1975, reveals much of this variety. Among the commercial enterprises are service stations, variety stores, beauty salons, and coin laundries. Institutional spending is often in the form of new church buildings and community halls. Local and senior governments invested in schools, water and sewer systems, municipal buildings, liquor stores, and post offices. Construction of this sort in towns and villages does not always result in new structures; a large share is in the form of renovations and expansions of existing buildings.

New Commercial and Public Construction in Nine Eastern Ontario Small Centers, 1961-1975

Commercial	
Service Station (2)	Insurance Office
Restaurant	Variety Store
Small Engine Shop	Coin Laundry (2)
Supermarket	Fast Food Outlet
Furniture Store	Beauty Salon (2)
Hardware Store	Real Estate Office
Auto Dealership	Bank
Public	
Municipal Office (2)	School (15)
Municipal Garage (2)	Telephone Exchange (5)
Community Hall (3)	Firehall (3)
Post Office (4)	Liquor Store (2)
Church Hall (2)	Medical Center
Church (4)	Water/Sewer Facilities (4)
Police Office	Senior Citizen Housing

*Numbers in parentheses indicate number of occurrences.

3. LAND USE PATTERNS IN TOWNS AND VILLAGES

Although no two towns look exactly alike, there are notable similarities in the arrangement and composition of their land uses. Characteristic of town and village land development are the following:

(1) The area occupied by the town is small in size.
(2) The density of development is low.
(3) There is considerable vacant land.
(4) There is, usually, a single, dominant commercial area.
(5) There is a juxtaposition of land uses.

Size. It is clear that a small center would not occupy a large amount of space, but it is important to grasp the actual scale of development in towns and villages. In area, few small towns reach one-half square mile in size (320 acres). Most are much smaller. A very common size of small town is one between 300 and 600 in population. Such a town tends to occupy about 200-250 acres. Consequently, all the different land uses within the town are small in extent. The commercial area may typically be only 8-12 acres in size, for example. The number of houses may total 100-150.

Density. It might be expected that places that are small in size would also be compact in their development, but this is generally not the case in towns and villages. Only those above 5,000 in population have densities approaching those found in suburban areas of cities. If one takes the area of a town or village which encompasses the bulk of development — its gross area — then it often turns out that the density of population in this area is about two to three persons per gross acre. The comparable gross density of population for contemporary suburbs is twelve persons per acre.

Vacant Land. The low densities that characterize land use in towns and villages are due to two factors. The first is simply a more widely spaced form of develoment in which many vacant building lots are scattered in the built-up portions of the town. The second, and more important factor, is large amounts of unbuilt-upon land — vacant land — in the community. Even excluding the land within a town's boundaries that may be farmed, for example, it is not uncommon to find as much as one-third of a small center's land to be vacant.

From a brief study of land use in ten small towns in various parts of Canada, obtained from planning maps, the extent of unused land and of other land uses can be grasped. In these towns, whose populations ranged from 200 to 2,700, the distributions were remarkably similar. The accompanying land use map for Fordwich, Ontario (Figure 7.1), typifies small-town land use patterns in Canada.

Distribution of Land Uses in a Sample of Canadian Towns and Villages

Residential	Commercial	Industrial	Public Park	Streets	Vacant
21.8%	3.0%	9.0%	11.4%	19.2%	35.4%

SOURCE: Planning Maps

Commercial Development. The "Main Street" or "King Street" of a Canadian small town is probably its most remembered part. The visually most dominant buildings are located there and it is usually the social center of the town. The number of commercial establishments is not large, usually less than twenty-five in a town of even 500, nor is there likely to be much diversity in the kinds of businesses. And even in towns of the same size one may not, today, find the same array of businesses. However, criteria such as the number of stores are only one measure of the street's importance. Main Street provides a social focus and the means of maintaining community cohesion through its post office, churches, municipal office, coin laundry, tavern, and doctor's office.

A frequent problem for small-town commercial areas, caused by the lack of growing local markets and the competition of urban shopping centers, is the existence of vacant buildings. Often, such buildings are not maintained

FIGURE 7.1
Typical Small-Town Land Use Pattern: Fordwich, Ontario

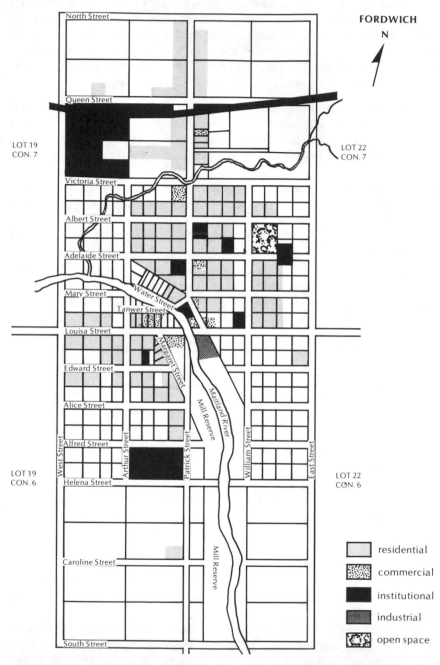

Source: Huron County Planning Department, *Howick Township Secondary Plan*

and become dilapidated. One of the most frequently expressed concerns of small-town residents is about the "ugly conditions" of some Main Street buildings. More recently, in towns of 5,000 and over, Main Street is often challenged by a shopping mall at the edge of the town. The long-term consequences for these towns are not yet known, but the characteristic small-town land use pattern of a single, prominent retail street or area is clearly being changed by these modern commercial developments.

Land Use Mixture. The small physical size of towns and villages, combined with the limited array of activities, typically leads to a juxtaposition of different kinds of land uses. On Main Street it is not uncommon to find stores, houses, service stations, a firehall, and churches all intermingled with fast-food outlets and the post office. While this wide mixture of land uses is not found in residential areas, something of the same diversity of uses exists there, too.

This mixed pattern of land use results from the small scale of development as well as from a lack of new development, a lack in both amount and pace. Land use patterns such as found in towns and villages seem to function satisfactorily. They provide a high degree of convenience; they offer opportunities for more interaction of people and activities than size alone would suggest; and they show that a high degree of tolerance is possible among diverse land uses. If there is a disadvantage, it is the absence of large-enough districts of similar uses to facilitate the use of normal zoning and planning tools. This may be a minor technical disadvantage.

4. HISTORIC BUILDINGS IN TOWNS AND VILLAGES

It is increasingly coming to be recognized by residents of small centers and by outsiders that most towns and villages possess many valuable examples of historic and architecturally significant buildings.[7] The lack of dramatic growth in small places, bemoaned by some, is also the reason that many older buildings still remain. Houses, churches, public and commercial buildings, and railway and industrial structures dating from halcyon days, often in the nineteenth century when every town's future seemed assured, provide a sense of tradition and stability to residents and visitors alike.

The accompanying sketches by Nicholas Hill, of towns in Huron County, Ontario are indicative of the architectural richness that abounds in towns and villages.[8] Some important buildings in small towns are in remarkably good repair, others are not. The realization that the heritage of a community is so bound up in its buildings has prompted numerous efforts from coast to coast in Canada to conserve particular buildings and entire streetscapes. St. Stephen, New Brunswick and Niagara-on-the-Lake, Ontario have undertaken almost town-wide restorations. Barriefield, a village near Kingston, Ontario, has been designated as a "heritage conservation district" in order to be eligible for grants from the province to

FIGURE 7.2
Typical Heritage Buildings Found in Small Ontario Towns

Clinton, Ontario

Belgrave, Ontario

SOURCE: Nicholas Hill, *Historic Streetscapes of Huron County.*

individual owners, and for the community to retain its historic flavor. Similar examples can be found in all provinces.

The existence of historic building resources may, however, be a mixed blessing for a town, especially a relatively small one. Take Bath, Ontario, for example, with less than 1,000 residents. A survey undertaken for the village council identified forty buildings dating from before 1850 and many more from the latter half of the nineteenth century.[9] But Bath is a town of modest resources, both publicly and privately, and has a dilemma about how, or whether, to proceed with broad scale building conservation and restoration. Almost one-third of the town's buildings are involved.

The old and frequently elegant buildings of a small community, now considered "significant," are often a paradox for the community. On the one hand, they are often a major reason for a town's persistence. On the other hand, they reflect the fact that little new growth has occurred in the town. Yet another consideration is that the old buildings represent a major resource of space that could not usually be built as inexpensively today, much less with the same character and meaning for the residents of the community. The issues that remain for many towns and villages with their abundance of good, old buildings are to find private users for them and to find funds for public use to be made of them. However, a growing number of small communities are finding solutions: special houses which become museums or senior citizen activity centers; railway stations which become dwellings or specialty shops; and Main Street buildings being refurbished under revitalization schemes. Fortunately, both the will and the means for preservation are emerging for towns and villages.[10] In some Ontario communities, municipal plans are now designating historic buildings for which town council approval must be sought before they can be altered.[11]

5. PHYSICAL DEVELOPMENT PROBLEMS

The concerns of town and village residents about the physical development of their community are seldom concerns about land use patterns. Rather, residents cite a set of discrete problems such as the following, elicited at public planning meetings in the villages of Fordwich, Gorrie, and Wroxeter in Ontario:

"install lights at the railway crossing"
"fix the bridge"
"resurface main street"
"repair the sidewalks"
"provide more street lights"
"better recreation facilities in the park"
"maintain empty stores on main street"
"repair the dam and clean up the mill pond"
"install better drains on main street."[12]

While the lists of physical development problems differ from one small community to another, they all possess similar features. First, the problems are quite specific; second, the issues are very pragmatic; and third, the solutions call for the resources and coordination of several levels of government. Regrettably, as direct as such an agenda of problems is, few of them seem to get solved. The reasons for this are discussed in a later chapter.

Looked at from a community planning perspective, the physical development needs of a town or village frequently also revolve around the solution to a set of specific problems. A report prepared for the Province of Newfoundland in 1968 on methods of preparing plans for small towns is probably still the most incisive rendering of land use planning issues in small communities:

> At the small-town scale some immediate problems may scarcely merit inclusion in a conventional municipal plan but can readily be included in a statement of problems and possible solutions. Problems caused by lack of care, including those of garbage disposal and the dumping of worn-out vehicles, are good examples of issues which may not fit the conventional mould and may not be recognized locally but which, if solved, could have immediate impact on the total environment in a small community.[13]

The problems they identify for Clarenville, Newfoundland, then a community of 1,800, are indicative of land use problems found to one degree or another in small centers throughout Canada:

  (1) The provision of an adequate water supply
  (2) The provision of a sanitary sewer system
  (3) Large areas of unsuitable building land
  (4) The scattered nature of existing development
  (5) The lack of industrial land
  (6) Problems of the town center
  (7) Access from the Trans-Canada Highway
  (8) Dangerous railway crossings
  (9) Poor access to some existing houses
  (10) Ugliness caused by lack of care, or indifference
  (11) Garbage disposal.[14]

A brief elaboration of several of these problems will help show their significance for small communities.

The Provision of Public Utilities. One seldom finds a town or village with five hundred or fewer residents that has a public waterworks system, much less a sewerage system. Not uncommonly, centers two and three times this size are in the same position. Services are generally privately initiated and maintained, for example, individual wells and septic tanks. The low-density development frequently found in small places is quite compatible with this form of servicing, although problems of polution may arise even then, depending upon underlying soil conditions. Higher-density development by filling-in vacant lots or districts, often propounded to conserve agricultural land and create more compact communities, may also involve costly collective utility systems.

Unsuitable Building Land. A problem typical of many small centers is the presence of unsuitable building land either within or adjacent to the community. Steep slopes and rocky, swampy, and low-lying areas frequently impede expansion and even infilling of towns and villages. They may make road building very expensive, make it too costly to provide utilities, and be difficult to drain. For small communities with few resources, these may be prohibitive costs. This puts a burden on remaining land, and the problem remains of how to use the unbuildable land.

Uneven Land Development. Most towns and villages have an uneven pattern of land development. Large areas in which houses are scattered are often combined with areas having little or no room for expansion, as well as with compact subdivisions. The scattered residences are difficult and costly to service and may not lend themselves to infilling, especially if (as is frequent) the existing development is on poor building land. At the same time, congestion may occur in the business, transportation, or industrial areas. There may be little room for expansion of such functions; thus, the need to consider outlying sites, which results in further scattering.

Traffic and Road Problems. Internally, both unsuitable land and scattered development may lead to unreasonable and costly road building and maintenance, or to the continuation of inadequate access to dwellings. Externally, small places are frequently burdened either by poor access to major highways or by the inconvenience of a major highway running through the community. An especially prevalent problem in towns and villages throughout Canada is the existence of dangerous railway crossings. Local roads must often approach rail crossings on steep grades and at sharp angles that restrict the vision of drivers.

Care and Maintenance of the Community. Towns and villages represent a clustering of people and activities that, although small, are sufficiently large to generate waste materials and the need for maintaining the condition of common-use areas. The dumping of car and truck bodies and other scrap may be haphazard; garbage dumps are often ugly and sometimes located on dangerous sites close to bodies of water. Unkempt cemeteries and derelict buildings are not uncommon problems in many small centers.

The array of problems affecting physical development in a town or village differs from one community to another. But evident in most small communities is a difficulty in finding solutions to their problems. The costs are often prohibitive, and the technical capability may not be available from senior governments. These issues are discussed further in the next two chapters.

6. DIMENSIONS OF PHYSICAL DEVELOPMENT

The picture of housing and land use patterns in towns and villages is, admittedly, a diverse one. Vigorous house building, deteriorating stores, historic buildings to conserve, construction of new public buildings, and scattered development are among the facets of physical development in most small centers. In general terms, these considerations also apply to urban situations, but towns and villages are not just scaled-down versions of a city. A need exists for a framework that can capture the nature of small-center development, and thus provide a better basis for comparison among small communities, and between small and large communities.[15]

Four dimensions of physical development will help in understanding the nature of an existing community and how it is changing. The dimensions are:

(1) *Scale* of development
(2) *Range* of types of development
(3) *Intensity* of development
(4) *Pace* of development activity.

Scale. The size of towns and villages is usually stated in terms of population, but these centers are usually small in area as well. As noted above, most small towns occupy less than one-third of a square mile of land. Even modest-size cities such as Prince Albert, Saskatchewan and Belleville, Ontario occupy only about five square miles each. It is important to grasp that, within the small area occupied by a town or village, a wide range of activities and buildings are accomodated. Thus, the components of the physical development are themselves small — for example, the number of houses or stores, and the areas they occupy — as is the overall area of a small center.

The scale dimension is notable not only in understanding the current pattern of physical development, but also in examining changes in development. Even the additions or changes to a small center's land use pattern are usually small in number (for example, houses), or small area required (for example, a new post office), or both. The generally small size of development and of land use changes should not be construed as being either less important or easier to deal with. The scale dimension can, however, place many problems in better perspective.

Range. The array of activities in a small community is, almost by definition, smaller than in a large town or city. While planners, for example, may classify a town's land uses by residential, commercial, or industrial, within these categories there will not be found a very wide array of types of development. Residential development in towns and villages usually means single-family houses. When an apartment building is built it is likely to be small one. Similarly, small varieties of development are found in a small center's commercial, industrial, and public land-use areas.

Moreover, when a town or village experiences growth, it is most likely to add more of the same kind of development that it now has, rather than embark on new forms of land use and buildings.

Intensity. Physical development can occur at varying degrees of intensity. Large areas may be covered with the same kind of development, such as large residential subdivisions. Or, intensity may come in terms of the degree to which development is concentrated in a small area, such as with a cluster of multistorey apartment buildings or a shopping center. In most small communities the development tends to be in discrete units and not concentrated in its location. The value of this dimension is in determining the effects that physical development has on a community, such as in the traffic generated, the need for larger public utilities, or the need for parks and schools.

Although most towns and villages might be characterized as having a low intensity of development, as seen, for example, in their low densities, some new development may be intense. New large industries or shopping centers are two types of intense development found in small communities. They may not change the overall density of the community, but they can put special demands on the center in terms of new services, better roads, or disruption of the established patterns of shopping and travel. Thus, this dimension may need to be applied both on a community-wide basis and with regard to new large development.

Pace. This dimension refers to the rate of growth in a community in terms of both the extent of growth and the continuity of growth. It is important in small communities not to view growth simply as a percentage rate of increase over, say, a five- or ten-year period. One needs to look at the *actual amounts* of growth. For example, when a town of 500 persons has experienced a 25 percent increase in the number of houses in the past decade, this means that only about thirty new houses were built in the ten years. This is undoubtedly very important for the community, but it does not involve a very large undertaking when compared with urban subdivisions of several hundred homes.

Further, for physical development in small communities one also needs to look at the *continuity* of growth. Using the example above, one should ask: was the 25 percent growth in houses and thirty new homes in the decade distributed evenly over the ten years at, say, three houses per year? Very frequently, one would find the answer to be No, for in small communities physical development tends to occur in discrete projects. A small builder, and in towns and villages most development firms are small, decides, for example, to build a single small subdivision of six to ten houses in one year. Because this would probably absorb most of the demand for houses in a small center for several years, such a project is not repeated either frequently or regularly.

This lack of continuous development distinguishes not only house building in towns and villages but also in commercial, industrial, and public buildings. A single town is likely to have one small apartment building, a new restaurant, a small industrial building, or a new motel, for example, over several years, but not several of each kind. Considered with the scale of population of small centers, this pace of activity is both understandable and appropriate.

These four dimensions — scale, range, intensity, and pace of physical development — allow one to view the land use of *individual* small communities on a comparable basis. This is essential because, as any resident or observer of small centers knows, *no two towns are completely alike*. Thus, to complete the picture it is necessary to identify where a community stands on each of these dimensions in terms of the *context* of the town or village. What is the economy of the place or of the region? Is the growth situation booming, moderate, or declining? How does the physical setting affect the community pattern? How far from a city is the center? These and similar questions need to be posed in order to explain qualitative differences in the physical development between any two small communities. Nevertheless, while towns differ from one another, experience has shown that small centers are more like each other in their physical development patterns and trends than they are like cities.

NOTES

1. The one hundred centers represent a 6 percent sample of all towns and villages, according to population. A complete discussion of the building activity surveys is found in Donald Nijsse, "Recent Physical Development in Small Towns and Villages in Canada" (Unpublished Master's Report, Queen's University School of Urban and Regional Planning, 1976).

2. Canada, Statistics Canada, *Building Permits*, Cat. No. 64-001 and 64-203.

3. The lack of data before 1962 prevented building activity being matched precisely with information from the regular decennial censuses of 1961 and 1971.

4. Housing growth is derived from an estimate of 1961 housing stock based on the census average of 3.6 persons per dwelling unit applied to the 1961 population.

5. There is an overlap of two years of the two decades used in this analysis. A comparison of the average annual increments of new housing shows significant differences: 1,760 per year for 1962-1972, and 2,700 per year for 1971-81; these need to be taken into account.

6. Data are for the same sample of one hundred small centers used to analyze housing trends. Nonresidential construction is reported only according to dollar value in Statistics Canada, *Building Permits*, Cat. No. 64-203.

7. Ralph Greenhill, Ken MacPherson, and Douglas Richardson, *Ontario Towns* (Ottawa: Oberon, 1974).

8. Nicholas Hill, *Historic Streetscapes of Huron County* (London, Ont.: Middlesex Printing, 1979).

9. Godfrey Spragge *et al.*, *History and Architecture of the Village of Bath, Ontario* (Kingston: Queen's University School of Urban and Regional Planning, 1976).

10. The Canadian experience in small-town historic conservation is not yet well-documented, but for a comparable American experience see *Small Town 7:9* (March 1977).
11. County of Huron, *Howick Township Secondary Plan* (Goderich, Ont., 1976), 39-40.
12. *Ibid.*, 39-50.
13. Newfoundland, Department of Municipal Affairs, *Planning for Smaller Towns* (St. John's: Project Planning Associates, 1968), 8.
14. *Ibid.*, 23.
15. This discussion derives from Gerald Hodge, *Planning for Small Communities* (A Report to the Ontario Planning Act Review Committee, Toronto, 1978, Background Paper No. 5).

TABLES/CHAPTER 7

TABLE 7.1

Growth in Housing and Population in Canadian Towns and Villages, 1962-1981

| | Percent Change 1962-1972 | | Percent Change 1971-1981 | |
	Dwellings	Population*	Dwellings	Population
Population of Center				
Under 1,000	18.2	3.5	40.4	14.3
1,001-2,500	17.6	5.7	37.9	20.4
2,501-5,000	26.4	13.2	45.0	18.5
5,001-10,000	32.9	19.7	40.3	8.8
Region				
Atlantic	17.1	8.9	17.5	−0.2
Quebec	19.8	15.2	39.1	21.9
Ontario	32.0	15.6	27.7	1.2
Prairies	36.6	14.0	66.7	34.9
British Columbia	36.1	14.6	59.6	12.0
CANADA	27.1	13.4	41.3	16.7

*Population change is for the period 1961-1971

SOURCE: Sample of centers drawn from Statistics Canada, *Building Permits*, 64-203.

TABLE 7.2

Composition of New Housing in Canadian Towns and Villages, 1962-1981

	Percent Distribution					
	1962-1972			1971-1981		
	Single Family	Two Family	Apartments	Single Family	Two Family	Apartments
Population of Center						
Under 1,000	75.6	0.9	23.5	75.0	5.6	19.4
1,001-2,500	76.7	7.2	16.1	72.6	4.2	23.2
2,501-5,000	68.2	6.0	25.8	57.5	5.3	37.2
5,001-10,000	47.2	6.5	46.3	60.8	4.3	34.9
Region						
Atlantic	76.2	6.3	17.5	54.6	2.8	42.6
Quebec	62.7	13.5	23.8	66.8	5.6	27.6
Ontario	45.7	1.7	52.6	74.5	4.6	20.9
Prairies	70.5	6.2	23.3	57.5	5.4	37.1
British Columbia	46.9	5.1	48.0	65.5	4.9	29.6
CANADA	60.1	6.1	33.8	63.0	4.7	32.3

SOURCE: Sample of centers drawn from Statistics Canada, *Building Permits,* 64-203

TABLE 7.3

Value of New Construction in Canadian Towns and Villages, 1962-1972

	Types of New Construction				
	Residential	Industrial	Commercial	Government/ Institutional	Total
	(dollars/capita)				
Population of Center:					
Under 1,000	681	94	430	328	1,523
1,001-2,500	622	165	167	270	1,224
2,501-5,000	889	171	456	441	1,957
5,001-10,000	936	302	305	664	2,207
Region					
Atlantic	518	78	249	518	1,363
Quebec	597	218	359	348	1,522
Ontario	921	65	174	391	1,551
Prairies	1,198	197	359	697	2,451
British Columbia	1,124	660	620	479	2,883
CANADA	839	217	336	487	1,879
	44.8%	11.4%	17.9%	25.9%	100.0%

SOURCE: Sample of centers drawn from Statistics Canada, *Building Permits,* 64-203

8 Community Needs

1. PERSPECTIVE ON COMMUNITY NEEDS

On a wintry night, residents of Burin, Newfoundland, kept a prayer vigil outside the local fish plant to avert its closure and prevent the transfer of its machinery to another town. The Premier of Newfoundland wired for federal help in an attempt to save five hundred jobs in the only industry of the town of 3,000.[1] This may be a dramatic example, but it illustrates vividly how private decisions become public concerns, and how an event can precipitate collective needs unsuspected before. Essentially this is the nature of community agendas and needs. They are intermeshed with individual needs and expectations.

Needs are undoubtedly "shaped by the social environment and involve values and judgments,"[2] but recognition of their sociocultural relationship should not imply that they are dispensable. Maslow has pointed out the hierarchical character of human needs in that the basic, lower-order needs (food, shelter, sex, and so on) must be satisfied before the higher-order needs come into full play.[3] Obviously a starving man cannot be concerned with self-actualization as long as he remains unfed. These are the intrinsic characteristics of human needs, and they underlie much of the theory that guides need-assessment methodologies.

Moroney identified four types of needs, each corresponding to an analytical perspective: (1) *normative needs* are derived from professional judgment, and objective standards about a specific situation, for example, water quality standards, and ratios of hospital beds per 1,000 population; (2) *perceived needs* are facilities and services felt by people to be necessary; (3) *expressed needs* are actually unmet demands, as observable from waiting lists or other registry points; and (4) *relative needs* are arrived at through the application of equity criteria, that is, how a group or community compares with others of similar characteristics in regard to provision of some facilities or services.[4] For example, does a community have a greater or smaller teacher/pupil ratio than comparable areas? This description suggests that there are two distinct approaches to identifying community needs: first, seeking people's opinions and judgments about their needs; and second, applying some objective standards or norms to the existing situation in a community. Not that these two perspectives always lead to conflicting inventories of needs, but they can be divergent.

Another issue that underlies the concept of community needs is the question of differentiating between "community" and "individual" needs. Do subsidized houses for senior citizens satisfy individuals' needs, or fulfill a community need? How do individual needs become community requirements? These questions confront politicians and public officials daily, and they have occupied the talents of welfare economists, political analysts, and sociologists for a long time. There are no clear-cut answers, but there are some illuminating concepts.

Economists view collective needs as being manifestations of "externalities and demand for public goods." Public goods fundamentally are such goods and services that are indivisible for consumption purposes, in that one person cannot obtain them without others receiving them as well. Further, they often require collective action for production.[5] Among the conventional examples of public goods are national defense, police protection, and pollution control. Even a "blue" Tory would concede that the market cannot provide national defense. It must be a collective (public) undertaking. If public goods constitute the baseline of community needs, then one has to examine their scope in modern times.

In postindustrial Canada, the scope of public goods has steadily expanded, almost consensually, to include provision for services such as education, welfare, old age pensions, highways, crime control, environmental preservation, and land use regulations; in sum, a variety of goods and services that may or may not fully meet the criteria of pervasive consumption externalities, indivisibility, and nonexclusion. The complexity and interdependence of modern life have fostered social expectations of collective (public) action in almost every area of life, often due to market inadequacies. These expectations generate paradoxes such as a demand for urgent public intervention when a fish plant closes at the same time that economic woes and individual difficulties are being blamed on too much government. Despite its apparent contradiction, the demand for public initiative on almost every community issue is not so unusual. It is an acknowledgment of the mediatory role of the government among competing interests in contemporary society. A community in present times is not a tribe. It is a shifting coalition of competing interests. Perhaps it is this realization that induced Steiner to conclude that "a collective good . . . is *not necessarily* a collective consumptive good. Collective goods arise whenever some segment of the public collectively wants and is prepared to pay for a different bundle of goods and services than the unhampered market will provide."[6] Such a notion of collective goods underlies what earlier have been described as normative and perceived needs.

Politically and socially, the idea of social justice (equity) provides the rationale of need for community facilities and services. In a society where production is sustained by tariffs, fiscal and monetary polices, and physical infrastructure, and where public policies ensure the viability of private corporations, wealth and income are not merely matters of individual enterprise. Similarly, poverty is not the result of bad luck or laziness. The system that produces affluence also creates poverty. These are the material and ideological realities of modern life, and they have become a part of the national ethos, thereby making equity a basis of community needs. When a sizable group or territorial community falls short on national norms in the provision of services, goods, and organizational arrangements, a presumption of collective needs is justified. This is the basis of relative and normative needs. Irrespective of whether or not a majority in a town or a city asks for a particular health, housing, welfare, education, or infra-structural service, a noticeable shortfall in its provision is taken to be an indication of community needs.

To sum up, community needs are goods, services, organizations, and regulations deemed necessary for the effective and equitable functioning of a group. There is a common stake in the availability of such a good or service, although some individuals may be the direct beneficiaries. Community needs are anchored in the institutional, economic, and techno-logical framework of a locality. With this perspective about community needs, we will proceed to look closely at towns and villages.

2. ASSESSING THE NEEDS OF TOWNS AND VILLAGES

In earlier chapters we have argued that contemporary Canadian towns and villages should not be viewed as folk communities where family, God, and virtue reign. Sociologically they recapitulate broader national trends, and include a variety of class and interest groups. These diverse groups may be more strongly linked together by sentiments of localism and interest in visibly shared territory, but such horizontal links do not bring about a consensual community. Further, Canadian towns and villages are truncated communities which greatly differ from each other, and reflect a high degree of uniqueness. These features imply that in probing for community needs we should not be expecting unanimity of demand and uniformity of collective objectives. Similarly, it should not come as a surprise that essentially community needs of small places are elements necessary for contemporary living.

In assessing community needs of small centers, we began with two assumptions. First, the needs should relate to the welfare of a group and are perceived or thought to be collective goods of some kind. Second, these needs should pertain to areas for which the public sector, be it local, provincial, or federal, bears primary responsibility. The second assumption is particularly necessary to maintain the manageability of the task, and to strike a level of discourse relevant for policy making. Community needs find expression through political and social processes. Leaders and informed persons articulate shared deprivations and necessities. In contemporary Canada, citizens' groups and local councils are the most common articulators of needs. Needs might be expressed in public meetings or articulated in the local media, or communicated through gossip or folklore. Also, they could be judged as functional necessities by prevailing standards and norms. We have sought empirical evidence to compose a generalized view of the towns' and villages' needs, and have relied on a nation-wide survey and findings of specific case studies as the main sources of information.

In 1976, we carried out a questionnaire survey of mayors, reeves, and other elected officials of a sample of small centers. The respondents were treated as community informants, and were specifically requested to respond on the basis of their knowledge about the facilities and services residents were demanding, and not merely report what they thought was needed by their communities. (The details of the selection procedures and estimates of the reliability of the sample are given in Appendix B.) Suffice it to say here that questionnaires were returned from 150 centers, thereby providing a fair cross-section of all centers of less than 10,000 population, in Canada. (It is a sample of a relatively low level of signficance in terms of size, that is, a 90 percent confidence level.) And it provides a fair basis to assess needs and problems of small centers.

We have also supplemented the survey data with secondary sources and published accounts of the needs of small communities. A few informal probes were also made through visits to selected places in Ontario, Nova Scotia, and Manitoba. From all these sources a profile of perceived and expressed community needs has been composed.

3. PRESERVING THE SMALL

There may have been times, such as during the era of Canada's settlement, when growing big was the ambition of towns and villages, but recently not many aspire to it. A genuine preference for staying small has emerged in postindustrial Canada. Despite its inherent ambiguities and apparent contradictions, there is a love of smallness. Towns and villages are viewed as peaceful, friendly, and healthy places in which to live. Regardless of whether or not these beliefs are entirely true, as long as people hold these beliefs they remain an element of small-community life. And the evidence about the pervasiveness of such beliefs is overwhelming.

Beliefs About Canadian Small Communities as Perceived by Their Citizens, 1976

	Most Common Beliefs About Small Communities	
	First Response	Second Response
Hamlets and Villages (under 1,000 population)	Peaceful, relaxing	friendliness free from crime
Small and large towns (1,000-10,000 population)	Peaceful, relaxing	community-minded

SOURCE: Authors' Survey, 1976

Before interpreting the above table, we should explain our coding and tabulation procedures. These responses come from an open-ended question phrased as: "What are the positive aspects of living in a small community such as yours?" Each response pertained to one community. Being an open-ended question, it often evoked more than one response. These responses were tabulated in seven categories (see Tables 8.1 and 8.2).* The order in which various characteristics were mentioned was taken to be the sequence of priorities. Table 8.1 reports the first-mentioned characteristics, and 8.2 the second-mentioned. Since the number of responses decreases precipitously beyond the two answers, we have not bothered to report them. A similar procedure has been followed for other open-ended questions, which are reported on later.

Returning to the above table, it is evident that residents of small centers consider their communities to have a peaceful, relaxing, and community-minded life-style, and that they consider these to be positive aspects of their habitat. Villages and towns show no difference in this regard. Even in the second set of responses (Table 8.2), "friendliness of neighbors," absence of crime, community spirit, and clean environment turn out to be the most commonly mentioned features of small centers.

It can be discerned from these responses that they reflect the converse of what have generally come to be called "urban problems." The emphasis on a cohesive social organization indicates that a high value is placed on the qualitative aspects of life, and on this score respondents consider small communities to be highly desirable. This finding is supported by our field work in Morden, Manitoba and Inverness County, Cape Breton Island. Interviewees in both these areas noted the friendly, relaxed life-style of their small centers and often couched their responses in terms of a contrast with "the city" and its more hectic pace. In a plan for Howick Township in the County of Huron, Ontario, the county planners have included the comments of residents of three villages regarding what they enjoy about their village. Almost uniformly the responses are: "friendly neighbors,"

---

*All numbered tables appear at the end of this chapter.

"the quiet way of life and slower pace," "the friendly community," "the fellowship," and "the quiet peaceful life."[7] These characteristics are quite evidently reflections of the small size.

Although the preference to stay small does not necessarily imply an antidevelopment bias, there is nothing that stirs up the divergent interest groups in villages or towns as much as a proposal to build an apartment block, factory, or large subdivision. Usually merchants, youth, landowners, and tax collectors favor such initiatives, whereas the newcomers and "the established families" oppose them. Despite such dissensions, there is often a consensus that the development should not be out of scale with the community. Small size is the foundation of a community's identity, and is regarded as an asset. To preserve this asset without becoming frozen into the *status quo* is the perpetual community need of towns and villages.

4. PERCEIVED AND EXPRESSED NEEDS

What comes as a surprise in assessing various pieces of evidence about the community needs pointed out by residents is the fact that people's concerns are modest, essentially relating to necessities of day-to-day living and to the quality of life. In our survey, a section of the questionnaire was set aside for open-ended questions about the problems and needs of communities. After scanning the answers, the responses were assigned to eight categories, and the initial two responses were tabulated. The results of these tabulations are presented in Tables 8.3 and 8.4. The main concerns of citizens are reported in terms of modal responses in the following table.

Main Problems of Canadian Small Communities as Perceived by Their Citizens, 1976

	Main (Modal) Problems Cited	
	First Response	Second Response
Hamlets and Villages (under 1,000 population)	Inadequate facilities for entertainment and recreation	Inadequate health facilities
Small and large towns (1,000-10,000 population)	Limited job opportunities and the outmigration of youth	Inadequate health facilities

SOURCE: Authors' Survey, 1976

The problems most enumerated by respondents are fairly familiar: the absence of public services, and unemployment. As the table shows, villagers complain of inadequate recreation and health facilities, and towns identify inadequacies of economic opportunities and health services as their major problems. On looking at the detailed responses in Tables 8.3 and 8.4, it becomes evident that inadequacies of employment opportunities and community services such as recreation and housing were the predominant problems identified in the villages as well as towns in the first instance (Table 8.3). Among the second-level problems (Table 8.4), insufficient health care and poor recreational facilities stand out as the most pressing. A point worthy of note is the low frequency of categories such as isolation, poor tax base, and lack of opportunities for women and the elderly in both tables. These are obviously problems of lower priority. Bearing in mind that these categories were derived from open-ended questions, it is also illuminating to note that educational and commercial issues have not been mentioned. It is tempting to deduce that their absence from the list of problems reflects a relative satisfaction with the *status quo* in these matters. It also indicates that with the universalization of these services they are taken for granted, and hence not perceived as urgent necessities.

From Tables 8.3 and 8.4 it may be observed that villages and small towns differ only slightly in terms of community problems. Generally, towns have a little larger range of problems, as indicated by a wider spread in their frequency distribution. Villages tend to show a clustered pattern of distribution, with most responses concentrated in two or three categories. This pattern can be interpreted to mean that small towns reach population sizes where needs for services are greater and aspirations for a more viable economic base are generated. It would also seem that hamlets and villages are not regarded as self-sustaining entities, economically and socially, and thus the levels of expectations among their residents are rather modest.

The indicator of small centers' problems so far has been the opinions of informed persons. We also incorporated a behavioral indicator in the questionnaire by asking about the "projects and/or improvements" undertaken in the past ten years. Responses to this question have been tabulated in Tables 8.5 and 8.6. The range of projects undertaken, as indicated by the tables, is impressive. Local public works predominate among them. These are essentially projects that, although initiated and/or executed at the local municipal level, operate within the parameters of provincial and federal programs and grants. Thus, provincial and federal policies become incentives for undertaking some projects and predispose local priorities toward certain services. This is also evident in the remarkable symmetry of the response distribution for villages and towns. Construction of community centers and organization of recreational programs are the modal categories for both (Table 8.5), followed by water purification and sewerage works.

As the second response (Table 8.6), recreational facilities again stand out as modal categories for villages as well as towns. It can be observed that recreational facilities have been the most frequently sought public project. This finding is partially confirmed by responses in the accompanying table to another question about the "major demands voiced by the members of your community in the past ten years."

Major Demands for Improvements by Citizens in Canadian Small Communities, 1966-1976

	Citizen Demands for Improvements (Modal)	
	First Response	**Second Response**
Hamlets and Villages (under 1,000 Population)	Hard services (water and sewerage services, roads)	Recreation facilities (parks, arenas, community centers)
Small and large towns (1,000-10,000 Population)	Recreation facilities (parks, arenas, community centers)	Hard services (water and sewerage services, roads)

SOURCE: Author's Survey, 1976

A further question was posed as to which public facilities were most commonly demanded by residents of the sample communities in the last ten years. Recreation facilities and public utilities, again, lead the list of responses and the demands are similar from both village and town residents. A close examination of Tables 8.7 and 8.8 confirms the lack of differentiation of villages and towns in terms of needs, although village demands tend to be clustered in a few categories. Town residents' demands are more diverse, thus supporting the proposition advanced earlier that towns are a bit more self-contained and have a wider variety of needs.

A very similar set of community needs emerged in a special background study conducted for this project with the people of Hunter River, a village in Prince Edward Island.[8] In a survey of 60 percent of the households in this village of about 300 people, it was revealed that persons associated with widely diverging interests agreed that the top-priority needs were for recreation facilities and programs, and for a community sewerage system. Other priority items for community improvement in Hunter River, in decreasing order were: new sidewalks, road improvements, a better garbage disposal site and collection system, dealing with unsightly premises, better fire protection, and a new community water system. Items such as housing, land planning, parking, and tax levels were far down the list.

A 1979 study of the development needs of small cities in the United States conducted by the Department of Housing and Urban Development affirms our findings. Sewer and drainage facilities were the first priority of towns and villages of less than 10,000 population in both metropolitan and nonmetropolitan settings.[9] Streets and roads were second-priority needs of small communities in nonmetropolitan areas, and water facilities were ranked similarly by metropolitan small towns.[10] The study concludes that "Cities of less than 10,000 population, in both metropolitan and non-metropolitan areas, gave a higher priority to sewer facilities, drainage facilities, water facilities, parks and recreation than did larger cities, reflecting the higher relative costs for smaller cities and their greater need because of more rapid growth."[11]

5. RELATIVE NEEDS

On assessing towns and villages by national standards for provision of (some) facilities and services, their hidden needs come to the surface. For example, the quality of well water in a village may be unacceptable by the standards of public health, but elderly residents may be resistant to incurring upgrading expenses, and may not see this as a necessity. "We have drunk this water for years and are still alive. Why bother now?" is often the response to suggestions for improving the water quality. Such situations frequently arise, and they point out the hidden needs of towns and villages arising from considerations of public health and welfare. Relative needs can also arise from considerations of spatial and social equity, and from unexpressed demands of special interest groups such as the poor, the handicapped, the unemployed, and the elderly. They may or may not be articulated in community forums, but their satisfaction is essential for the functioning of towns and villages, all the same.

Relative needs surface in many forms. Perhaps the most common manifestation is the feeling pervasive in towns and villages about the discrimination and neglect practiced by "city-based" corporations and public bureaucracies. Excessive electricity rates, closing of bus lines and rail routes, telephone districting arrangements which turn "local" calls into long-distance calls, the dumping of a city's garbage nearby, and restrictive legislatures that are insensitive to the scale and resources of small communities, are some examples of the relative needs arising from a sense of inequitable treatment.[12]

Relatively poor states of facilities and services for the disadvantaged segments of local populations is the source of many unacknowledged relative needs. The physically and mentally handicapped, the poor, the welfare dependent, the exceptional children, and the unemployed youth are poorly served. To the extent that traditional ways of providing care and support through family and friends are eroding, the need for formal services increases. Imagine the plight of a person requiring psychotherapy but living in a village in Northern British Columbia or Eastern Quebec. Services that have not been universalized are increasingly needed in towns and villages. Similarly, facilities for music, drama, and art, though increasing, are largely unavailable in towns and villages. All these are potentially relative needs. No doubt the small size of towns and villages poses difficulties in the delivery of such services, such as the absence of thresholds of demands and economies of scale, but underserved populations of towns and villages will continue to feel deprived of necessities.

6. SMALL-COMMUNITY NEEDS: A MODEST AGENDA

This chapter indicates that the problems and needs of small communities are modest. Granted, villages and towns have needs that are urban in character — roads, sidewalks, street lights, and sewers — but by all evidence, it is a list of modest proportions.

Recreational and entertainment facilities, water and sewerage services, and job opportunities are the most frequently expressed needs in small communities. They are reflections of the urban ethos that characterizes contemporary Canada. Indeed, people in small communities acknowledge that the strength of these places lies in their life-style. Their peaceful environment and relaxed pace of life are highly regarded, especially in the context of what is perceived as turbulent urban society. There are only minor variations in public demands between villages and towns. The most interesting difference is the greater variety of services requested in towns (pop. 1,000-10,000). Villages and hamlets tend to be more selective in needs, and usually need fewer services and facilities.

The moderate scope of the problems and needs of small communities is due, in no small measure, to the realistic expectations of residents. They want to preserve smallness and maintain community identities, yet not be deprived of essential civic amenities.

Most standard community services and facilities, such as the post office, schools, and electricity, have been universalized, although questions of scale, appropriateness, and equity continue to arise. At the same time, the demand for modern necessities such as recreation arenas, subsidized housing, and special education programs is increasingly being voiced by small communities. Not only are there aspirations for more contemporary facilities and programs; recreation needs also are increasing, due to the changing living patterns of shift workers and working mothers.

The community needs of residents of towns and villages are no less urgent than those of city dwellers. It should not be assumed that the needs of small communities can be easily met. The resources of small communities are meager, and their dependence on senior government all the more acute.

NOTES

1. "Town Prays for Only Industry to Survive Relocation Plans," *The Whig Standard*, Kingston, 3 January 1983, 5.
2. Robert M. Moroney, "Needs Assessment for Human Services," in Wayne Anderson and B. Frieden, eds., *Managing Human Services* (Washington, D.C.: International City Management Association, 1977), 133.
3. Abraham Maslow, *Motivation and Personality* (New York: Harper & Row, 1954), 80-106.
4. *Ibid.*, 136-37.
5. Public Goods are characterized by joint consumption, nonexclusion, and indivisibilities. For a discussion of these characteristics in the urban situation,

see Werner Z. Hirsch, *Urban Economic Analysis* (New York: McGraw-Hill, 1973), 297-99.

6. Peter O. Steiner, "The Public Sector and the Public Interest," in Robert H. Haveman and Julius Margolis, eds., *Public Expenditures and Policy Analysis* (Chicago: Markham, 1970), 25.

7. County of Huron, *Howick Township Secondary Plan* (Goderich, Ont., 1976), 39.

8. John Blakney, "Planning for Small Rural Communities: A Case Study of Hunter River, P.E.I." (Unpublished Master's Report, Queen's University School of Urban and Regional Planning, 1977).

9. United States Department of Housing and Urban Development, *Development Needs of Small Cities* (Washington, D.C.: Housing and Urban Development Department, 1979) 44, Table 3.5.

10. *Ibid.*

11. *Ibid.*, 4.

12. For example, the Regional Planners of the Greater Vancouver Regional District were surprised to learn that what concerned farmers in the region were conditions such as "fencing-off of roads" or "prohibition of slow-moving vehicles on other main roads," which compelled them to make long detours, "seepage of sewage in their fields," "intricate regulations of various public agencies," etc., and not the agricultural reserve boundaries that planners were expecting to be the issue. See Harry Lash, *Planning in a Human Way* (Ottawa: Ministry of State for Urban Affairs, 1976), 36-37.

TABLES/CHAPTER 8

TABLE 8.1

Positive Aspects of Living in Canadian Small Communities — First Response by Citizens, 1976

		Hamlets and Villages		Towns	
Lifestyle Aspects		Number	Percent	Number	Percent
a)	Peaceful & Relaxing	25	36.8	14	32.5
b)	Community Spirit	21	30.9	11	25.6
c)	Clean & Healthy Environment	2	2.9	4	9.3
d)	Proximity to Nature	3	4.4	2	4.6
e)	Beauty & Amenity	1	1.5	1	2.3
f)	Desirable Social Environment, Friendliness, No Crime	8	11.7	5	11.6
g)	Other	8	11.7	6	13.9
	Total	68	100.0	43	100.0

SOURCE: Authors' Survey, 1976

TABLE 8.2

Positive Aspects of Living in Canadian Small Communities — Second Response by Citizens, 1976

Lifestyle Aspects		Hamlets and Villages		Towns	
		Number	Percent	Number	Percent
a)	Peaceful & Relaxing	5	8.9	0	0.0
b)	Community Spirit	7	12.5	12	37.5
c)	Clean & Healthy Environment	15	26.8	4	12.5
d)	Proximity to Nature	9	16.1	5	15.6
e)	Beauty & Amenity	0	0.0	1	3.1
f)	Desirable Social Environment, Friendliness, No Crime	16	28.6	8	25.0
g)	Other	4	7.1	2	6.3
	Total	56	100.0	32	100.0

SOURCE: Authors' Survey, 1976

TABLE 8.3

Problems of Small Communities in Canada — First Response by Citizens, 1976

Community Problems		Hamlets and Villages		Towns	
		Number	Percent	Number	Percent
a)	No problems	2	2.9	2	4.6
b)	Limited job opportunities, out-migration of youth	20	28.5	15	34.1
c)	Lack of opportunities for women, and elderly	0	0.0	2	4.6
d)	Inadequate community facilities, housing, etc.	7	10.0	10	22.7
e)	Inadequate health facilities	7	10.0	3	6.8
f)	Inadequate recreation and entertainment	27	38.6	10	22.7
g)	Poor tax base and little industrial incentive	3	4.3	0	0.0
h)	Isolation and loneliness	2	2.9	2	4.6
i)	Unstable, transient population	2	2.9	0	0.0
	Total	70	100.0	44	100.0

SOURCE: Authors' Survey, 1976

TABLE 8.4

Problems of Small Communities in Canada — Second Response by Citizens, 1976

	Community Problems	Hamlets and Villages		Towns	
		Number	Percent	Number	Percent
a)	No problems	1	1.7	0	0.0
b)	Limited job opportunities, out-migration of youth	6	10.3	2	5.9
c)	Lack of opportunities for women, and elderly	5	8.6	3	8.8
d)	Inadequate community facilities, housing, etc.	11	18.9	6	17.6
e)	Inadequate health facilities	16	27.6	8	23.5
f)	Inadequate recreation and entertainment	10	17.2	7	20.6
g)	Poor tax base and little industrial incentive	3	5.1	3	8.8
h)	Isolation and loneliness	4	6.9	4	11.8
i)	Unstable, transient population	2	3.5	1	2.9
	Total	58	100.0	34	100.0

SOURCE: Authors' Survey, 1976

TABLE 8.5

Projects Undertaken in Canadian Small Communities, 1966-1976 — First Response by Citizens, 1976

	Local Projects	Hamlets and Villages		Towns	
		Number	Percent	Number	Percent
a)	Street Paving	6	10.3	4	10.5
b)	Road Building	7	12.1	0	0.0
c)	Water Purification and/or Sewerage	19	32.7	8	21.1
d)	Educational Facilities	2	3.5	1	2.6
e)	Community Centers and/or Recreation Programs	20	34.5	19	50.0
f)	Municipal Building and/or Services	2	3.5	2	5.3
g)	Health Facilities	1	1.7	1	2.6
h)	Others	1	1.7	2	5.3
	Total	58	100.0	38	100.0

SOURCE: Authors' Survey, 1976

TABLE 8.6

Projects Undertaken in Canadian Small Communities, 1966-1976 — Second Response by Citizens, 1976

Local Projects		Hamlets and Villages		Towns	
		Number	Percent	Number	Percent
a)	Street Paving	6	13.6	4	11.4
b)	Road Building	4	9.1	6	17.1
c)	Water Purification and/or Sewerage	5	11.4	7	20.0
d)	Educational Facilities	1	2.3	4	11.4
e)	Community Centers and/or Recreation Programs	18	40.9	9	25.7
f)	Municipal Building and/or Services	10	22.7	4	11.4
g)	Health Facilities	0	0.0	1	2.8
h)	Others	0	0.0	0	0.0
	Total	44	100.0	35	100.0

SOURCE: Authors' Survey, 1976

TABLE 8.7

Community Demands for Improvements in Small Communities in Canada, 1966-1976 — First Response

Community Demands		Hamlets and Villages		Towns	
		Number	Percent	Number	Percent
a)	Education & Cultural Facilities	4	6.6	1	2,4
b)	Recreational Facilities and Programs	10	16.4	18	42.9
c)	Industry & Employment	1	1.6	3	7.1
d)	Provincial Support and Grants	9	14.8	3	7.1
e)	Health Services and Pollution Control	1	1.6	1	2.4
f)	Housing Services	2	3.3	3	7.1
g)	Strengthening Linkages and Promotion of Local Commerce	2	3.3	0	0.0
h)	Hard Services — Water and Sewerage, Roads, etc.	32	52.5	13	31.0
	Total	61	100.0	42	100.0

SOURCE: Authors' Survey, 1976

TABLE 8.8

Community Demands for Improvements in Small Communities in Canada, 1966-1976 — Second Response

Community Demands		Hamlets and Villages		Towns	
		Number	Percent	Number	Percent
a)	Education & Cultural Facilities	3	7.9	1	2.9
b)	Recreational Facilities and Programs	9	23.7	8	22.9
c)	Industries & Employment	4	10.5	0	0.0
d)	Provincial Support and Grants	4	10.5	1	2.9
e)	Health Services and Pollution Control	4	10.5	6	17.1
f)	Housing Services	0	0.0	4	11.4
g)	Strengthening Linkages and Promotion of Local Commerce	6	15.8	2	5.7
h)	Hard Services — Water and Sewerage, Roads, etc.	8	21.0	13	37.1
	Total	38	100.0	35	100.0

SOURCE: Authors' Survey, 1976

9 Planning Approaches to Small Towns

A basic agenda of small-community needs has been established; it is now appropriate to explore the role and capability of towns and villages as problem-solving units. Obviously, their small size allows them fewer resources to call upon when they want to solve problems. Further, more than 80 percent of all Canadian towns and villages have no self-governing apparatus. Many of these, in turn, exist within the context of rudimentary rural local government. The aim of this chapter is to assess the effectiveness with which small-community problems as well as aspirations are addressed at present, and to suggest some more appropriate means where they are needed.

Towns and villages are, by and large, in a *dependent* position. We have alluded to their generally meager resources. Whether the resources be financial, administrative, technical, or human, towns and villages have fewer options to exercise than urban areas. Most small centers are, as well, removed from locations of extensive economic development; 75 percent are beyond easy commuting distance of a metropolitan area, for example. Many are in regions where the staple resource is, at best, economically slow growing. Their economic prospects are not for self-generating growth; they cannot depend on the scale and diversity of economic activities enjoyed by large centers. Although, as we noted, there are a considerable number of job opportunities in the regions surrounding small centers, these tend not to be very high-income jobs and the places of employment tend not to be "growth industries." In sum, most towns and villages lack the revenue sources that would make it possible for them to consider having a high level of services.

Thus, towns and villages are generally very dependent upon senior governments — federal, provincial, county, and regional — to provide both the stimulus for economic development and much of the funding for physical infrastructure and community services. Even in the realm of community planning, which every province has established, the small incorporated centers and rural municipalities are expected to perform in the same milieu as large centers. Because they lack resources, towns and villages are more noticeably on the *receiving end* of senior government policy than are cities and large municipalities. That policy is delivered in a great variety of ways; this chapter will examine several key aspects of it as well as examining how towns and villages fare in this dependency relationship.

First, we shall look at the capacity of senior government programs to satisfy the felt needs of towns and villages. In particular, the experience of Hunter River, Prince Edward Island will be described. Second, the framework of community planning will be examined for its relevance and effectiveness for small centers, using the situation in Ontario as the primary focus. Third, the impact of the extensive arrays of senior government programs, services, and projects on towns and villages will be discussed; policy arrays from Nova Scotia and Manitoba are used as examples.

1. RESPONSES TO SMALL-TOWN NEEDS

When one probes the felt needs of the residents of towns and villages about the improvements they would like for their communities, what is most often revealed is a modest set of demands. The problems are usually discrete in nature, such as the installation of street lighting or a sewer system. Compared to the complex problems of cities, where the solution of any one problem usually requires that many others be addressed, small-community problems are readily solvable if the resources and authority are available. It is, of course, the "if" that is so crucial in responding to community needs and aspirations.

In a spatial study conducted in Hunter River, Prince Edward Island in 1976, the ability of a small community to solve its problems was addressed. Hunter River is an incorporated village of 322 persons (1981). More than just a simple inventory of community problems was sought in the study. The question was asked whether the problems could be solved by the community with help from senior governments. A total of seventeen problems or needs were identified in a survey of village residents.[1] All these problems were beyond the capability of the village council to solve, either because of resources or jurisdiction. The accompanying table arrays them in the order of priority assigned by community residents, and shows where help might be obtained.

Of seventeen community needs identified as significant by village residents, only four could be readily satisfied through extant provincial government sources of assistance to small communities; three problem areas were not under provincial jurisdiction. Of the three problem areas to which federal government programs might have applied, none could assist the village.

Needs for Community Improvement in Hunter River, Prince Edward Island, and the Responsiveness of Senior Governments, 1976

Community Needs in Order of Priority	Ability of Senior Governments to Respond	
	Provincial	Federal
1. (a) Sewerage System	No	No
(b) Recreation Program	Yes	**
2. (a) Sidewalks	No	**
3. (a) Road Improvements	Yes	**
4. (a) Garbage Disposal	Yes	**
(b) Fire Protection	No	**
(c) Unsightly Premises	No	**
5. (a) Water System	No	No
(b) Speeding Traffic	No	**
6. (a) Police Protection	No	**
7. (a) Pond Water Control	No	**
(b) Lower Taxes	**	**
8. (a) Railway Crossing Lights	Yes	**
(b) Parking Facilities	**	**
9. (a) Rental Housing	No	No
10. (a) Land Planning	No	**
11. (a) Additional Housing	**	**

Yes = program available
No = no program available
** = no jurisdiction

SOURCE: Blakney, 1977.

A more detailed look at this disparity between the promise and performance of senior government policy reveals the following. Three of the four provincial programs that could help the community — building sidewalks, establishing a garbage disposal site, and installing railway crossing lights — could not be brought to bear on problems by the community itself. Implementation was not only at the discretion of, but also carried out by, a provincial ministry. Only one community need, improved recreation services, could proceed through community initiative to implementation. Three problems dealing with acquiring a new water system, sewerage, and sidewalks were potentially solvable with provincial and federal programs but were not practicable for Hunter River to initiate. They involved a shared-cost approach and the village's portion of the cost would prove prohibitive given the community's meager tax base. Finally, the need to provide rental housing in the community could not be satisfied because the federal and provincial funds would only be supplied to communities with water and sewer services.

The situation of Hunter River is not unique among the towns and villages that seek to improve their communities; only the set of problems may differ. Nor is it a recent symptom of central government performance. Two decades ago, Saskatchewan community development officers began cataloging some of the persistent shortfalls in the delivery of central government policies and programs to small communities.[2] One of the foremost concerns was with the *standardized* approaches of many provincial and federal programs of assistance to small communities. Another was the lack of local control allowed over implementation of proposed improvements and, especially, the remoteness and infrequent contact between senior government staff and the people of the community.

The character of a community should be taken into account in the assistance programs of senior governments, for it influences both the form of assistance and the ability of the community to obtain it. As Baker noted, "what one community can do very easily, another may find very difficult."[3] Communities having a high proportion of elderly citizens may, despite their size, be inhibited in taking advantage of programs that favor town or village expansion. Some programs, such as those for providing improved recreational facilities in small communities in Ontario, require strong local leadership and the capability to formulate a "community recreation plan" before receiving funds. Many programs, such as those for providing public utilities and housing, call for matching contributions; many small communities simply cannot meet the initial costs of their share. The towns and villages that cannot meet the requirements of these various programs usually have to struggle along for long periods without a solution, even though they may be in greater need of the service or facility than communities that meet the requirements.

A point also needs to be made of the not-infrequent frustration and confusion in towns and villages from coast to coast over shortfalls in services and programs rendered directly by senior government ministries and other public agencies and corporations. Cost overruns and interminable delays on public utilities projects authorized and supervised by provincial departments are common newspaper items in small centers. Site inspection by provincial and federal housing officials of subsidized housing projects has often been found wanting in "remote" towns and villages.

The following quotation about an Ontario community may suffice to encompass the general issue:

> Reeve William Halligan of Loughborough Township wants action on the proposed reconstruction of the combined bridge and dam in Sydenham Lake at the lake's outlet to Millhaven Creek in Sydenham (village).
>
> Reeve Halligan expressed concern over the continued delays in starting the project. . . . He noted it had first been scheduled to begin in June, then July and now August.
>
> "If we keep getting this sort of run-around the work will never get done this year," he said.
>
> "I don't care who is to blame for the delay; what I want to know is who is at fault — is it the consulting engineers, Cataraqui Conservation Authority or the Ontario Ministry of Transportation and Communications," he declared.[4]

Unfortunately, the lack of coordination of central government programs in the field is accepted by small centers, cynically, as a normal part of the service.

2. THE MYTH AND REALITY OF SMALL-TOWN PLANNING

Every municipality in Canada is empowered to undertake community planning. That is, it is empowered to plan for its physical environment — residential areas, main streets, parks, roads, industrial areas, and so on. This power is contained in a province's Planning Act or similar statute, which permits communities to prepare plans and regulate land use. The statute prescribes the format for local land-use planning: the type of plans to be prepared, the allowable land-use controls such as zoning, and the administrative arrangements to be used. All provincial planning statutes apply these provisions universally to both large municipalities and small ones. Herein lies a flaw, as we shall see.

Handicaps to Small-Town Planning

The various provincial Planning Acts have their genesis in a concern about the ills of rapid and large-scale growth of *cities*. The problems of urban congestion, slums, land use conflicts, and premature subdivision of vast areas around cities, especially just prior to and just after World War I, led to the promulgation of such legislation. All provinces had Planning Acts by 1930. As cogent as the need for planning powers were, and still are, for cities, scant attention was paid to the situation in small communities. The planning needs of towns and villages may appear to be much the same as those of larger centers when looked at as general categories of problems: land use conflict, sprawl, traffic problems, inadequate services, or deteriorating housing. But they are different — in scale, intensity, and pace of change — and this means they are seldom compatible with the prescribed planning formula of the provincial Act.

It cannot be assumed, as the various Planning Acts do, that small communities also need planning because they face a high demand for land, rapid growth, and major changes in the character of their development. There are of course some that are thus affected: resource towns such as Fort MacMurray, Alberta come to mind as do towns on the fringes of metropolitan centers such as Lumsden near Regina and Georgetown near Toronto. But these latter types of town and village development are exceptions, perhaps not numbering more than a few hundred among the over-9,000 towns and villages. To them the standard Planning Act approaches pertain.

In most towns and villages in Canada, the land development situation is not very different from that discerned in a study of several dozen small communities in Eastern Ontario.[5] First, in terms of scale, it was found that absolute growth was only in the order of 15-20 new dwellings per year, consuming only four or five acres of land. Even in centers experiencing relatively rapid growth the increment of change is modest by urban standards, 60-150 homes in any one year. Second, in terms of intensity, over three-quarters of the new development in towns and villages is in the form of housing. Usually it is single-family detached houses, most frequently in the form of relatively compact subdivisions on the edge of the community. Large-scale facilities such as big factories, shopping centers, or apartment buildings are things most small communities do not have to plan for. Third, in terms of pace of change, new development in towns and villages tends not to be continuous year after year. A modest subdivision of 20-30 houses built in one year is not likely to be repeated for several more years. The same holds true for the addition of new commercial outlets and public facilities in towns and villages. In other words, the demand is readily satisfied in small centers, and this is understandable given their small size.

The land use patterns of towns and villages, such as were described in Chapter 7, do not fit the typical mold assumed by land use control regulations found in most Planning Acts. Zoning, the most common regulatory tool, assumes the existence of extensive areas of similar land uses in a community, each requiring protection from intrusion of land use with conflicting characteristics, for example, industry in residential areas. But in small communities the amount of development in any one use seldom results in extensive "zones" of similar uses for which zoning regulations would be appropriate. The intermingling of land uses in towns and villages is the common situation. Where this causes conflict and annoyance to residents, which seems seldom, the typical form of zoning would not be practicable. (Later in this chapter we shall explore solutions to this matter.) Only as towns reach population levels of 2,000 or more do fairly large districts of similar land uses appear. Even then the distinctions are very general: the residential district, the business district, and possibly, the industrial district. Elaborate regulations will still not be helpful in such situations.

Another key assumption of the provincial Planning Acts is that all communities are capable of establishing a workable planning function. Here, again, the small size of towns and villages fails to support such an assumption. In small communities, the job of making planning policy falls to a small group of people on a planning board or council where one is unlikely to find anyone with experience in town planning or even with a clear understanding of the purposes of a plan. Further, the burden of making most technical and administrative planning judgments falls frequently to only three officials: the town clerk, the building inspector, and the roads superintendent. The latter positions may be covered by fewer than three persons and one or all of them may work at their municipal job only part-time. Rarely does one find a community of less than 20,000 with its own professional staff planner. Planners who work for regional planning commissions, counties, or the like may be able to offer local planning services. Where they do, their work is often characterized by "inventing" appropriate planning tools for the small centers rather than indiscriminately applying conventional planning methods.

In general, the provincial Planning Acts are not highly regarded by small communities; they often carry the stigma of centralized government's interference in local affairs, besides being seen as frequently irrelevant to local needs. It is not uncommon for the Act's provisions to be disregarded for a variety of reasons. On the one hand, there may be no very compelling changes taking place in the community's land development. On the other hand, there may be no persons able to grasp the technical and administrative needs of a regular planning activity. Few small municipalities actively seek official plans of the kind prescribed by provincial planners; and when they have plans they seldom consult them. Not a small factor is the high cost of having plans and zoning bylaws prepared and, of necessity, maintaining planning consulting services thereafter if no local planner is available.

A final matter not be overlooked is that most towns and villages do not have their own individual local government. That is, the vast majority of these centers are unincorporated and cannot, therefore, undertake to plan officially for their future under provincial Planning Acts. Such planning, as limited as it may be, is only available to the rural municipality, township, county, or district in which the unincorporated town or village is located. The small center in this situation is, thus, dependent on the council of the "parent" incorporated area not only to appreciate the planning problems of the small center but also to be willing to undertake planning. Most of the above-cited handicaps to local planning for incorporated towns and villages also apply to rural municipalities and townships: conventional planning tools are of doubtful value and resources are meager.

Major Types of Planning Problems in Small Towns

The "kit of tools" prescribed by provincial planning statutes has not proved to be very cogent in either content or scope for small centers. This is a serious handicap to place on the achievement of effective planning for towns and villages, especially when one considers the array of very real and insistent problems these small places must cope with. A brief examination of key problem areas of towns and villages will more readily indicate the special planning needs of small centers.

The Lack of Water and Sewer Systems. Probably three-quarters of Canada's towns and villages lack a public waterworks system, and even fewer have sewer systems. Community-wide systems carry high capital costs for the water purification and sewage treatment plants, and even when the costs are shared by the province small communities find them to be burdensome. Moreover, the small scale of growth in most towns and villages means that the costs of amortization do not become much easier to bear. On the other side, small size and low density of development could mean that towns and villages could employ "intermediate technologies" for less elaborate and less costly solutions in providing basic utilities.

Achieving Coherent Land Use Patterns. In most towns and villages, buildings tend to be scattered over large areas. Whether the context is the plethora of small lots in many prairie villages or the random lot pattern of many maritime communities, the effect is one of both low density and uneven development. Paradoxically compactness, which could be achieved with the relatively small number of dwellings involved, often gives way to an overly generous use of the land. The absence of both a functioning land market and effective land use controls contributes to this situation. Yet planning solutions must take towns and villages on their own terms rather than applying conventional land use controls and planning concepts. For example, in-filling town lots and promoting compactness in fringe areas may lead to the dilemma of having to acquire costly utilities.

Conserving Rural Land Resources. Too often, rural land is regarded as a residue of other development or even as a limitless resource. However, good farmland, high-quality woodlands, lands with aggregate (sand and gravel) potential, as well as lands suited for water conservation and recreation are not only limited but also often inextricably linked to the economic well-being of nearby small towns. Land planning in rural areas must consider the land base as a resource tied to the performance of particular economic functions, an economic "factor of production." Farmers, foresters, resort owners, and cottagers are customers of a village's shops as well as being part of the social fabric of the total rural community. Planning in rural areas should be for the rural "region," including both town and country.[6] For its part, the small center can promote more viable rural communities by reducing scattered development and taking care not to pollute surrounding land and water resources.

Providing Satisfactory Housing. Despite the vigorous growth in housing stock in towns and villages, there is an obvious lack of variety in the housing being provided. Dwellings are produced a few at a time in a context that features a very small market and small builders. The single-family house is frequently the only type of housing available, and few dwellings can be rented. Only at population levels above 2,500 does the range of housing choice broaden significantly. Yet the demand for housing is often diverse even in fairly small centers; provision must be made for individuals, young and growing families, older retired couples, and farm families. The large old homes that many villages possess might be converted to apartments for senior citizens, for example, but adaptive-use programs need to be developed. In theory, mobile homes offer another kind of solution, but in practice they are usually treated as "exceptional" and are either "quarantined" or badly sited or both. Some small centers in metropolitan regions face inundation by new housing to satisfy the demands of urbanites for lower-cost housing and/or a rural atmosphere; in the process, they may lose their historic character and social cohesion. Providing housing in towns and villages is a complicated matter and one for which there is a paucity of applicable public and private resources.

Refurbishing "Main Street." The portion of a town or village that probably provides the most lasting image is its "Main Street" commercial section. Unfortunately, in many small towns the growth in population and housing has not been matched in the old business district. Commercial growth, when it does occur, is likely to be found on the periphery of the town, either in a shopping plaza or along the highways serving the community. Main Street's shops frequently are vacant or deteriorating; where they are active, there is almost inevitably inadequate parking. However, there are some hopeful signs that Main Street may be revitalized through programs such as those now underway in Saskatchewan and Ontario. In addition, many communities have taken the initiative in refurbishing their own downtown areas, perhaps none more successfully than High River, Alberta.

Preserving the Natural Environment. Small centers offer a natural advantage against pollution: by virtue of their size, they tend not to generate pollutants in large amounts. Not infrequently, however, their rudimentary means of water supply and sewage disposal, and haphazard building practices, lead to serious local water pollution. Another common source of pollution is garbage disposal. A casual approach to their environment often leaves small centers visually unattractive and odoriferous, and allows them to pollute sources of water supplies. Further, many small centers also have large industrial establishments with high effluent characteristics that may be detrimental both to local and regional environments. The proper disposal of mine tailings, liquid effluents, and air emissions is a sophisticated process requiring a good deal of technical capability and political persuasiveness. Small communities not only lack the expertise for this task but also may be dubious about "disturbing" the town's major employer. Provincial and federal governments, who license these projects, should not leave the nearby town to bear undue burdens of pollution.

The foregoing list of community problems encompasses more than normal community or physical planning activity. Provincial and federal development assistance programs may be involved. Efforts must be made to integrate the efforts of different functional agencies toward the common end of community improvement. This added dimension of planning, of course, increases the volume and complexity of planning action that must be undertaken by an already meager administration in the small community. Support and advice will be needed from senior governments if small communities are to cope with the intricacies of planning. And the planning tools the communities themselves must use should be devised to allow a simpler, more direct approach to problem solving.

3. TOWARD MORE APPROPRIATE SMALL-TOWN PLANNING

Community planning is a complex and expensive activity, and the smaller the community the more difficult it is to marshall the resources, both technical and financial, to tackle planning. Added to this is the questionable value of the approach to local planning advocated in provincial Planning Acts in regard to the needs and capabilities of towns and villages. Every year, as more experience is gained, there is an inevitable increase in the volume and complexity of provincial legislation related to planning, a trend that runs counter to the needs of small centers. As with every community, planning is most effective for small communities when their plans and other planning instruments can be used to help solve *their own* local problems.

Conventional physical planning for communities is based on concepts of *city* development (land use patterns, density, and traffic circulation) and the problems that cities experience. It has little direct relevance to the small scale, small growth, and diverse land-use situations of most towns and villages. Small centers tend to see their development in terms of a number of specific problems such as the ones cited in this and the previous two chapters. An insightful report prepared for the Newfoundland government stressed this problem-solving approach:

> If day-to-day problems can be solved with the aid of a plan then, even if these are of minor importance in themselves, the value of planning is established. . . .[7]

This report advocated that plans for smaller towns focus on a statement of the community's problems and possible solutions, many of which, if solved, could have an immediately beneficial effect on the small center's physical environment. Further, such plans should be "simply written without jargon" in order to be understandable to those who have to administer them in towns and villages — the hard-pressed, often untrained local clerk. The frustration of trying to deal with a complicated plan and its attendant regulations may simply lead to ignoring it.

If we are to engage in planning that will be effective for small communities, then we must utilize "appropriate technology" for the task. Two major dimensions must be addressed in this regard. First, the availability of tools that can assist in solving the planning problems of *small* communities. Second, the capability of local people to utilize the tools. In other words, proper planning tools for small communities must address *both* the problems and skills characteristic of towns and villages. We shall now look at each of these dimensions, which could be called respectively the "technical" and the "management" dimensions. It will be seen from the examples provided that there is a symbiotic relationship between the two.

Basic Components of the Toolkit

The planner's toolkit contains four planning components that are basic for all communities, large and small: (1) community plans; (2) plan-preparation tools; (3) plan-realization tools; and (4) public participation. The difference between those tools appropriate for small communities and those not so suited is perhaps best described as the difference between a large and a small wrench in a mechanic's toolbox: each is peculiarly suited for its task. One might add that the planner's toolkit for a small town need not contain as many or as wide a range of tools as is needed in city planning. Fortunately, over the past half-dozen years, planning tools have been devised specifically for small communities. Examples of these will be cited to capture both the kind of inventiveness needed for small-town planning and the basic principles that need to be applied. The most important should be stated here: the uniqueness of each town and village needs to be respected in the application of planning tools!

(a) Community Plans

The cornerstone of any community's planning activities is a community-wide plan. It is designed to provide both an image of the future physical development of the community and a policy commitment to solve problems and make public investments that will help in achieving the desired future. The community plan for a small community deals with land uses, circulation, recreation facilities, and parks, just as does a plan for a large city. But because the small-town planning situation is simpler and less subject to massive change, its community plan can be simpler and more direct. This shows up in the set of community objectives that is the heart of the plan, such as the objective that leads the plan for High River, Alberta, a town of 4,800 south of Calgary:

> To retain and reinforce the town's uniqueness, its friendliness; the personal
> service of its shopowners; the peace and quiet, and freedom from most kinds
> of pollution; most of all its park-like setting with The Trees, The Rivers and
> Streams, The Open Space, The Mountain Views, The Chinooks.[8]

While the balmy winter winds, the Chinooks, are well beyond planning regulation, this goal does reveal the sort of things the residents of the community consider vital. Indeed, many small-community plans contain a similar goal, usually at the top of their list, that can be paraphrased as: "to preserve the quality of small-town life for present and future residents." It seems fair to say that this reflects an awareness on the part of small-town residents of their town's vulnerability to change. There is another sort of awareness small-town residents possess about their community; that is the

FIGURE 9.1
**An Approach to Illustrating the Planning Problems of a Small Town:
Clarenville, Newfoundland (1968)**

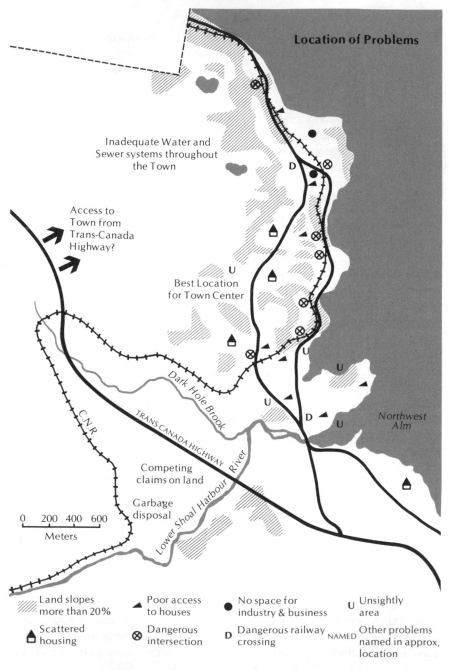

SOURCE: Newfoundland, Department of Municipal Affairs, *Planning for Smaller Towns*

detailed knowledge they have about the various parts of the community environment. It follows, therefore, that plans for small communities should convey a sense of immediacy and directness both in content and style.

Fortunately, the small size of a town or village makes it possible for a community plan to take a very direct approach to needs and problems. In a prototype small-town plan for Clarenville, Newfoundland prepared for the provincial government, a map of the entire community of 1,700 shows the location of the major problems the residents would like to solve.[9] It shows the dangerous railway crossings, the scattered housing, the town center problems, and so on. This plan, moreover, provides photographs of the problem situations, and then addresses itself to the solution of these problems. The above-mentioned plan for High River provides its citizens with a map showing a long-range plan that uses vivid graphic techniques to get its ideas across. New facilities such as a golf course, information center, town farm, and regional museum are indicated by prominent, eye-catching symbols, and the five major districts of the town each have a brief description on the map of their main problems and proposed solutions. A series of municipal plans prepared with the assistance of the County of Huron Planning Department for towns and villages in the western part of Ontario included many well-executed sketches of streetscapes and individual buildings, some of which are reproduced in Chapter 7.[10]

The concern over the style of presentation of plans for small communities is cogent, for it is through its presentation that a plan achieves relevance for the populace. A community plan is a way of demonstrating consensus among community members about their goals and the actions they are prepared to take to improve the community. It is both a *record* of what was decided by those involved at the time of preparation *and* a *compact* with future members of the community. It goes without saying that a community plan should communicate its ideas clearly regardless of the size of community. But it is probably more serious if a small-town plan does not communicate clearly at the outset. There are likely to be few, if any, professional planning, administrative, or public media skills and resources available in the small community to interpret the plan when issues arise later. If there is frustration in attempting to understand the plan on the part of citizens, municipal councillors, or local officials, the community will lose interest in its plan and either ignore it or pay only lip-service to it.

When one raises the possibility of developing more relevant forms of community plans for towns and villages in Canada there is an inevitable consternation evident in professional planning circles. Planning practice in Canada is conducted within an elaborate statutory framework that increasingly thrives on formal procedures, documentation, and legalisms. Thus, the small-town plans discussed above and their innovations regarding content and style, not surprisingly, are exceptions to conventional planning practice. Typically, a plan for a small community in Canada is lengthy, given to jargon, and repetitious. Two examples illustrate something of the conventional approach for small-community plans — one for a New Brunswick town of just over 400 persons is fifty pages long, and another for an Ontario town of just under 1,000 residents is ninety pages long. Despite the care and attention lavished by the professional planners on these plans and others like them, one has to wonder who, besides the planners, will read them? Such plans can, therefore, be self-defeating for the planners because people will, with justification, "put the plan on the shelf."

The elaborate planning statutes have not prevented good-quality and useful plans from being made for and by small communities, even though the instances are relatively few. Especially notable are a series of town and village plans for small centers in the region surrounding Calgary, Alberta. These plans have a format wherein all the component parts — community objectives, land use analysis, population and land forecasts, land use plan, and development policies — are printed on one large poster-size sheet. These poster plans, of which a portion of the one for the Village of Acme (pop. 411 in 1977) is illustrated, are simply and attractively presented, and designed specifically for each community.[11] They amount to only the equivalent of sixteen letter-size pages in total, can be folded for easy distribution, and when fully open have all the necessary elements of the community plan within a glance of one another. Professional planners from the staff of the Calgary Regional Planning Commission assist the communities to prepare their plans and ensure that they meet the criteria for General Municipal Plans called for in the Alberta Planning Act.

Opportunities also exist to make plans appropriate to small-community needs after the basic statutory requirements have been satisfied. Very often, the crucial planning issues for a community revolve around some special area — its business district, its waterfront, or some cluster of historic buildings, for example. Special-area plans may carry statutory provisions in some provinces but, in general, they are much less subject to conventional formats and lend themselves to innovative approaches. One common planning situation among towns and villages which lends itself to a special-area plan is the elaboration of proposals for small unincorporated centers. Most such places are usually given only cursory attention in the plans for the rural municipalities, counties, or districts in which they are located. This despite the fact that they may be the most important centers in their locale, regardless of their small size. More than 80 percent of Canada's towns and villages fall into the unincorporated category.

Indicative of the type of plan that could be prepared in a small unincorporated village is that done in conjunction with the village of Sydenham, Ontario (pop. 500 in 1976) by graduate planning students at nearby Queen's University. This plan, called a "Plan for Community Enhancement," is based on residents' perceptions of problems and solutions.[12] It is brief (ten pages) and concentrates on practicable

FIGURE 9.2
Land Use Proposals from a Poster Plan Prepared for a Small Town:
Acme, Alberta

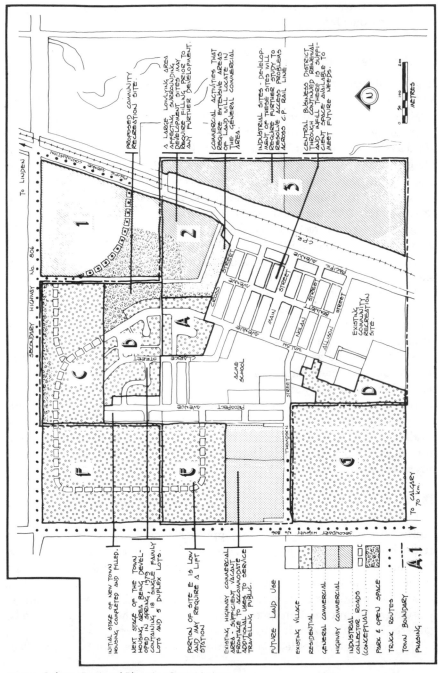

SOURCE: Calgary Regional Planning Commission

recommendations which try to capitalize on the community's assets. Suggestions are made regarding street and commercial signs, sidewalk needs, pedestrian pathways, off-street parking, and park improvement. Simple drawings showing some of the suggested village improvements accompany the plan.

(b) Plan Preparation Tools

Community planning is essentially a logical process of working from a knowledge of present conditions, making prognoses of how conditions might change in the future, and then proposing the future conditions the community desires and which are achievable. A community plan is only as good as the knowledge it is based on and the prognoses that are made, or as planners call them, respectively, "surveys" and "forecasts." On the one hand, the surveys and forecasts are the basis of decisions about how much is required for development and the roads and other public utilities and services needed in the community. On the other hand, the surveys and forecasts are the means by which the community comes to understand itself, its prospects, and the validity of planning proposals for its future. The plan preparation phase can be characterized as a learning phase for both citizens and planners singly and mutually.

Plan preparation tools should be appropriate for the scale and conditions of small communities. Many tools developed for city planning are simply not needed in planning for small centers. Thus, it is not just a matter of scaling-down planning tools, it is also a matter of choosing the appropriate ones. The first and most important question in this regard is, what kind of information is needed for a small-town situation? Elaborate studies of land use and the economic base will probably be irrelevant. Statistical analyses involving correlations, sampling, and so forth cannot provide reliable estimates because of the small overall populations involved. However, the small size of community can facilitate the collection of information about housing, population, and jobs, very often in a "richer" form than would be possible in cities.

The Community Profile. A particularly appropriate approach to obtaining and presenting planning data for towns and villages is the Community Profile. As the name suggests, the approach is to consolidate the various data about the community's environment, population, economy, and regional setting, usually in a single document so that an integrated picture of the community is presented. Separate analyses often give a fragmented view while residents have a fairly unified view of their town or village. Moreover, the information on existing conditions in the community can be gathered by local citizens in many cases.

The Community Profile as a community self-survey can be an excellent way of involving the public in the planning process. In one excellent example from three small villages in rural New York state, everyone from school children to adults in service clubs participated in gathering the necessary data.[13] One other ingredient useful for planning that can also be incorporated in the profile is the identification of problems in the community and the aspirations of residents for the town or village. Also worth incorporating is an historical overview of the community that provides a sense of the place and the phases of its development. This, too, serves to make certain that the planning process is linked to the people and their cultural background. The Municipal Plan for Alma, New Brunswick, although prepared by outside consultants, is admirable in its inclusion of a substantial history and the use of historic photographs.[14]

Analyses and Forecasts. Fundamental in the planning of a community of any size is information related to population and housing. The planner needs to know the size, composition, and trends in both these factors as well as the occupancy characteristics of people in dwellings. In cities these may be estimated with reasonable accuracy from average values and ratios of such things as household size. In small communities, as we have noted, there is often such variability in the composition of population and housing that average values and ratios are "unstable" indicators. An accurate field survey of all households is the only sure way to acquire reliable data to analyze. In forecasting future levels of population and housing it is best to use the simplest method of projection. The linear extrapolation, which projects *absolute increments* of change — numbers of additional people/year, new houses/year — rather than percentage rates of change, has been found to be the best method.

Two kinds of economic analysis can prove useful in small-community planning. One is a locational analysis of the places of employment of residents. The extent to which residents commute to other places for work and the kinds of jobs they hold in outside communities will indicate the ways in which the town or village is economically dependent. This could, in turn, be used to forecast possible impacts on the community of changes in the region surrounding the town or village, such as the starting-up or closing of a large plant.

A second kind of economic analysis relevant to small communities has to do with the prospects for business establishments. These firms provide not only goods and services but are also one of the main sources of employment in the community. A method called Threshold Analysis can be used to determine whether new businesses might be viable. As used in a study of small centers in North Dakota, it calculates the population required, in the town and the trade area, to support additional retail trade and service firms.[15] Given the diverse and overlapping shopping and business pattern of rural and small-town residents (as described in Chapter 4), it is necessary to take a regional view of business thresholds.

(c) Plan Realization Tools

Once the community's plan has been prepared, it is necessary to have ready the tools for implementing the plan, for bringing it to realization. The two most common implementation tools are land use regulations and capital-spending strategies. But, as with other planning tools to be used in small-town situations, one must ask at the outset, what problems are they aimed at solving? Zoning is the most familiar regulatory tool for land use, but zoning grew up in the city. It has a good deal to commend it in the large common-use districts of cities and in establishing the dimensions for the rapid and large-scale growth frequently experienced in cities. But might not the diverse, dispersed development of small communities require a more flexible approach? There is also the question about the technical and administrative skills required for the successful use of the tools. Whatever implementation tools are chosen, they carry with them the obligation to be administered rigorously and continuously.

Zoning: Its Uses and Limitations. Zoning is based on the evidence that as communities grow in size, land uses tend to sort themselves into districts of similar uses, and types and arrangements of structures. Different uses and structures may prove disruptive or even unsafe and inequitable when introduced into an already-established district such as a residential neighborhood. Zoning, therefore, specifies the land uses that may be located within each district of the community as well as specifying the size and placement of structures in which the use occurs. In communities that anticipate the building-up of large districts of land, either through new development or redevelopment, zoning can also prove helpful in specifying the kind of environment and uses the community expects will be the outcome. From an administrative point of view, zoning's minimum specifications leave to the proponent of a development the choice to proceed. The zoning bylaw can do much to prevent the worst kind of development but it cannot promote the best, and it is relatively inflexible to new ideas about development.

In general, not until a town reaches a population of about 2,500 does its development separate into very extensive, homogeneous districts of different land uses. (Even at this size, a town's residential area will contain only about 800 houses occupying 150 acres of land and its business district will barely encompass 75 acres.) The districts that become evident in this size of town and larger will be few in number and probably accommodate a variety of uses. If a zoning bylaw is appropriate, it should probably have only a small number of relevant districts: residential, commercial, industrial, and rural. Some larger places may develop the need to control commercial development along highways or in special areas such as a waterfront; these may warrant a separate zone and regulations.

Because most towns and villages do not develop extensive land use districts and because their new development comes in discrete, comprehensible, but diverse projects, a general zoning bylaw may be ineffective. It may not be able to anticipate the array of possible development without being unrealistic from the outset. Moreover, what may be clearly incompatible land use in a city suburb may not be considered inimical to a small town. A more flexible, direct, case-by-case approach commends itself for land use regulation in small towns and villages, rather than predetermining what uses will or will not be allowed. More important than actual use is the effect, or impact, the use has on surrounding areas: does it generate traffic congestion, have abnormal hours of operation, or create much noise, odor, or other dangerous effluents? This approach, which has already come into use in many small towns in the United States, is called Performance Zoning because it regulates land use on the basis of its external effects, or performance.[16]

Performance zoning may treat the entire town as a single zone and establish the criteria for performance of all new or changed land uses, criteria such as off-street parking requirements, external signs, hours of operation, and size of structures. Or, several zones may be designated and separate criteria drawn up for each. In many ways, this kind of performance regulation of land uses in communities is analogous to the development permits used in Interim Development Control, which has been employed in several Canadian cities. Ontario planning legislation allows the development permit to be used in parts of a community that the local council has designated for Site Plan Control. In both these instances, the local government does not automatically grant permission for development in advance of receiving a proposal and plans for the project. This allows the project to be judged on its own merits as well as leaving the final approval to the community.

Subdivision Regulation. The concern in small communities may not be the land uses that occur on particular parcels of land; rather, the concern may be that the parcels have adequate roads, fire access, utilities, and sanitary conditions. Preceding these concerns should be those about the buildability of all lots that are sold, and making certain that steep slopes and floodplains are protected from erosion and pollution. Subdivision regulations address such matters. Subdivision proposals should be the subject of thorough scrutiny by local officials, even though in many provinces the final authority for their approval lies with the provincial government. The long-term commitments and implications of any subdivision fall to the local government. Of particular concern are the relationships of the subdivision to the overall community plan, the provision of roads, parks, and utilities, and the treatment of unique and hazardous topography. Since many technical building and engineering questions arise with subdivisions, a small community may be advised to convene a review committee of people with knowledge in such matters or to seek advice from a regional planning agency if one exists. Several provinces have also produced handbooks on the principles of good subdivision design, which a community can use to assess proposals. More will be said later about the important role of such technical assistance in planning for small communities.

(d) Public Participation

It should not be assumed that the relatively tight-knit social milieu of a small community will automatically provide for involvement of the public in the planning program of their town or village. Unless some crisis situation faces the community, the participation of residents may have to be encouraged. Small-town planners, the local council or commission, as well as the professional planners, must be aware that a number of factors may make the public reluctant to participate in the planning affairs of small communities: no urgency is perceived, the subject has highly technical aspects, the feeling that the planning program is being "forced on them" by a provincial or regional government, or the attitude that "the news will get around fast enough." The very attributes of small size that should make for vigorous public participation may constrain it. But, properly approached, it can be a very rich planning experience for both the public and the planner.

There are two crucial elements in a public participation program for planning in a small community. The first is the time frame, and the second is the amount of opportunity to participate. Regarding the time element it is important that the planning process not be rushed into and that once begun it not become protracted. For most residents the planning process begins with the first public meeting about the new plan or the amendment to the zoning bylaw. Ample time should be allowed before such a meeting is scheduled, say up to two months if it is the very beginning of planning or the complete revision of a plan. Then a schedule of all the meetings to be held should be drawn up. Most provincial Planning Acts set the number of meetings required for various planning decisions; they are minimal and could, advisedly, be extended. The approach taken by planners who consult primarily to small communities in the interior of British Columbia is instructive. For Valemount, British Columbia (pop. 1,300 in 1981) planners set out the following sequence of steps: a first public meeting to discuss planning issues and problems, a second public meeting (three months later) to discuss the first draft of the community plan, then a formal public hearing prior to council adopting the plan.[17] In addition, the planners distributed information bulletins to all community residents and property owners several times during the planning program. The first such bulletin requested the views of citizens on problem areas and planning issues.

Beyond the stimulus of public meetings, questionnaires, and media coverage, there should be provision for direct participation by residents of all ages. The community self-survey for a Community Profile, mentioned above, is one such way. In addition to the regular planning board or commission it can prove helpful to appoint a number of committees to represent particular interests (for example housing, recreation, waterfront, and historic buildings) or particular geographic areas. In the situation of the unincorporated town or village whose plan is prepared by the surrounding rural municipality, township, or county, it seems especially important to have an advisory planning committee drawn from the interests of the small center. Although the unincorporated town or village may be the business and governmental focus of the rural municipality, and the location of its most pressing planning problems, too often the aspirations of the townspeople are overlooked. People often enjoy serving on committees concerned with the future of their community; by involving residents in the planning process, planners can stimulate a valuable interchange of information and opinion with those most affected.

4. SUPPORTIVE PLANNING FRAMEWORKS FOR SMALL TOWNS

Several times in this chapter we have asked whether planning tools are amenable to small-town needs and whether they were manageable with local resources. However, a basic dilemma is often present in small-town situations, regardless of the appropriateness of the planning tools. In the majority of small communities, resources are simply too meager to permit a satisfactory planning process to be administered locally or to hire outside professionals. Meanwhile, the intricacies of planning are increasing. Seven provinces have revised their Planning Acts during the past seven years, for example. Emerging legislation on environmental assessment, agricultural land preservation, pits and quarries, and coastal zone management will further impinge on the planning interests and resources of small communities. Means are needed whereby towns and villages as well as most rural municipalities may be assisted not only to employ basic planning tools but also to become effective participants in broader planning processes.

Fortunately, it is possible to report that supportive frameworks for small-community planning are more and more a reality throughout Canada. The past decade has seen the emergence of field services, financial support programs, self-help manuals, and other technical assistance from provincial ministries. In addition, there has been considerable development of regional support services in planning and economic and social development for towns, villages, and rural areas. The variety in these undertakings bespeaks the diversity of needs in rural regions. A sampling of emergent planning support activities, such as we present below, will indicate positive directions in the development of these "bridges," but is in no way an exhaustive listing. There is much unheralded innovation in this realm.

Provincial Support

Ministries in many provinces which are in charge of promoting planning and administering the provincial Planning Act are actively developing support services for small municipalities and rural areas. The most direct form of support is the provision of professional planning assistance in the regions where the towns and villages are located. The Manitoba Department of Municipal Affairs operates community planning field offices in several centers across the province. Ministry staff planners will assist communities to prepare various planning instruments and will also act as advocates for a municipality in planning issues requiring formal hearings. In Prince Edward Island, Land Use Service Centers of the parent ministry, located in regional centers outside Charlottetown, perform similar functions for small centers and rural areas. The New Brunswick approach assigns planners from the ministry office in Fredericton to assist rural areas and has established regional planning commissions in some areas, which are staffed by planners employed by the ministry. Variations on these approaches are used in several other provinces.

Another tool which many provinces are using to assist small communities in their planning and development is the provision of financial support programs either for general planning or for specific kinds of development. Ontario has a program of "community planning study grants" which are available only to small municipalities. It allows them to obtain the services of consultants to conduct the necessary studies for the preparation of community ("official") plans, zoning bylaws, and so forth. Special planning situations such as seasonal residential areas, Main Street development, or waterfront areas requiring planning studies in small communities are also eligible under this program. Saskatchewan's Main Street Development Program offers grants to municipalities to improve their business districts, and combines this with technical assistance from provincial ministries.

A feature of the latter program is its self-help nature; grants are available as incentives to communities but improvements are seen as best when initiated by the local government and business community. This approach has much to recommend it in terms of the traditional self-reliance of towns and villages. It does, however, raise the issue about whether the initiatives will be forthcoming from the local level: are the incentives great enough? Is the protocol for becoming involved too awesome? It is never possible to know whether a broad-scale program such as a Main Street program will stimulate local involvement, given the diversity of community situations and attitudes. But the Saskatchewan manual provided to towns and villages tries to encourage participation with the use of down-to-earth language, simple diagrams of possible improvements, and explanations of the technical details of topics such as architecture, paving, and design principles.[18] As the guide says, "It has been designed and printed to be *used*, not merely read"; it is an example well worth following.

Other useful types of self-help planning manuals have been appearing with increasing frequency and sensitivity to small-community needs in recent years. One of the earliest and best, from the Newfoundland Provincial Planning Office, provides residential subdivision design criteria with the express aim of helping those municipalities which "may never become involved in a planning scheme larger than a subdivision."[19] Considerable effort is made to reduce jargon and to provide simple diagrams and examples from various communities in the province, while still maintaining the rigor and integrity of the planning process. Similar manuals on subdivision design also of high quality are available from the Ontario Ministry of Housing[20] and the Prince Edward Island Department of Municipal Affairs.[21] The Ontario planning ministry, in addition, initiated in 1980 a series of "planning guidelines" for all its municipalities, dealing with issues such as mobile homes, land severances, private roads, planning for cottage areas, and official plan and zoning amendments. These publications in concise terms provide background planning information, information on the nature of extant legislation, topics for local discussion, and instructions for making formal planning decisions. These publications are admirably brief and coherent, and the plans are well within the capabilities of small communities.

Valuable steps have been taken by most of the provincial ministries responsible for planning to assist small centers and rural areas in their planning, but are they sufficient? Technical assistance programs and services demand continuity and progressive integration of elements. In planning, especially, the processes that are stimulated do not reach a final conclusion. Even the completion of a major step like the adoption of a community plan only opens the door to a longer-term process of implementing it. It is important, therefore, that provincial efforts do not diminish or languish after the publication of a few manuals. Indeed, as small communities become actively involved in planning their need for personal contact with planning professionals increases. Provincial support programs should anticipate this stage and provide easy access of communities to planners. And, to the greatest extent possible, there should be continuity in professional personnel in order to cultivate the idea that a community has "their" planner. This personal association will not only benefit planning activities but also serve to facilitate contacts with other senior (provincial and federal) agencies. The actions of these other agencies tend to have the greatest impact on small communities. This is seldom adequately recognized, except in the communities themselves. This issue is more fully dealt with in the concluding section of this chapter.

Regional Support

Over the past decade, an increasing number of efforts have been made in Canada to provide supportive planning services to towns, villages, and rural areas at the regional level. These are indigenous efforts, in contrast to the operations of a "branch" office or field service of a senior government ministry or agency. A regional planning commission comprised of all the communities, large and small, within some appropriately defined area is the oldest and, in many ways, the most successful format. Such commissions can provide the continuing professional staff support for individual small communities as well as the planning perspective for the facilities and services needed by all communities. Alberta's regional planning commissions, of which there are eight each covering several thousand square miles, are admirable examples in this regard. The assistance of the Calgary Regional Commission staff planners in preparing village plans was mentioned above. It should be noted that this commission will do planning work for all municipalities in its region, regardless of their membership (the example cited is one such instance). Two other Alberta planning commissions have made notable contributions: the Oldman River Commission (near Lethbridge) addressed itself to the difficult task of planning for the provision of services in its rural region, services such as libraries, ambulance, and garbage collection.[22] The Peace River Commission (in northwestern Alberta) addressed itself to fashioning a plan that would meet citizens' desires for growth within a context of small towns and rural areas.[23]

Regional planning commissions usually work through a loose coalition of municipalities; the commission has very few powers either to ensure conformity with the plan by the actions of member municipalities or to obtain coordination in the actions of other agencies. Rural regional planning linked to a governing function, and thus with more power to implement plans, is a feature of, for example, the regional district of British Columbia and the county planning operations in Ontario and Nova Scotia. This type of planning arrangement provides the constituent municipalities with their "own" staff planner, or at least a close approximation of it. There is no viable substitute in an ongoing community planning process for the regular, frequent contact of a professional planning advisor. The permanent planning staff of a county or regional government goes a long way to assuring this for small communities unable to afford such assistance.

The regional planning approaches described here have been set in place largely to achieve conventional land use planning in small-town and rural communities. Although they may incorporate necessary components such as access to professional staff, technical assistance, and opportunities for participation, these may not be sufficient to produce effective land use planning, as the experience all too frequently confirms. Planning techniques and approaches often still bear the stamp of their urban origins emphasizing, as they usually do, land use regulation. Such regulations are often seen by rural people as preventing the development of land rather than encouraging it, or as being imposed by outside forces in their interests, or as creating unmanageable local government workloads, or as all three combined. In the end it is not enough to establish a formal planning support framework unless it can overcome these perceived, and often real, limitations.

Moreover, it appears from the few fully effective planning efforts in rural areas in Canada that there must be as much emphasis placed on developing a planning *process and milieu* suited to each area as on completing official plans and zoning bylaws. The approach of the Peace River Regional Planning Commission in Alberta during the 1970s exemplifies this tack. The commission actively sought participation of regional residents and as a result its 1973 policy statement strongly reflects the citizens' views. The plan did not attempt to forecast growth of population or to allocate land uses. Rather, it attempted

> to apply a set of guiding policies, and establish a process which will give significant leverage on the big structural decisions to the Commission and the municipalities involved.[24]

The Peace River region's approach is essentially a cooperative effort of the commission, the citizens, and their local governments, and is multidisciplinary as well. That is, it incorporates elements of several disciplines: land use planning, rural community development, economic development, and public education. The best-documented case study of a successful rural regional planning effort embodying these same principles is from rural New York State. If a "recipe" for a viable regional planning option for rural areas is sought, the Tug Hill region experience is worthy of note. Its approach is summarized as follows:

> reliance on local decision-making is the essence of this approach, coupled with an extensive effort to bolster decision-making through broadly based local assistance. The key principles of this method are flexibility and diversity.[25]

The broadly based, diverse approach of the Tug Hill and Peace River commissions makes it much more likely that the planning and resource development problems encountered by small communities in rural regions, such as cited earlier in this chapter, will be tackled. The supportive, participatory nature of these commissions' work, coupled with their staff and organizational capability, means that small communities will have both an ally and buffer when dealing with the developmental initiatives of senior governments and large corporations.

5. THE IMPACT OF SENIOR GOVERNMENT POLICY ON SMALL TOWNS

Planning for the physical setting of towns and villages, as important as it is, could just be "window dressing" for most small communities unless complemented by planning for economic development and social services. But the latter planning is usually done *for* small communities by senior governments at the provincial and federal level. Senior governments are obliged, of course, to pursue policies for the greater good of the total population. Some policies are aimed at the welfare of all settlements, large and small; some are aimed at small communities particularly; and some are aimed at regional well-being, where the region may, and usually does, contain small centers. These policy areas are extensive, varied, and ubiquitous, provincially and federally. They range from transportation, farm support, and regional development to national and provincial parks, school consolidation, and environmental protection.

One feature that most of these central government policies have in common is that they disregard the effects on the small community. The problem is twofold. First, the aim of the policy is usually sectoral rather than spatial; that is, in satisfying a particular activity or function, the needs and capabilities of the affected area are an afterthought, if considered at all. Second, little thought is given to the impact on small communities of either the form in which policy is delivered (grants, projects, services, and so on) or the means of dispensing the policy (for example, the agency). There are "what," "how," and "where" dimensions to policy delivery of central governments which become increasingly crucial in their effect the smaller and more rural the setting of the small center. Some general examples may help to illustrate these issues.

Industrial development programs are not usually set up to take into account the costs incurred by local residents and local municipalities. The industrial incentives are a relatively small part of the public costs associated with locating a new plant. A good many other costs fall upon the community in which the plant is located. New employees will require housing and in most towns and villages no large housing surplus exists; this means that new housing must be built and the land developed and serviced. The latter costs alone can run to more than $10,000 for each additional household to provide the roads, utilities, public maintenance, and other services. There is probably no better example of the diversity and severity of problems induced in small communities through federal and provincial industrial development promotion than in those small centers along the Strait of Canso in Nova Scotia.

Port Hawkesbury, which tripled in population from just over 1,300 in 1961 to nearly 3,900 in 1981, was the main center of the Strait of Canso area and the only one with a local government.[26] It was urged to prepare for growth to possibly as much as 10,000 population. Not only was the provincial government's forecast far in excess of the town's actual growth, but also an additional 3,000 persons were allowed to sprawl into adjacent rural areas, where no plans were made to provide them with necessary services. Port Hawkesbury, in the meantime, had undertaken huge borrowing for capital projects — sewers, roads, water, community center — to accommodate the forecasted growth. There were, as well, many social costs due to social instability, human dislocation, and the resulting increased demand for social services and facilities. It is the local community that bears these costs and they are often the most burdensome.

Major energy projects that aim to satisfy the needs of metropolitan industrial areas in Canada (and abroad) have their most direct impact in the rural and nonmetropolitan regions where the resource is usually located. Construction workers throng into these areas for a few years, straining housing and social services. The employees of the completed project, who are usually fewer than the construction workforce, may either require the expansion of an existing town or disperse among surrounding communities. The aftermath may be local pollution problems of considerable magnitude. Dealing with these impacts of energy projects is often left to the small community, whether it be the huge coal strip-mining operations at Michel, British Columbia, the Tar Sands plant at Fort MacMurray, Alberta, or the nuclear generating station at Goderich, Ontario. In the realm of energy projects the policy is often dispensed through a public corporation or regulatory agency, which is less accessible than a line ministry. A prolonged public hearing on a heavy-oil plant in the rural Cold Lake area of Alberta and Saskatchewan showed how interested the public was in being involved in the decision-making and how frustrating the formalities were for them.[27] On the other hand, the Columbia River power project by B.C. Hydro in the 1960s, which flooded several small communities in the Arrow Lakes valley, allowed its staff planners (upon their urging) to work closely with villagers to re-establish their communities.[28]

Small communities encounter two recurring facets of senior government programs. The first of these is the *sheer number of different agencies* employed to deliver policy. In our field studies of towns and villages in Nova Scotia and Manitoba in 1976, it was determined that to serve nine activities or functions, a small community in Nova Scotia was required to deal with at least sixteen different provincial agencies. In Manitoba the comparable number was thirteen different provincial agencies. Nine different federal government agencies were involved in programs at the local level in both provinces. And, as the accompanying table shows, in some activities and functions as many as six different agencies are involved. The issue here is the pragmatic one of being able to match the complexity of the central government policy delivery system with sufficient administrative and technical resources in small communities. The typical small local government has only a half-dozen employees, and seldom does this include any trained professionals.

Ministries and Agencies of Provincial and Federal Government Pursuing Programs in Small Communities, Nova Scotia and Manitoba, 1976

Activities and Functions	Nova Scotia		Manitoba	
	Provincial Involvement	Federal Involvement	Provincial Involvement	Federal Involvement
Water and Sewers	(1) Dept. Municipal Affairs (2) Dept. Environment	(1) DREE	(1) Dept. Municipal Affairs (2) Water Services Bd. (Agric.)	(1) DREE (ARDA) (2) PFRA
Recreation	(1) Dept. Lands & Forests (2) Dept. Recreation (3) Dept. Development	(1) DREE	(1) PEP	(1) DREE
Protection	(1) Dept. Mun. Affairs (2) Dept. Att. Gen.	(1) RCMP		(1) RCMP
Planning	(1) Dept. Municipal Affairs	(1) CMHC (2) DREE	(1) Dept. Municipal Affairs	(1) CMHC
Housing	(1) Nova Scotia Housing Corporation (2) Dept. Social Services	(1) CMHC	(1) Manitoba Housing & Renewal Corp.	(1) CMHC
Social Welfare and Health	(1) Dept. Public Health (2) Dept. Public Works (3) Dept. Social Services (4) Mun. Hospital Loan Fund	(1) Dept. National Health and Welfare	(1) Dept. Health & Social Development	(1) Dept. National Health and Welfare
Education	(1) Dept. Education (2) School Loan Fund	(1) Min. Manpower & Immigration (2) DIAND	(1) Dept. Education (2) Dept. Colleges (3) Dept. Agriculture	(1) Min. Manpower & Immigration (2) DIAND
Industry and Tourism	(1) Dept. Development (2) Dept. Tourism	(1) DREE (2) Min. Manpower and Immigration	(1) Dept. Industry & Commerce (2) Dept. Tourism (3) Dept. Mines (4) Man. Development Corp.	(1) DREE (2) Min. Manpower and Immigration
Transportation	(1) Dept. Highways (2) Dept. Municipal Affairs	(1) CNR (2) Nat. Harbours Board (3) Ministry of Transport	(1) Dept. Highways	(1) CNR (2) Min. Transportation

The second facet is the problem of coordination of central government programs. This has a field component, which we have already referred to, and a substantive component. By the latter we mean the "package" of policies put together from the programs of one or more agencies that are aimed at, say, creating a better level of well-being for small towns and rural areas. Such undertakings are notoriously difficult to implement and, again, the burden of the shortfall is usually borne at the "receiving end" of the policy, that is, in the rural area or small center. These problems tend to occur when the coordination of constituent programs is left to chance. Duplication, interdepartmental conflict, and competition among programs and personalities are all too readily detected by citizens of the community. This is considered to be one of the main variables influencing the impact of large new investments on small communities in their vicinity.[29]

Baker describes the multiprogram milieu he encountered in Saskatchewan small communities over twenty years ago. Distressingly, it could be replicated just as easily in almost every nonmetropolitan region in Canada:

> a series of meetings were held, on a district basis, which brought together all the (provincial) government field staff who carry on a program in each of several small communities. It was found that approximately twenty-five field workers were available to each community. In each district they met with a group of key leaders representing all the active organizations in a community. Several interesting observations were made:
> (1) Although the field workers were all helping to service the same community, they frequently did not know each other personally (indicating a segmentation of services);
> (2) after each field worker described his or her programme to the community group, leaders sometimes had to ask for the differences between two programmes, they sounded so similar;
> (3) on occasion, leaders asked whether a particular programme had been available some years earlier, when they could have used it (indicating they simply had not known such help existed);
> (4) a number of field workers found it hard to see what their programme had to do with the "individual" community (indicating inadequate insight into the social phenomenon involved).[30]

Despite the extensive restructuring of central government departments and local government units that has been taking place over the past two decades, the effort put into achieving more effective policy delivery has almost always been confined to devising means of central office coordination; improvements at the field level, at the end-point of administration, receive little more than lip service. Sometimes, it seems, the most appropriate small-town stance is that of an official in a small Prairie community:

> We don't give a hoot what they do in the Capital as long as they leave us alone.[31]

This expression of opinion contains the seeds of two concerns townspeople and villagers have about central government programs — are they really needed, and do they fit the situation? It cannot be said too forcefully that solutions to small-town problems should be *small-town solutions!*

NOTES

1. John Blakney, "Planning for Small Rural Communities: A Case Study of Hunter River, P.E.I. "(Unpublished Master's Report, Queen's University School of Urban and Regional Planning, 1977).
2. H.R. Baker, "The Impact of Central Government Services on the Small Community," *Canadian Public Administration* 3: 2 (1960): 97-106.
3. *Ibid.*
4. *The Whig-Standard*, Kingston, 16 July 1977, 26.
5. As reported in Gerald Hodge, *Planning for Small Communities* (A Report to the Ontario Planning Act Review Committee, Toronto, 1977, Background Paper No. 5).
6. An excellent example of such an approach is James F. MacLaren Ltd., *Countryside Planning* (Toronto, 1975, A Study Prepared for the Province of Ontario and the County of Huron).
7. Newfoundland, Department of Municipal Affairs, *Planning for Smaller Communities* (St. John's: Project Planning Associates, 1968), 7.
8. Alberta, Task Force on Urbanization and the Future, *High River, Alberta* (Edmonton, June 1973), 7.
9. Newfoundland, Department of Municipal Affairs, *op. cit.*
10. See for example, County of Huron, *Village of Brussels Secondary Plan* (Goderich, Ontario, 1976).
11. Acme, Alberta, *General Municipal Plan* (July 1979).
12. Queen's University School of Urban and Regional Planning, *Sydenham Ontario, A Plan for Community Enhancement* (A COPLAN Project, April 1982).
13. Institute on Man and Science, *Community Profile: The Revitalization of Stump Creek* (Rensselaerville, N.Y., 1975).
14. Alma, New Brunswick, *Municipal Plan* (Prepared for the New Brunswick Department of Municipal Affairs, Fredericton, 1974).
15. United States, Federal Reserve Bank of Minneapolis, *A Regional Economic Analysis of the Turtle Mountain Indian Reservation: Determining Potential for Commercial Development* (Grand Forks, N.D., 1978).
16. A discussion of the advantages and disadvantages of performing zoning in small communities is found in Judith Getzels and Charles Thurom, eds., *Rural and Small Town Planning* (Chicago: American Planning Association, 1979), 89-95.
17. Urban Systems Ltd., *Planning Program for the Village of Valemount* (Kamloops, B.C., January 1979).
18. Saskatchewan, Department of Industry and Commerce and Municipal Affairs, *Guide to the Saskatchewan Main Street Development Program* (Regina, 1979).
19. Newfoundland, Department of Municipal Affairs and Housing, *Residential Subdivision Design Criteria for Newfoundland* (St. John's, 1975).
20. Ontario, Ministry of Housing, *A Guide to Residential Planning and Design in Small Communities* (Toronto, 1980).

21. Prince Edward Island, Department of Municipal Affairs, *Residential Subdivision Design Handbook* (Charlottetown, 1979).
22. *Cf.*, Oldman River Planning Commission, *Intermunicipal Services, Library* (Lethbridge, Alta., 1974).
23. Peace River Planning Commission, *The Preliminary Regional Plan* (Grande Prairie, Alta., 1973).
24. Len Gertler and Ron Crowley, *Changing Canadian Cities: The Next 25 Years* (Toronto: McClelland and Stewart, 1977), 207.
25. Cynthia D. Dyballa *et al., The Tug Hill Program* (Syracuse, N.Y.: Syracuse University Press, 1981), 148.
26. A. Paul Pross, *Planning and Development: A Case Study of Two Nova Scotia Communities* (Halifax: Dalhousie University Institute of Public Affairs, 1975). Pages 29-71 summarize the Port Hawkesbury experience.
27. Brian Plesuk, ed., *The Only Game in Town* (Edmonton: Alberta Environment, July 1981).
28. James Wilson, *People in the Way* (Toronto: University of Toronto Press, 1973).
29. Pross, *op. cit.*, 90. See also in this regard Roy T. Bowles, *Big Industries and Small Communities* (Toronto: Butterworths, 1982).
30. Baker, *op. cit.*
31. *Ibid.*

10 Toward a Viable Future for Small Towns

1. PERSPECTIVE ON THE FUTURE

Although Canada is mostly an urban country, a condition that will no doubt continue to prevail in the future, it is important to remember that the most numerous settlements are towns and villages. There are almost 9,500 small centers, compared with about 150 small and medium-size cities and two dozen metropolises. As the 1980s begin, over 4.7 million people call towns and villages home.

These data bear repeating because, as one ponders the future of our communities, there is a tendency to be mesmerized by forecasts of the vast scale and continued growth of our metropolitan areas. As the accompanying table shows, Canada's metropolitan areas are expected to accommodate almost another four millon people by the end of this century. But it is also worth noting that nonmetropolitan areas (in which small towns are included) are likely to add close to two million people by the year 2001. By our estimates, about half of this growth will occur in towns and villages; the remainder will accrue to small cities and rural areas. Thus, by the end of the century, almost one million more people will choose to reside in small centers than in 1981, or close to 5.7 million Canadians in all.

Urban growth in Canada over the next two decades will total about five million persons. It will be shared among our large metropolitan areas and small and medium size cities. Some of the latter will grow to metropolitan size (over 100,000) in this period. But, overall, the number of cities in Canada, large and small, will likely not increase much from the present level.

Most significant from the point of view of this study is that towns and villages will experience vigorous growth in the two decades up to 2001. Not all small centers will expand in population, but it is likely that more than half will, and growth will be experienced in almost all regions and in all sizes of center from the smallest to those of 10,000 population. Although the total population of towns and villages will expand by upwards of one million people, when distributed over the 9,500 small centers the average growth will be modest — perhaps no more than one hundred people in those places that experience growth.

213

Actual and Forecasted Population for Nonmetropolitan and Metropolitan Areas in Canada, 1961-2001

	Actual				Forecast	
	1961	1971	1976	1981	1986	2001
Canada						
Total Population (000s)	18,238	21,569	22,992	24,343	25,990*	29,735*
Percent	100.0	100.0	100.0	100.0	100.0	100.0
Nonmetropolitan						
Towns & Villages (000s)	3,749	4,232	4,471	4,742	5,015	5,700
Percent	20.5	19.6	19.4	19.5	19.4	19.2
Small Cities/Rural (000s)	5,196	5,463	5,725	5,945	6,313	6,664
Percent	28.5	25.3	24.9	24.4	24.1	22.3
Metropolitan						
Census Metro Areas (000s)	9,293	11,874	12,796	13,656	14,662*	17,371*
Percent	51.0	55.1	55.7	56.1	56.5	58.5

*Canadian and metropolitan-area forecasts prepared for the Ministry of State for Urban Affairs, as cited in Leonard O. Gertler and Ronald W. Crowley, *Changing Canadian Cities: The Next 25 Years* (Toronto: McClelland and Stewart, 1977), 89-91.

It is, however, not the overall scale of new population growth in towns and villages that is so important, but rather where it occurs, its composition, and its source. The answers to these issues are not easily predicted, but the implications of each deserve to be noted. The *location* of small-town growth is paramount for what it means to the affected centers, especially in their ability to cope with it. Senior governments will also be involved in responding to town and village growth, and for them it will matter whether growth is occurring on the fringes of metropolitan centers or in the more distant countryside, resource frontier, or tourist region. The *composition* of new growth is also important, because of the past tendency of towns and villages to attract many elderly people. Closely related is the matter of the *source* of new growth: will it be due to the retention of townspeople, villagers, and open-country residents in their local communities? Or will it be due to a "backflow" of urbanites to small communities?

We should not, of course, overlook those small centers that will not grow in population and may even decline. If we are not well-equipped to deal with town and village growth, it is safe to say that we are even less well-equipped to deal with their decline. One thing is certain, however, and that is that the growth or decline of small communities cannot be dealt with — in tools, policies, or concepts — as one would deal with urban growth or decline. For towns and villages, both their smallness and their individuality, one proceeding from the other, must be appreciated in designing policies and programs. This notion underlies all the observations and suggestions made in the remainder of this chapter.

IMPORTANT

2. THE STAYING POWER OF SMALL COMMUNITIES

A major thrust of the evidence presented in the foregoing chapters is that Canadian towns and villages can no longer be considered a "dying breed" of settlement, as our urban media and social scientists often lead us to believe. There is a *renascence* of Canada's small centers. It is not necessarily, or even normally, associated with rampant population or economic growth in a town or village. But for the past two decades, since 1961 it seems, there has been an obvious resurgence in the fortunes and roles of small centers. In the recessionary times that have plagued the early 1980s small communities seem to have a peculiar resiliency; perhaps they have always had such a tendency. It seems due to a host of reasons, many of which are not yet clear, but the milieu of towns and villages today is clearly a picture of persistence.

The data and various probes of this study present a view of the reality of the current situation of towns and villages. They do not directly provide the source of the resurgence; however, several parameters of these tendencies may be discerned to give better direction in seeking the reasons:

(1) Town and village persistence is a general phenomenon throughout the nation, occurring with comparable vigor in all regions;

(2) The capacity of small centers to add to their population, housing stock, or commercial base is found among all sizes of center;

(3) Growth in population, housing, and commercial base in towns and villages may occur in any of these realms independently;

(4) A small center's growth is not a function of proximity to a metropolis, except when located within thirty miles of a metropolis; and

(5) Small-center populations possess social and economic characteristics very similar to those of city populations.

In addition, the recent town and village revival is not due to any concerted effort to directly promote small-center growth by senior governments. With the exception of the Manitoba "Stay Option" policy of the early 1970s, there have been no such national or provincial government initiatives. It is also clear from the trends of several key variables that the shift in the fortunes of small centers was taking shape in the early 1960s. Four censuses later, we are able to confirm this, but it should not distract us from the fact that the persistence of towns and villages is real and not a fleeting thing.

What accounts for this new-found staying power of small centers? The answer, Bourne notes, is "unlikely to submit to any single act of explanatory variables . . . what is needed perhaps is some moulding of aspects of various interpretations."[1] The three "aspects" that seem most likely to combine for a fruitful explanation are: (1) the national societal context; (2) the local functional context; and (3) the community context. A brief review of each context follows.

Towns and villages exist and function within the *societal context* of contemporary Canada. Although we urge the recognition of the unique features of small centers within the array of settlements, the small communities of Canada are just as subject to the forces, tensions, and trends of modern society as are the cities. Indeed, in many ways it is because the people, the businesses, and the institutions of towns and villages are now so firmly linked to the larger society that small centers have persisted. For example, since 1950, better roads, telephone service, television, and electric power grids have all become available on a widespread basis and have helped transform life in small communities, as did better schools, health insurance, welfare services, and improvements in water supply. On the commercial side, the main streets of small towns now reveal nationally-known supermarkets, fast-food outlets, and automobile establishments. On the cultural side, one finds branches of national service clubs, the Canadian Cancer Society, and the Women's Institute, all of which send delegates to provincial, national, and even international conventions. Of course, sports and arts groups with their outside connections and interests also help to keep towns and villages "plugged in" to national systems of cultural, commercial, and policy information.

This rendering of small-community life caught in the web of national society appears to echo an "information model" of urbanization propounded by John Friedmann.[2] He conceived of a situation in which modern (urban) forms, values, attitudes, behavior, and institutions are propagated among the centers of a country according to their potential to receive and exploit information. Historically, cities provide high communications potential, which fosters change in technology, commerce, and public institutions. In turn, these improvements reduce the impediments to communications with other, smaller settlements, and previously peripheral areas become attractive to new activities. A good deal of the societal context today supports a dispersed, decentralized pattern of settlement in towns, villages, and rural areas by encompassing it within what Friedmann called a "communications-modernization web."

The local or subregional *functional context* reveals several behavioral transformations in shopping and work patterns that are associated with small town resurgence. More and more, rural residents conduct their shopping in ways that do not correspond to the regular hierarchical arrangements envisioned by central-place theory. They may, for example, shop for groceries in a nearby village, patronize a restaurant in another, and buy building materials in yet another. This affects the mix of business establishments in rural towns, the particular mix differing from town to town. The pattern already evident in rural Canada is one in which a number of small places *collectively* provide the needed goods and services to the residents of a rural district, possibly several hundred square miles in extent.

Home-to-work commuting patterns show many parallels with those for shopping. The two main features of rural and small-town job commuting are: (1) considerable commuting in and out of small centers; and (2) commuters finding jobs usually within a driving time of one-half hour or less of their homes. The result is an area of interchange of people and jobs which is quite compact within rural regions, and does not show a great deal of dependence on the presence of a nearby city. The fact that people can find jobs locally is a major reason that towns and villages persist.

In short, the emergent spatial format in rural regions is a *complex* of small centers, each providing its own distinctive array of stores, jobs, services, institutions, and social activities for the residents of small towns and the countryside. This new format implies a great deal of autonomy for small-town and rural residents. While this is true, it is important that it not be construed as self-sufficiency and self-containment for these areas. It seems more likely that this is a spatial manifestation of the integrative tendencies present throughout Canadian society. The societal context supports unique geographical arrangements in rural Canada which, in turn, enhance the staying power of small communities.

The two contexts within which small-town persistence is occurring — the national and the subregional functional contexts — are necessary to provide the conditions for the resurgence of towns and villages. They provide the *facilitating mechanisms* — the roads and other physical infrastructure, the health, education, and social infrastructure, and the locational situations — necessary for small places to persist. But when one asks why the resurgence occurs in one small center and not in another, or why it takes different forms, it is clear that the national and the regional contexts are not sufficient to explain town and village persistence. Clearly, there must be an impetus from people and communities, acting in conjunction with the facilitating mechanisms of the two larger contexts, to allow a town or village to persist.

In other words, the staying power of a small center depends very much on the actions of people in the community — the individuals, groups, firms, and institutions — that is, on the *community context*. The historical, cultural, and social circumstances of every small community differ. These, in turn, influence the disposition of individuals and groups in a community, indeed the community as a whole, to behave in unique ways. Thus, the patterns of shopping, commuting, and of socializing, as well as the ways in which social concerns are handled, the degree of cooperation in the community, and the care shown for the community, are a reflection of the choices that individuals and groups feel inclined to make.

There is no easy or satisfying theoretical explanation of *community staying power*, but experience shows that it exists. Two examples of small-town persistence in different parts of Canada demonstrate its reality. One is the little Ottawa Valley village of Forfar that fought back when a conglomerate bought and then closed its 120-year-old cheese factory. The community cooperated to reopen it, and today the cheese factory employs fourteen people and ships Forfar Cheese all over the country. Another example is Wanham, in Alberta's Peace River Country. With a population of just over 300, Wanham in 1970 saw its lumber yard close and the building being sold without warning. This helped trigger the idea of consolidating the energies of the many small clubs and organizations (a common and often perplexing thing about small communities) to bring projects to fruition for the benefit of all in a democratic and planned way.[3] They formed COCO, the Committee of Coordinating Organizations, and have been able to put artificial ice in their arena, rebuild the ball diamond, construct a tennis court, and start a museum. This helped to stimulate other projects in the town.

It may be argued that the community context of town and village persistence is an ephemeral thing, but this would be too limited a view. It seems to be based on values such as optimism about the future, self-reliance, individualism, and equality of opportunity. These are, unquestionably, the values of several successive generations in rural Canada. That they persist in today's towns and villages is not surprising. To explain how these values are nurtured and expressed from community to community is much more difficult. But what is quite clear is that they will be expressed in a great variety of ways. The outcomes may not be as dramatic as those of Wanham or Forfar. Rather, persistence may show itself in the establishment of a new business, the building of a small subdivision, the renovation of the town hall, or the organization of a "mobility club" to provide transportation for senior citizens.

Perhaps classifying this aspect of town and village persistence cannot be any more precise than to note the pervasive disposition of individuals and groups to sustain a sense of *community*. This is not a new tendency among people in small centers; it was present at the outset of the founding of a town or village. What is new is that the seemingly inexorable centralizing and spatial-consolidation tendencies of Canadian society of two and more decades ago are considerably less prominent. Whereas sustaining not only a sense of community but also a physical community seemed then an improbable goal for rural residents, today it is being achieved. In some ways it is paradoxical that as rural and small-town Canadians become more socially and institutionally integrated into the national milieu, the more they are able to sustain distinctive small communities. Is it as simple as towns and villages wanting to persist, nowadays can persist.

3. TOWNS AND VILLAGES IN CONTEMPORARY CANADA

The preceding chapters have probed for answers to two general questions: (1) What has been happening to Canadian small communities recently? (2) What socioeconomic characteristics distinguish them in contemporary times? The first question brought forth the answer that small communities are tenacious entities, which have not only persisted but also undergone robust growth in the past decade. The second question revealed the social convergence that has swept through both small and large communities of Canada. This suggests that it is the industrial-urban milieu of the society at large that supports all sizes of settlements. Contemporary towns and villages cannot be a world apart from other Canadian settlements. It is not likely that the preindustrial social and economic orders will continue to exist in small communities in the midst of an integrated megapolitan society. Distinct though towns and villages may be, they are subject to national and provincial laws; they are woven into regional school and health boards, their residents also marry by choice and for love, and are exposed to the same television, radio, and newspapers. The material, technological, and institutional bases of Canadian society have been homogenized, as well as standardized.

Even agriculture is now a corporate business, and farming is almost as technologically complex as industrial activity. A prairie farmer plows his fields sitting in an air-conditioned and stereo-equipped tractor cabin. Already, computers and microelectronics have found their way into the homes and businesses of small communities. This is the social milieu that shapes the character of cities, towns, and villages, and even the country-side. These findings suggest a theoretical stance with which towns and villages must be viewed.

National and regional social systems play a primary role in determining the forms and characteristics of territorial units such as cities, towns, or villages. Like a stellar system, individual settlements assume shapes, roles, and even sizes through the interplay of elementary forces that for the most part originate from the system at large. They do acquire individual characters, but those characters are variations on common themes, and manifestations of a particular configuration of national and regional institutions. This realization changes the focus of an inquiry meant to uncover the distinguishing characteristics of towns and villages. In order to distinguish these characteristics, we are better-advised to look at a center's mix of institutions, specific local conditions, and relative position in the regional and organizational framework. The same approach applies to towns and villages as a class or category of settlements.

The task of differentiating towns and villages from cities and metropolises ceases to be one of positing one as an opposite of the other. One has to look for unique ways in which common institutions and organizations combine to produce a distinct socioeconomic configuration, be it a city or a village. In searching for differentiating features of towns and villages, one must look for individual characteristics arising from unique combinations of standard institutions, much like one set of building blocks producing a myriad of forms. Thus the distinguishing features of towns and villages are their smallness, their diverse mix of institutions and activities, their truncated social structure, and their subordinate role in national decision-making arenas. These features — not the indices by which rural and urban areas have been conventionally differentiated — distinguish them as a group.

At this juncture, it may be pointed out that equally important are our findings as to what contemporary towns and villages are not. They are not folk communities or tribal settlements unspoiled by industrialism, where simplicity, solidarity, and the love of nature reign. They are milltowns, minetowns, and railtowns, and often single-industry communities. They are also frontier settlements, farm-service centers, retirement and resort villages, and ex-urban bedroom communities. Though peripheral to the loci of power, they are economically and culturally integrated into national and regional systems. Much of the folklore about the countryside and villages is the product of an era when such communities were largely isolated.

A substantial proportion of contemporary transactions take place within large corporate organizations, be those public bureaucracies or the Loblaws supermarket chain. These practices have further eroded the problems of distance. In these times, a territorial community cannot help being drawn into the economic and cultural mainstream. The distinctive ways of life bred in relatively isolated villages of the nineteenth and early-twentieth centuries have not survived in full force in modern times. Contemporary villages and towns are microcosms of modern Canada, and to expect them to be the "folk" communities of a bygone era is more an expression of hope and belief than of the empirical reality. They are neither models of social harmony and peace, as back-to-the-land enthusiasts are inclined to believe, nor are they dreary and dull places to live, as urbanities believe them to be. Community life in Canada is no longer based on territorial loyalties, but on organized economic interests, social networks, and shared lifestyles. This is as true of towns and villages as of cities, though the smallness of the former creates an aura of familiarity across the whole social spectrum.

The Distinction of Being Small

The most significant attribute of towns and villages is their smallness, territorial as well as demographic. What are generally regarded as their distinguishing characteristics are directly attributable to smallness. Being small, they can be readily comprehended and related to by individuals. They are "imageable," as Lynch defines them, on account of their relatively sharp edges and well-defined nodes.[4] Those who live in a village can be readily distinguished from those who live outside, and this facilitates the crystallization of a sense of belonging that is often very diffused in metropolises.

The smallness of a center contributes to the visibility and observability of its residents. This may not necessarily engender emotional closeness or friendships, but it does promote mutual acquaintances and personalized dealings. A birth or marriage may not result in a communal feast, but in a village it is inevitable that almost everybody would know about it. Similarly, a death is the passing-away of an acquaintance, even if there was little contact with that person. These features of small-community life differentiate small centers from the "lonely crowds" that cities are sometimes called. The pervasive mutual acquaintance of small centers is often mistaken for harmony and friendliness, but even if contemporary Canadian towns and villages are not convivial burgs, they offer greater opportunities for mutual empathy and face-to-face relations.

Because of their small size, towns and villages are unable to sustain many professional and commercial services. Most small communities do not have hospitals, fire departments, colleges, public housing, and bus or taxi services. To live in these places one has to learn to rely on another's help, so volunteerism and mutual help are functional necessities. It is not uncommon to drive neighbors and even mere acquaintances to doctor's appointments, or to rescue strangers in a snowstorm. To render and expect such help is part of the ethos of small-community living, and to the extent that it prevails it makes towns and villages self-reliant and participatory communities.

Despite their disposition towards face-to-face relations and a participatory ethos, contemporary towns and villages have become communities of interests, although the territory serves as a strong shared interest whose preservation and management pull various social segments together. Social relations proceed along kinship, class, and occupational lines. The poor may be known to everybody, but it does not necessarily follow that they are any more integrated into the local social structure. The professionals associate with each other, and the blue-collar workers have their own social circuits. The point here is that the shared interests and life-styles provide anchors for local social organization — a typical basis of modern community life. However, mutual acquaintance reduces the distance between various social networks, and the territory serves as an interpenetrating interest linking various groups together.

Towns and villages correspond to the neighborhoods or districts of a city, except that in their case the "neighborhood" is free-standing. They have the same functions and a similar degree of self-containedness, and are often devoid of higher-order activities. But, unlike neighborhoods, they are physically separated from other elements of the larger system, and thus susceptible to a truncation of their social structures. The absence of higher-order activities and powerful positions in towns and villages generally deny them an upper class and access to the establishment. This condition not only truncates their social structures, but also breeds a sense of insecurity which finds expression both as adversarial sentiment and as local boosterism. Other economic and demographic forces also contribute to the process of truncation. For example, while in the 1950s and 1960s the youth were leaving towns and villages for better opportunities in cities, by the late 1970s the elderly had started to be drawn to them for convenient retirement, particularly to hamlets and villages. One way or the other, towns and villages do not capture the full cast of actors that characterize Canadian society. The process of truncation only defines their relative status in the national social hierarchy, and acts as a constraint on the realization of their full potential as communities. It is a structural condition, but not necessarily a drawback. It does not appear to have detracted from their viability.

Towns and Villages in the Settlement System

Conventionally, a hierarchical arrangement of central places is assumed to be the key feature of a settlement system. But such hierarchies have been scrambled in recent times with the emergence of multiple channels of accessibility, and with the rise of national (and multinational) organizations and corporations which, by internalizing transactions, link remote villages directly with metropolitan centers. Towns and villages are not necessarily nodes of low-level activities that serve as central places for the surrounding countryside. Generally towns and villages have come into their own as places of residence, daily activities, and even jobs for their respective populations. Functionally a set of towns or villages is the "building block" of contemporary settlement systems. Even in the Prairie Provinces, an individual village or town is no longer the basic settlement unit; "several centres, each differing in size and in the role they serve for rural residents, go together to form a system."[5] This view of the structure of settlement systems, particularly of its lower layers, suggests that the preservation and development of towns and villages is not a matter of "doing-up one place," but requires a careful balancing of inter-linked roles and functions of a set. A cluster of towns, villages, and intervening countryside must be treated as a spatial unit, not as a single community; yet the uniqueness of each one must be given proper attention. These are the challenges of local planning.

The physical separateness of towns and villages gives an impression of their autonomy, but in fact they are integrated into regional and national economies. Their fortunes are determined as much by local activities as by distant forces. A protective tariff on tin or copper in Europe may destroy the economic base of a somnolent mining village in Quebec. This may not spell doom for the village, because of the safety net of the modern welfare state and on account of the resilience of people; but such a situation illustrates the web of forces within which contemporary small communities are enmeshed.

Towns and villages are increasingly being strung into Canadians' family life-cycles. Just as most households move from place to place in search of jobs and preferred lifestyles, between suburbs and central cities and from apartments to houses and back as families expand and shrink, similarly an increasing number are "doing time" in the country, either as a result of postings and transfers, or by choice in search of community and nature. This phenomenon of being "cycled" through the country in one's lifespan is recent, and it may have contributed to the counterurbanization trends sweeping the western world. It is a reflection both of increased mobility and new social values. How this phenomenon will be affected by the microelectronic revolution and information-processing economies are intriguing questions. Will these forces further dissipate clustered settlements and accelerate the formation of communities without propinquity,[6] or will they merely strengthen decentralizing trends, thereby drawing more people away from cities and into towns and villages? These questions need to be answered in order to formulate future settlement policies. So far, towns and villages have held their ground because they provide the basic requirements of modern living, and are integral elements of the broader social system.

4. PRINCIPLES FOR THE DESIGN OF POLICIES AND PROGRAMS

Not without justification, one might observe that the power of small communities to persist seems very often to be thwarted by the policies and actions of national and provincial governments. The closing of community schools and the discontinuation of railroad passenger services are but two examples. That such a large amount of housing construction does occur in small towns and rural areas is due more to "sweat equity" than to housing policy.[7] This may say a lot for the spirit of self-reliance among rural Canadians, but it says little for equity in policy delivery. Moreover, nonmetropolitan Canada has weathered a wide variety of senior government programs and projects which threatened to "improve" towns and villages right out of existence, from the Arrow Lakes of British Columbia to the outports of Newfoundland.[8]

As more and more Canadians decide to live in towns and villages, perhaps senior government approaches to small communities will become more sensitive to these distinctive habitats. It is desirable that they do, because small communities depend to a large extent upon their provincial and national governments to provide the funding for physical infrastructure and community services, and the stimulus for economic development. In this section we distill some general principles for the design of programs, policies, and projects of senior governments which affect towns, villages, and other rural communities.

The first principle stems from the observation that solutions to small-town problems should be small-town solutions. That general axiom bears much repeating:

(1) **Senior governments' policies, plans, and programs for small centers should be consistent with the scale, nature, and needs of towns and villages.**

The maintenance or revitalization of small towns demands a distinctive approach. Most tools of research, planning, and development are urban in nature. Take, for example, the current concern over the future of commercial areas in small centers: the Ontario program for Downtown Revitalization[9] exemplifies the "citified" approach, while the Saskatchewan Main Street Development Program[10] respects the fundamental characteristics of towns and villages, and their residents. Another positive effort is the Community Management Development Program in Manitoba, which provides technical assistance directly to rural businessmen. In Newfoundland, the Rural Development Authority has funded nearly 1,000 local development projects submitted by individuals and groups in small communities: "These are not projects that were decided upon by government officials, but rather the projects resulted from 'felt needs' of people at the local level."[11] Efforts like these help small communities to maintain their functional identities, and work against the almost relentless centralizing tendency evident in senior government programs.

The crucial first step in framing policies for small towns is to recognize that they are not just scaled-down versions of cities. The second step, and almost as crucial, is to recognize that small communities do not readily fit into neat aggregates. They are not readily observable through analytical indicators, especially *per capita* indexes. They very often differ significantly from one another. By their very smallness, the social, economic, and physical ingredients of which all communities are comprised are fewer in number and more dispersed in their distribution. There is not, when designing policy or devising research, the flexibility provided by the existence of groupings of, say, land uses, income groups, decision-makers, or resources. Thus, as a second principle:

(2) **Policies, programs, and research regarding towns and villages should be capable of responding to differences among individual small centers.**

As we noted when referring to community needs, the list of community "problems" usually differs from one town or village to another. Our policies and programs should be capable of solving these different problems rather than require communities to "fit" some universal norm. In general, programs that elicit community needs and deal with them, as do those cited in Alberta, Manitoba, and Newfoundland, should be more successful (and at least less disruptive).

There are, of course, those policies and programs whose scope is national or regional, and in which small centers are only the *incidental* recipients of assistance. While towns and villages are often directly affected by programs such as industrial development, park expansions, energy projects, and school consolidation, seldom are their effects on small centers allowed for at the outset of the program.[12] Just as we now know that we should ascertain environmental impacts and social impacts when formulating programs, so should the impact on small communities be examined.

(3) **Programs and projects for economic, social, physical, and energy development should be designed to take into account all their impacts on towns and villages.**

The inconsistencies among senior government programs are often apparent to small-town and rural local government officials. The quotation at the end of the last chapter is almost certain to have arisen in one of those frustrating situations in a small center when several senior government agencies (representing the same or different governments) seemed to be stumbling over each other to promote their own programs, meanwhile solving nothing. It is as if the potential policy and program resources of senior governments far exceed the capability of delivering them effectively to small communities. Duplication of effort, interagency conflicts, and competition among programs are all-too-often discerned by townspeople and villagers.

(4) **Means should be established to integrate the efforts of all nonlocal agencies and governments toward common objectives in the development of towns, villages, and rural regions.**

Even if the reforms suggested above are put into effect, it should not be assumed that small communities will be able to cope with the intricacies of planning and development all alone. Many will need support and advice from technically qualified people. The mode of delivery of such technical assistance may vary. It may be made available: (1) through a government agency, such as the Community Planning Assistance Branch of Ontario's Ministry of Housing; (2) through persons seconded to locally based programs, such as the Regional Resources Project No. 1 in south-central Alberta; or (3) through new regional institutions such as Brandon University's Community Resources Centre, which is aimed at assisting "rural people, groups, and communities [to] get information and assistance to help them deal with the problems of change that they are experiencing."[13]

(5) **Technical and professional assistance should be readily available to towns and villages to help them solve, or to cooperate in solving, their own problems.**

Closely akin to the need for technical assistance is the need for planning and administrative tools that are simpler and more in keeping with the problems and capabilities of small communities. Much needs to be done in this realm. A little-known study of possible planning instruments for small communities was explored in a Newfoundland report over a decade ago.[14] It advocated town plans that focused on a statement of community problems and possible solutions, rather than on an abstract arrangement of land uses. Further, it proposed that such plans be written without the usual planner's jargon so that they would be understandable to those who have to administer them in towns and villages — the hard-pressed, and often untrained, town clerk or building inspector.

Finally, the bulk of the planning concerns of towns and villages are not those of physical planning, but of social services and facilities. The provision of housing for senior citizens, recreation facilities, and health care services are among the highest items on the agenda in rural communities. It is important to grasp that such concerns tend to raise complex issues in small towns about community functioning, even more so than they might in urban areas. The reason is twofold: first, the usual meager array of services in rural areas means that few support services will be available; and second, the greater distances and lower densities of population almost automatically call for transportation solutions as well. Typically, it seems that little concern is ever shown about these facets of the situation; often the result is anxiety and pessimism over rural social services planning. One rural health council in Ontario has noted this issue this way: "The challenge of understanding the balance point between having *people* transported and having *services* transported is a central issue in service planning in rural areas."[15] Putting it another way, the provision of services in small communities is much more involved with the integral functioning of the entire *community* and the available resources. To round out our set of principles:

(6) **In planning for social services in towns and villages, it is vital to take into account the milieu of the community, its existing resources, and its transportation situation.**

NOTES

1. Larry S. Bourne, "Alternative Perspectives on Urban Decline and Population Deconcentration," *Urban Geography* 1 (1980): 39-52.
2. John Friedmann, "An Information Model of Urbanization," *Urban Affairs Quarterly* 4 (1968): 235-44.
3. Wallace Transem, "Community Organization: The Wanham Experience," in Frank Jankunis and Barry Saddler, eds., *The Viability and Livability of Small Urban Centres* (Edmonton: Environmental Council of Alberta, 1980), 103-06.
4. Kevin Lynch, *The Image of the City* (Cambridge, Mass.: Harvard University Press, 1960).
5. Canada, Ministry of State for Urban Affairs, *Human Settlement in Canada* (Ottawa: Ministry of State for Urban Affairs, 1976), 76.
6. Melvin M. Webber, "Order in Diversity: Community without Propinquity," in Lowdon Wingo, ed., *Cities and Space* (Baltimore: Johns Hopkins University Press, 1963), 23-56.

7. See, for example, New Brunswick, Department of Municipal Affairs, *A Study of Sprawl in New Brunswick* (Fredericton, 1980); and Andy Rowe, "The Financing of Residential Construction in Newfoundland," *Canadian Public Policy* 7 (1981): 119-22.
8. James Wilson, *People in the Way* (Toronto: University of Toronto Press, 1973); and Ralph Matthews, *There's No Better Place Than Here* (Toronto: Peter Martin Associates, 1976).
9. Peter Barnard Associates and Proctor and Redfern Ltd., *Revitalizing Ontario's Downtowns: Guildelines for a New Program*. A Report to the Province of Ontario, March 1975.
10. Saskatchewan, Department of Industry and Commerce, and Municipal Affairs, *Guide to the Saskatchewan Main Street Development Program* (Regina, 1979).
11. Remarks made by J. O'Reilly, Deputy Minister of Rural Development of Newfoundland, at the Fifth Summer Institute in Urban and Regional Planning, Queen's University, Kingston, 17 June 1977.
12. Boyce Richardson, *James Bay* (Toronto: Clarke, Irwin, 1972); and Wally Smith, "P.E.I.'s Tiny Schools, Throwing It All Away," *Axiom* 3:1 (December 1976): 18-22.
13. *This is West — Man*, Brandon, Issue 11, April 1976.
14. Newfoundland, Department of Municipal Affairs, *Planning for Smaller Communities* (St. John's: Project Planning Associates, 1968).
15. Sandra Mark, *Community Dialogue on the Needs of the Elderly in Lanark, Leeds and Grenville (Counties)* (Smiths Falls, Ont.: District Health Council, 1981), 62.

Appendix A

TOWNS AND VILLAGES CONTAINED IN THE SAMPLE OF 100 CENTERS USED FOR ANALYSIS OF HOUSING AND COMMERCIAL SERVICES

	Province	Town/Village	1971 Population
1.	Newfoundland	Englee	1,050
2.		Wesleyville	1,142
3.		Fogo	1,155
4.		Freshwater	1,562
5.		Burin	2,586
6.		Grand Bank	3,476
7.	Prince Edward Island	Murray Harbour	367
8.		Murray River	478
9.		Borden	624
10.		Georgetown	767
11.		Alberton	973
12.		Kensington	1,086
13.	Nova Scotia	Annapolis Royal	758
14.		Clarks Harbour	1,082
15.		Mahone Bay	1,333
16.		Berwick	1,412
17.		Parrsboro	1,807
18.		Middleton	1,870
19.		Windsor	3,775
20.		Westville	3,898
21.		Antigonish	5,489
22.		North Sydney	8,604
23.	New Brunswick	Milltown	1,893
24.		St. Stephen	3,409
25.		Sussex	3,942
26.		Grand Falls	4,516
27.		Dalhousie	6,255
28.	Quebec	Duparquet	786
29.		St. Germain de Grantham	1,104
30.		Barraute	1,288
31.		Labelle	1,492
32.		Melocheville	1,601
33.		Ste. Thècle	1,725
34.		Normandin	1,823
35.		Ferme Neuve	1,990
36.		Ville Marie	1,995

Province	Town/Village	1971 Population
37.	Rimouski Est	2,069
38.	Varennes	2,382
39.	Beaupré	2,862
40.	Clermont	3,386
41.	Port Cartier	3,730
42.	Marieville	4,563
43.	La Providence	4,709
44.	Bagotville	6,041
45.	Lac Mégantic	6,770
46.	Chibougamau	9,701
47. **Ontario**	Woodville	473
48.	Belmont	798
49.	Bath	810
50.	Iron Bridge	874
51.	Grand Valley	904
52.	Brussels	908
53.	Jarvis	965
54.	Athens	1,071
55.	Watford	1,400
56.	Frankford	1,862
57.	Keewatin	2,112
58.	Bancroft	2,276
59.	Brighton	2,956
60.	Geraldton	3,178
61.	Caledonia	3,183
62.	Petrolia	4,044
63.	Meaford	4,045
64.	Petawawa	5,784
65.	Espanola	6,045
66.	Stoney Creek	8,380
67. **Manitoba**	Benito	479
68.	St. Pierre	846
69.	Beausejour	2,236
70.	Minnedosa	2,621
71.	Morden	3,266
72.	Dauphin	8,891
73. **Saskatchewan**	Wapella	518
74.	Cabri	737
75.	Carlyle	1,101
76.	Battleford	1,803
77.	Humboldt	3,881
78.	Weyburn	8,815
79. **Alberta**	Irricana	139
80.	Kitscoty	320
81.	Bassano	861
82.	Stony Plain	1,770
83.	Redcliff	2,255
84.	Lacombe	3,426
85.	Hinton	4,911
86.	Wetaskiwin	6,267
87. **British Columbia**	Tofino	461
88.	Harrison Hot Springs	598
89.	McBride	658
90.	Abbotsford	706
91.	Greenwood	868
92.	Enderby	1,158

Province	Town/Village	1971 Population
93.	Oliver	1,615
94.	Warfield	2,132
95.	Hope	3,153
96.	Rossland	3,896
97.	Duncan	4,388
98.	Merritt	5,289
99.	Quesnel	6,252
100.	Chilliwack	9,135

Appendix B

SAMPLING PROCEDURES FOR THE COMMUNITY-NEEDS SURVEY OF SMALL CENTERS

The following procedures were used to formulate a sampling frame.

(a) All Census Divisions were classified by the rate of population change for the 1961-71 period. As the national rate of population growth for this period was 13 percent, this figure and its multiples were used as cut-off points for five categories of the rate of change. The five categories of the population change were:
- (1) less than 0 percent
- (2) 0 - 12 percent
- (3) 13 - 20 percent
- (4) 21 - 39 percent
- (5) 40 or more percent

(b) As a proxy for the regional economic base, the modal sectoral occupation of a division's labor force was used. All Census Divisions were classified as specializing in agriculture, manufacturing, or services.

(c) Combining (a) and (b), a three-by-five matrix was designed; all Census Divisions were classified in appropriate cells of this matrix.

(d) A proportionate random sample of Census Divisions was drawn from each cell. Some adjustments were made for underrepresented cells.

(e) All incorporated centers of less than 10,000 population in sampled Census Divisions were included in the final sample; selected unincorporated centers were also included.

Thus, a two-step proportionate random sample was drawn with some adjustments for underrepresented areas, including British Columbia, which presented difficulties of cross-tabulation in the sampling matrix.

Size of the Sample

We sent out 407 questionnaires to 207 incorporated and 200 unincorporated small centers selected by the above-described procedures.

Requiring a 95 percent confidence limit for the sample, it was calculated that this number would be sufficient, as suggested by the following calculation.

$$n = \frac{N}{(N+1)(.05)^2}$$

where n = sample size

N = Total Universe = 8,000

Therefore $n = \dfrac{8000}{(8001)(.05)^2} = 381$

Thus, our aim of obtaining a sample of 400 centers would have met the size requirements at a 95 percent level of significance.

The response to the mailed questionnaire was very good as far as this procedure goes. We got back about 150 (37 percent) filled-in questionnaires. Another attempt was made to obtain responses from centers that had not sent back the questionnaires, but the response was meager. Limitations of time and resources did not permit a vigorous follow-up.

By size, the final sample has about a 91 percent confidence limit, as indicated by the following calculations:

$$150 = \frac{8000}{(8001)(x)^2}$$

$$x^2 = \frac{8000}{8001 \times 150} = .007$$

$$x = .085$$

Overall, the sample includes centers of all sizes, and from almost all functional regions of Canada.

It must be borne in mind that about three-quarters of the 8,000 centers have less than 200 population, and frequently they are merely a designation covering the jurisdiction of a post office or an electoral district. If we were to consider only the functioning small centers, then our sample would turn out to be highly significant.

Bibliography

Abramson, Jane A. *Rural Non-Farm Communities and Families: Social Structure, Process and Systems in Ten Saskatchewan Villages.* Saskatoon: Canadian Centre for Community Studies, 1967.

Adams, Thomas. *Rural Planning and Development.* Ottawa: Commission of Conservation, Canada, 1917.

Adler, H.J., and D.A. Brusegard. *Perspectives Canada III.* Ottawa: Statistics Canada, 1980.

Alberta. *Town of St. Paul.* (Pamphlet) St. Paul, Alberta, 1973.

Alberta Human Resources Development Authority. *Socio-Economic Analysis of Isolated Communities in Northern Alberta.* Edmonton, 1970.

Alberta, Task Force on Urbanization and the Future. *High River, Alberta.* Edmonton, June 1973.

Alma, New Brunswick. *Municipal Plan.* Prepared for New Brunswick Department of Municipal Affairs, Fredericton, 1974.

Armstrong, Marcia B., and Anthony Fuller. *Profile of the Transportation Disadvantaged in a Rural Area of Southwestern Ontario.* A Report to the Urban Transportation Research Branch. Montreal: Transport Canada, 1979.

Baker, H.R. "The Impact of Central Government Services on the Small Community." *Canadian Public Administration* 3:2 (1960): 97-106.

Basavarajappa, K.G., and J. Lindsay. *Mortality Differences in Canada, 1960-62 — 1970-72.* Ottawa: Statistics Canada, 1976.

Baskin, John. *New Burlington, The Life and Death of an American Village.* New York: Norton, 1976.

Bernikow, Louise. " 'Alone' Yearning for Companionship in America." *New York Times Sunday Book Review,* 15 August 1982, 25.

Berry, Brian J.L. "The Counterurbanization Process: How General?" In *Human Settlement Systems,* edited by N. Hansen, 25-50. Cambridge Mass.: Ballinger, 1978.

Blakney, John. "Planning for Small Rural Communities: A Case Study of Hunter River, P.E.I." Unpublished Master's Report, Queen's University School of Urban and Regional Planning, 1977.

Blau, Peter M., ed. *Approaches to the Study of Social Structure.* New York: The Free Press, 1975.

Blumenfeld, Hans. "Continuity and Change in Urban Form." In *Internal Structure of the City*, 2nd ed., edited by Larry S. Bourne, 47-56. New York: Oxford University Press, 1982.

Bourne, Larry S. "Alternative Perspectives on Urban Decline and Population Deconcentration." *Urban Georgraphy* 1 (1980): 39-52.

Bowles, Roy T. *Social Impact Assessment in Small Communities*. Toronto: Butterworths, 1981.

Bowles, Roy T., ed. *Big Industries and Small Communities*. Toronto: Butterworths, 1982.

Brinkman, George L. *The Development of Rural America*. Lawrence, Kansas: University of Kansas, 1974.

Bryant, C.R., and L.H. Russwurm. "The Impact of Non-Farm Development on Agriculture: A Synthesis." *Plan Canada* 19: 2 (June 1979): 122-139.

Bullock, Nicholas. "Time Budgets and Models of Urban Activity Patterns." *Social Trends* 5 (1975): 1-19.

Bunce, M. *Rural Settlement in an Urban World*. London: Croom Helm, 1981.

Burnet, Jean. *Next Year Country: A Study of Rural Social Organization in Alberta*. Toronto: University of Toronto Press, 1951. Reprinted 1978.

Burnford, Sheila. *Without Reservation*. Toronto: McClelland and Stewart, 1970.

Burton, I. "Retail Trade in a Dispersed City." *Transactions of the Illinois State Academy of Science* 52 (1959): 149-50.

Buttel, Frederick H., and Howard Newby, eds. *The Rural Sociology of the Advanced Societies: Critical Perspectives*. Montclair, N.J.: Allanheld Osmun, 1980.

Canada, Ministry of State for Urban Affairs. *Human Settlement in Canada*. Ottawa: Ministry of State for Urban Affairs, 1976.

Canadian Council on Rural Development. *Commitment to Rural Canada*. Fifth Report and Review, 1973.

Chisholm, Michael. *Rural Settlement and Land Use*. London: Hutchinsons, 1962.

Coates, Vary, and Ernest Weiss. *Revitalization of Small Communities: Transportation Options*, vol. 1. Washington, D.C.: United States Department of Transportation, 1975.

Cohen, Richard A. "Small Town Revitalization: Case Studies and a Critique." *Journal of the American Institute of Planners* 43: 1 (January 1977): 3-12.

Corporation of the Town of New Liskeard. *Town Profile* (Mimeographed.) New Liskeard: Clerk-Administrator, 1975.

County of Huron. *Howick Township Secondary Plan*. Goderich, Ontario, 1976.

County of Huron. *Village of Brussels Secondary Plan*. Goderich, Ontario, 1976.

Coward, Raymond T., and William M. Smith. *The Family in Rural Society.* Boulder, Colo.: Westview, 1981.

Dahms, Fred. "Declining Villages?" In T.A. Crowley, ed., *Proceedings: Second Annual Agricultural History of Ontario Seminar,* University School of Part-time Studies and Continuing Education, University of Guelph, 1977, 50-65.

Dahms, Fred. "Small Town and Village Ontario." *Ontario Geography* 16 (1980): 19-32.

Dahms, Fred A. "The Evolving Spatial Organization of Small Settlements in the Countryside — An Ontario Example." *TESG (Journal of Economic and Social Geography)* 71: 5 (1980): 305.

Day, Lee M. "Community Facilities and Services: An Economic Framework for Analysis." *American Journal of Agricultural Economics* 50: 5 (1968): 1195-1205.

Denman, Anne Smith, ed. "Design Resourcebook for Small Communities." Special Issue of *Small Town* 12: 3 (Nov.-Dec. 1981).

Douglas, Lloyd H., and Scott Shelley. *Community Staying Power.* Manhattan, Kansas: Kansas State University, Agricultural Experiment Station, Research Publication 171, February 1977.

Drewett, Roy, and A. Rossi. "General Urbanization Trends in Western Europe." In *Dynamics of Urban Development,* edited by L.H. Klaassen *et al.,* 119-36. Aldershot: Gower, 1981.

Drewett, Roy, John Bodelard, and Nigel Spence. "Urban Britain: Beyond Containment." In *Urbanization and Counterurbanization,* edited by Brian J.L. Berry, 43-80. Beverly Hills: Sage, 1976.

Dyballa, Cynthia. *The Tug Hill Program.* Syracuse, N.Y.: Syracuse University Press, 1981.

Elkin, Frederick. *The Family in Canada.* Ottawa: Vanier Institute, 1968.

Ellenbogen, Bert L. "Service Structure of the Small Community: Problems and Options for Change." In *Communities Left Behind: Alternatives for Development.* Ames, Iowa: Iowa State University Press, 1974.

Falcocchio, John C., and Edmund J. Cantelli. *Transportation and the Disadvantaged.* Lexington, Mass.: Lexington Books, 1974.

Feldbruegge, David. "Newburgh, Ontario: An Historical Analysis of Village Growth." Unpublished Master's Report, Queen's University School of Urban and Regional Planning, 1977.

Forcese, Dennis. *The Canadian Class Structure,* 2nd ed. Toronto: McGraw-Hill Ryerson, 1980.

Friedmann, John. "An Information Model of Urbanization." *Urban Affairs Quarterly* 4 (1968): 235-44.

Friedmann, John. *Regional Development Policy.* Cambridge, Mass.: M.I.T. Press, 1966.

Friedmann, John. "The Urban Field as Human Habitat." In *Systems of Cities,* edited by L.S. Bourne and J.W. Simmons. New York: Oxford University Press, 1978.

Fuguitt, Glenn V. "The City and the Countryside." *Rural Sociology* 28 (1963): 246-61.

Fuguitt, Glenn V., Paul R. Voss, and J.C. Doherty. *Growth and Change in Rural America.* Washington, D.C.: Urban Land Institute, 1979.

Fulton, David, ed. *Design for Small Communities: A Report of Interdesign.* Toronto: Macmillan, 1975.

Gardner, Bruce L. "Distribution of Gains and Losses from Economic Growth in Rural Areas." In *Benefits and Burdens of Rural Development.* Ames, Iowa: Iowa State University Press, 1970.

Gertler, Len, and Ron Crowley. *Changing Canadian Cities: The Next 25 Years.* Toronto: McClelland and Stewart, 1977.

Getzels, Judith, and Charles Thurow, eds. *Rural and Small Town Planning.* Chicago: American Planning Association, 1979.

Gilg, Andrew W. *Countryside Planning.* London: Methuen, 1978.

Glazebrook, G.P. de T. *Life in Ontario — A Social History.* Toronto: University of Toronto Press, 1968.

Gold, Gerald, and Marc-Adelard Tremblay, eds. *Communities and Cultures in French Canada.* Toronto: Holt-Rinehart, 1973.

Gold, Gerald L. *St. Pascal.* Toronto: Holt, Rinehart and Winston, 1975.

Government of Canada, Department of Regional Economic Expansion. *Single-Sector Communities.* Ottawa, 1979.

Green, R.J. *Country Planning — The Future of Rural Regions.* Manchester: Manchester University Press, 1971.

Greenhill, Ralph, Ken MacPherson, and Douglas Richardson. *Ontario Towns.* Ottawa: Oberon, 1974.

Hahn, A.J. "Planning in Rural Areas." *Journal of the American Institute of Planners* 36:1 (January 1970): 44-49.

Hansen, Niles M. *The Future of Non-Metropolitan America.* Lexington, Mass: Lexington Books, 1973.

Hansen, Niles M. "Preliminary Overview." In *Human Settlement Systems,* edited by N.M. Hansen, 1-22. Cambridge, Mass.: Ballinger, 1978.

Harp, John. "Canada's Rural Poor." In *Poverty in Canada,* edited by John Harp and John R. Hotley. Scarborough, Ont.: Prentice-Hall, 1971.

Hart, J.F. *et al.* "The Dying Village and Some Notions About Urban Growth." *Economic Geography* 44 (1968): 343-49.

Hart, John Fraser. *The Look of the Land.* Englewood Cliffs, N.J.: Prentice-Hall, 1975.

Healy, Robert G., and James L. Short. *The Market for Rural Land: Trends, Issues, Policies.* Washington, D.C.: Conservation Foundation, 1981.

Heller, Ursula. *Village Portraits.* Toronto: Methuen, 1981.

Hewes, Lawrence. *Rural Development: World Frontiers.* Ames, Iowa: Iowa State University Press, 1974.

Hibbs, John. "Maintaining Transport Services in Rural Areas." *Journal Transport Economics and Policy* 6 (1972): 10-21.

Hill, Nicholas. *Historic Streetscapes of Huron County.* London, Ont.: Middlesex Printing, 1979.

Hirsch, Werner Z. *Urban Economic Analysis.* New York: McGraw-Hill, 1973.

Hodge, Gerald. "Do Villages Grow? Some Perspectives and Predictions." *Rural Sociology* 31:2 (June 1966): 183-96.

Hodge, Gerald. *Planning for Small Communities.* A Report to the Ontario Planning Act Review Committee. Background Paper No. 5. Toronto, 1978.

Hodge, Gerald. *Domestic Energy Use in Rural Ontario: Some Findings from Frontenac County.* Kingston: Queen's University School of Urban and Regional Planning, 1982.

Honigman, John J. and Irma. *Arctic Townsmen.* Ottawa: Canadian Research Centre for Anthropology, Saint Paul University, 1970.

Institute on Man and Science. *Community Profile: The Revitalization of Stump Creek.* Rensselaerville, N.Y., 1975.

Irving, John. "Trying to Save Peggy Sneed." *New York Times* Book Review section, 20 August 1982, 20.

Jackson, John D. "Community Studies: The Traditional Approach Contrasted with a Class Approach." *International Journal of Urban and Regional Research* 4: 4 (1980): 578-79.

James F. Maclaren Ltd. *Countryside Planning.* A Study Prepared for the Province of Ontario and the County of Huron. Toronto, 1975.

Jankunis, Frank J., and Thomas Menard. *Small Business in Southern Alberta: A Case Study Approach.* Lethbridge: University of Lethbridge Department of Geography, n.d.

Lamb, Richard. *Metropolitan Impacts on Rural America.* Research Paper No. 162. Chicago: University of Chicago Department of Geography, 1975.

Lash, Harry. *Planning in a Human Way.* Ottawa: Ministry of State for Urban Affairs, 1976.

Lash, Harry. "Where Do We Start on a National Settlement Policy." *Plan Canada* 16:2 (June 1976): 94-101.

Lassey, W.R. *Planning in Rural Environments.* New York: McGraw-Hill, 1977.

Lewis, G.J. *Rural Communities.* London: David and Charles, 1979.

Leyton, Elliot. *Dying Hard.* Toronto: McClelland and Stewart, 1975.

Lingeman, Richard. *Small Town America.* Boston: Houghton Mifflin, 1980.

Lloyd, Anthony John. *Community Development in Canada.* Ottawa: Canadian Research Centre for Anthropology, Saint Paul University, 1967.

Lotz, Jim. *Northern Realities.* Toronto: New Press, 1970.

Lotz, Pat and Jim. *Cape Breton Island.* Vancouver: Douglas, David and Charles, 1974.

Lotz, Jim. *Understanding Canada.* Toronto: NC Press, 1977.

Lucas, Rex A. *Minetown, Milltown, Railtown.* Toronto: University of Toronto Press, 1971.

Lynch, Kevin. *The Image of the City.* Cambridge, Mass.: Harvard University Press, 1960.

MacDonald, John. *Rural Life in Canada.* Toronto: University of Toronto Press, 1973.

Mackintosh, W.A., and W.L.G. Joerg, eds. *Canadian Frontiers of Settlement.* 8 vols. Toronto: Macmillan, 1934-36.

Mark, Sandra. *Community Dialogue on the Needs of the Elderly in Lanark, Leeds and Grenville Counties.* Smiths Falls, Ont.: District Health Council, 1981.

Martindale, Don, and Galen R. Hanson. *Small Town and the Nation.* Westport, Conn.: Greenwood, 1969.

Maslow, Abraham. *Motivation and Personality.* New York: Harper & Row, 1954.

Matthews, Ralph. *There's No Better Place Than Here.* Toronto: Peter Martin, 1976.

McGahan, Peter. *Urban Sociology in Canada.* Toronto: Butterworths, 1982.

Meredith, M.L. "The Prairie Community System." *Canadian Farm Economics* 10 (1975): 19-27.

Moline, Norman T. *Mobility and the Small Town, 1900-1930.* Research Paper No. 132. Chicago: University of Chicago Department of Geography, 1971.

Moroney, Robert M. "Needs Assessment for Human Services." In *Managing Human Services,* edited by Wayne Anderson and B. Frieden, 128-154. Washington, D.C.: International City Management Association, 1977.

Mozersky, Kenneth A. "The Structural Determinants of Individual Perceptions to Social Change in Western Canadian Communities." *Canadian Journal of Agricultural Economics* 21:1 (1973): 27-40.

Munro, Alice. "Thanks for the Ride." In *The Penguin Book of Modern Canadian Short Stories,* edited by Wayne Grady, 70-83. Harmondsworth: Penguin, 1982.

New Brunswick, Department of Municipal Affairs. *A Study of Sprawl in New Brunswick.* Fredericton, 1980.

Newfoundland, Department of Municipal Affairs. *Planning for Smaller Towns.* St. John's: Project Planning Associates, 1968.

Newfoundland, Department of Municipal Affairs and Housing. *Residential Subdivision Design Criteria for Newfoundland.* St. John's, 1975.

Nicholls, W.M. *Views on Rural Development in Canada.* Ottawa: Canadian Council on Rural Development, 1968.

Nijsse, Donald. "Recent Physical Development in Small Towns and Villages in Canada." Unpublished Master's Report, Queen's University School of Urban and Regional Planning, 1976.

North, Douglass C. "Location Theory and Regional Economic Growth." *Journal of Political Science* 67 (June 1955): 243-58.

Ontario, Ministry of Housing. *A Guide to Residential Planning and Design in Small Communities.* Toronto, 1980.

Pahl, R.E. *Whose City?* Harmondsworth: Penguin, 1975.

Paterson, Lesley, and Patricia Malone. "Small Towns and Villages in Canada and Population Stablity." Unpublished Master's Report, Queen's University School of Urban and Regional Planning, 1977.

Peace River Planning Commission. *The Preliminary Regional Plan.* Grande Prairie, Alta., 1973.

Peter Barnard Associates, and Proctor and Redfern Ltd. *Revitalizing Ontario's Downtowns: Guidelines for a New Program.* A Report to the Province of Ontario, March 1975.

Philbrook, Tom. "Regional Development and Social Change." *Canadian Journal of Agricultural Economics* 15 (1967): 80-89.

Plaskin, Robert. "A Stake in the Future." *Globe and Mail*, Toronto, 9 October 1978, 11.

Plesuk, Brian, ed. *The Only Game in Town.* Edmonton: Alberta Environment, July 1981.

Porter, John. *Canadian Social Structure.* Toronto: McClelland and Stewart, 1967.

Prince Edward Island, Department of Municipal Affairs. *Residential Subdivision Design Handbook.* Charlottetown, 1979.

Pross, Paul A. *Planning and Development: A Case Study of Two Nova Scotia Communities.* Halifax: Dalhousie University Institute of Public Affairs, 1975.

Qadeer, Mohammad A. "Issues and Approaches of Rural Community Planning in Canada." *Plan Canada* 19:2 (June 1979): 106-21.

Queen's University School of Urban and Regional Planning. *Sydenham, Ontario: A Plan for Community Enhancement.* A COPLAN Project, April 1982.

Redfield, Robert. *The Primitive World and Its Transformation.* Ithaca, N.Y.: Cornell University Press, 1953.

Regional District of Nanaimo Planning Department. "Nanoose Bay: Local Residents and Interest Group Viewpoints" and "Lighthouse Country: Local Residents and Interest Group Viewpoints." Nanaimo, B.C., 1981.

Regional Municipality of York. *Interim Policy on the Urban Settlements in Rural York Region.* Interim Policy Paper, June 1974.

Richardson, Boyce. *James Bay.* Toronto: Clarke Irwin, 1972.

Robertson, Heather. *Grass Roots.* Toronto: James Lewis & Samuel, 1973.

Robertson, James, and Carolyn Robertson. *The Small Towns Book.* New York: Anchor, 1978.

Robinson, Ira M. *New Industrial Towns on Canada's Resource Frontier.* Research Paper No. 73. Chicago: University of Chicago Department of Geography, 1962.

Robinson, John P., Philip E. Converse, and Alexander Szalai. "Everyday Life in Twelve Countries." In *The Use of Time*, edited by Alexander Szalai. The Hague: Mouton, 1972.

Rowe, Andy. "The Financing of Residential Construction in Newfoundland." *Canadian Public Policy* 7 (1981): 119-22.

Russell, Anthony J. *The Village in Myth and Reality*. London: Chester House, 1975.

Russwurm, Lorne H. *The Surrounding of Our Cities*. Ottawa:' Community Planning Press, 1977.

Saskatchewan, Department of Industry and Commerce. *Community Profile — Weyburn*. Regina, 1974-75.

Saskatchewan, Departments of Industry and Commerce and Municipal Affairs. *Guide to the Saskatchewan Main Street Development Program*. Regina, 1979.

Saskatchewan, Royal Commission on Agriculture and Rural Life. *Service Centres*. Regina: Queen's Printer, 1956.

Schumacher, E.F. *Small is Beautiful*. London: Abacus, 1974.

Simmons, James W. *Canada: Choices in a National Urban Strategy*. Research Paper No. 70. Toronto: University of Toronto Centre for Community Studies, 1975.

Sinclair, Peter R., and Kenneth Westhues. *Village in Crisis*. Toronto: Holt-Rinehart, 1974.

Smith, Wally. "P.E.I.'s Tiny Schools Throwing It All Away." *Axiom* 3:1 (December 1976): 18-22.

Sorokin, Pimtrim, and C.G. Zimmerman. *Principles of Rural-Urban Sociology*. New York: Kraus Reprint, 1969.

Spelt, Jacob. *Urban Develoment in South-Central Ontario*. Toronto: McClelland and Stewart, 1972.

Spragge, Godfrey. *History and Architecture: Village of Bath, Ontario*. Kingston: Queen's University School of Urban and Regional Planning, 1976.

Stabler, Jack C. "Regional Economic Change and Regional Spatial Structure: The Evolving Form of the Urban Hierarchy in the Prairie Region." In *The Future of Small and Medium-Sized Communities in the Prairie Region*, edited by B. Wellar, 1-26. Ottawa: Ministry of State for Urban Affairs, 1978.

Statistics Canada. *Building Permits*. Cat. No. 64-001 and 64-203.

Statistics Canada. *Crime and Traffic Enforcement Statistics — 1978*. Ottawa, 1978.

Statistics Canada. *Federal Government Employment in Metropolitan Areas*. Cat. No. 72-205. Ottawa: Ministry of Supply and Services Canada, 1981.

Steiner, Peter O. "The Public Sector and the Public Interest." In *Public Expenditures and Policy Analysis*, edited by Robert H. Haveman and Julius Margolis, 21-58. Chicago: Markham, 1970.

Sternlieb, George, and William Hughes. "New Regional and Metropolitan Realities for America." *Journal of the American Institute of Planners* 43:3 (July 1977): 227-40.

Stone, Leroy O. "Small-Community Aspects of Demographic Processes in a Steady-State Economy." *Proceedings of the Conference on Approaches to Rural Development*. Guelph: University of Guelph, May 1981.

Swanson, Bert E., and Richard Cohen. *Small Towns and Small Towners*. Beverly Hills: Sage, 1979.

Tiebout, Charles E. *The Community Economic Base Study*. New York: Committee for Economic Development, 1962.

Todd, Kenneth R. "Transportation in Rural Areas: A Case Study of North Frontenac County." Unpublished Master's Report, Queen's University School of Urban and Regional Planning, 1981.

Toennies, Ferdinand. "From Community to Society." In *Social Change*, edited by Amitai Etzioni and Eva Etzioni-Halevy, 54-62. New York: Basic Books, 1973.

"Town Prays for Only Industry to Survive Relocation Plans." *Whig Standard*, Kingston, 3 January 1983, 5.

Transem, Wallace. "Community Organization: The Wanham Experience." In *The Viability and Livability of Small Urban Centres*, edited by Frank Jankunis and Barry Sadler, 103-06. Edmonton: Environmental Council of Alberta, 1980.

Tremblay, Marc-Adelard, and W.J. Anderson. *Rural Canada in Transition*. Ottawa: Agricultural Economics Research Council of Canada, 1966.

Troughton, Michael J. *et al.*, eds. *The Countryside in Ontario*. Proceedings of the Countryside in Ontario Conference. London: University of Western Ontario, 1974.

Tweeten, Luther. "Emerging Issues for Sparsely Populated Areas and Regions Under a National Growth Policy." *American Journal of Agricultural Economics* 55:5 (1973): 840-50.

Tweeten, Luther, and George L. Brinkman. *Micropolitan Development*. Ames, Iowa: Iowa State University Press, 1976.

United States, Department of Housing and Urban Development. *Development Needs of Small Cities*. Washington, D.C., 1979.

Urban Systems Ltd. *Planning Program for the Village of Valemount*. Kamloops, B.C., January 1979.

U.S. Federal Reserve Bank of Minneapolis. *A Regional Economic Analysis of the Turtle Mountain Indian Reservation: Determining Potential for Commercial Development*. Grand Forks, N.D., 1978.

Vidich, Arthur J., and Joseph L. Bensman. *Small Town in Mass Society*. New York: Garden City, 1968.

Warren, Roland. "Towards a Reformulation of Community Theory." In *Perspective on the American Community*, edited by R. Warren, 69-78. Chicago: Rand McNally, 1966.

Webber, Melvin M. "Order in Diversity: Community Without

Propinquity." In *Cities and Space,* edited by Lowdon Wingo, 23-56. Baltimore: Johns Hopkins University Pres, 1963.

Whebell, C.F.J. "Corridors: A Theory of Urban Systems." *Annals of the Association of American Geographers* 59:1 (March 1969).

Whiting, L.R., ed. *Communities Left Behind: Alternatives for Development.* Ames, Iowa: Iowa State University Press, 1974.

Whiting, L.R., ed. *Rural Industrialization: Problems and Potentials.* Ames, Iowa: Iowa State University Press, 1974.

Whitney, V.H. "Economic Differences Among Rural Centres." *American Sociological Review* 12:1 (1974): 50-57.

Wilson, James. *People in the Way.* Toronto: University of Toronto Press, 1973.

Wirth, Louis. "Urbanism as a Way of Life." *American Journal of Sociology* 44:1 (July 1938): 8-20.

Wood, K. Scott, and Harold Verge. *A Study of the Problems of Certain Cape Breton Communities.* Halifax: Dalhousie University, Institute of Public Affairs, 1966.

Woodruffe, B.J. *Rural Settlement Policies and Plans.* London: Oxford University Press, 1966.

World Bank. *The Assault on World Poverty: Problems of Rural Development, Education and Health.* Baltimore: Johns Hopkins University Press, 1975.

Zimmerman, C.C., and G.W. Moneo. *The Prairie Community System.* Ottawa: Agricultural Economics Research Council, 1972.

Subject and Location Index

Place names are indicated by asterisks.

A

Acme,* 194-195
Age of Household Head, 104
Automobile Use, 8, 85-91, 95-97

B

Bancroft,* 54
Barriefield,* 157
Bath,* 159
Beiseker,* 149
Belgrave,* 158
Beliefs about Life in Small Communities, 131-132, 170-171
Broadview,* 9
Burin,* 167

C

Census Subdivision, definition, 14
Churchill Falls,* 43
Clarenville,* 160, 192-193
Clinton,* 158
Commercial Development, 35-36, 86-91, 153-154
Committee of Coordinating Organizations, 218
Community Management Development Program, 224
Community Need Thresholds, 175
Community Plans, 191-196
Community Profile, 196-197
Community Staying Power, 5, 217-218
Commuting, 77, 91-95
Counterurbanization, 9-11
Crime Rates, 142

H

Health and Recreational Needs, 172
Hanna,* 41, 117
Heritage Buildings, 157-159
High River,* 191
'Horizontal' Dimension, 133
Household Income, 57, 60
Housing
    age, 152-153
    conditions, 142
    growth, 35-36, 149-153, 186
    types, 151-152, 188
Howick Township,* 171
Hunter River,* 174, 182-183

I

Inverness,* 9, 171

K

Kitimat,* 43

L

Labor-Force Participation Rates, 55
Land Use, 154-157, 188
Lansdowne,* 149
Life Expectancy, 140
Location Quotients (LQ), 45-46
Lumsden,* 185

M

"Main Street," 155-157, 189, 202, 224
Metropolitan Area Influence, 76-84
Metropolitan and Rural Time Budgets, 138-139
Minimum Requirements Measure, 47
Modular Society, 50-51, 62, 119
Morden,* 171